"Richard Erskine's book blends theory and practice in a comprehensive and complementary way. It is an excellent guide for those who want to understand and practice relational-focused integrative psychotherapy. You will find in every paragraph of this book a creative synthesis of knowledge and method, an inspiring resource for all psychotherapists."

Dr. Şafak Ebru Toksoy, *Istanbul Bilgi University, Institute of Graduate Programs: Trauma and Disaster Mental Health*

"This book is a treasure to help psychotherapists understand clients unconscious process and non-verbal communication. Richard Erskine skilfully demonstrates the theory and practice of a relationally-focused and developmentally-based psychotherapy that facilitates the integration of the fragmented parts of the self. This book is a must read to every psychotherapist, from beginners to the very experienced ones"

Ruth Birkebaek, MD, *psychotherapist, supervisor, and international trainer, London, UK*

"Each chapter provides a richly coloured tapestry of Integrative Psychotherapy. The presentation of client material helps to give the reader a vibrant image of how in-depth psychotherapy looks in practice. This book is a wonderful, essential creation, beautifully crafted, with many practical ideas and concepts interwoven and interconnected."

Sally Openshaw, *President, International Integrative Psychotherapy Association (IIPA); UKCP Registered Psychotherapist; COSRT Accredited Sexual and Relational Therapist and Supervisor*

"Richard Erskine is a much-respected innovator and developer of integrative psychotherapy, well known for his writings and teaching on Inquiry, Attunement, and Involvement in the therapeutic relationship. The various chapters in this volume offer vivid case vignettes that provide useful examples of the methodology involved in conducting in-depth psychotherapy. In addition to the chapters addressing individual psychotherapy, there are chapters focusing on couple as well as group therapy, and supervision. This book is an ideal resource for those who wish to gain a deeper understanding of a developmentally-based, relationally-focused integrative psychotherapy."

Ray Little, *author of several articles and book chapters on the theory and methods of psychotherapy, Edinburgh, Scotland*

Essays on Integrative Psychotherapy

This book is a distinctive collection of essays on the theory and methods of a developmentally based, relationally focused Integrative Psychotherapy.

In an easy-to-read style, Richard Erskine elaborates on a relationally focused psychotherapy for acute and cumulative neglect, dissociation, alcoholism, obsession, prolonged grief, as well as psychotherapy with couples. Detailed examples of actual psychotherapy sessions illustrate the therapeutic methods of both phenomenological and developmental inquiry as well as the significance of the psychotherapist's interpersonal involvement through acknowledgment, validation, normalization, and presence. Each chapter takes the reader into further depths of understanding the complexities of an in-depth psychotherapy. Erskine writes from the heart while drawing from over 50 years as a psychotherapist, supervisor, and trainer.

Essays on Integrative Psychotherapy vividly illustrates the interpsychic struggle of clients who engage in the schizoid process of relational withdrawal and live in loneliness, and will be essential reading for psychotherapists and psychoanalysts in practice and in training.

Richard G. Erskine, PhD, is a licensed clinical psychologist, licensed psychoanalyst, certified transactional analyst, and group psychotherapist. His professional background includes training in Gestalt therapy with both Fritz and Laura Perls, client-centered therapy, emotional and cognitive development, body-oriented psychotherapy, object relations therapy, and psychoanalytic self-psychology. Since 1976 he has served as the Training Director at the Institute for Integrative Psychotherapy in New York City and Vancouver, Canada; he is Professor of Psychology on the Faculty of Health Sciences at Deusto University, Bilbao, Spain; and he conducts professional development seminars in several countries, both in person and via the internet. His website is www.IntegrativePsychotherapy.com.

Essays on Integrative Psychotherapy

Developmental and Relational Perspectives

Richard G. Erskine

Routledge
Taylor & Francis Group

LONDON AND NEW YORK

Designed cover image: Getty

First published 2025
by Routledge
4 Park Square, Milton Park, Abingdon, Oxon OX14 4RN

and by Routledge
605 Third Avenue, New York, NY 10158

Routledge is an imprint of the Taylor & Francis Group, an informa business

British Library Cataloguing in Publication Data
A catalogue record for this book is available from the British Library

Library of Congress Cataloging-in-Publication Data
A catalog record has been requested for this book

ISBN: 9781041040712 (hbk)
ISBN: 9781041040705 (pbk)
ISBN: 9781003626718 (ebk)

DOI: 10.4324/9781003626718

Typeset in Times New Roman
by Taylor & Francis Books

To my children and grandchildren who have given special meaning to my life; to Karen for her constant support, editing skills, and enthusiasm for life; and to my clients who have been phenomenal teachers about the intricacies of psychotherapy.

Contents

Figures

When

When you listen to me
I hear the stirring in my heart
When you whisper to me
I see the brightness in my mind
When you speak to me
I feel the warmth in my soul
When you meet me
I sense the life in my world
When you answer me
I believe the strength in my self

David Forrest,
February 2002,
West Bridgford, UK

Contributors

Richard G. Erskine, PhD, is a licensed clinical psychologist, licensed psycho-analyst, certified transactional analyst, and group psychotherapist. His professional background includes training in Gestalt therapy with both Fritz and Laura Perls, client-centered therapy, emotional and cognitive development, body-oriented psychotherapy, object relations therapy, and psychoanalytic self-psychology. Since 1976 he has served as the Training Director at the Institute for Integrative Psychotherapy in New York City and Vancouver, Canada; he is Professor of Psychology on the Faculty of Health Sciences at Deusto University, Bilbao, Spain; and he conducts professional development seminars in several countries, both in person and via the internet. His website is www.IntegrativePsychotherapy.com.

Preface

As I reread the various chapters in *Essays on Integrative Psychotherapy: Developmental and Relational Perspectives*, I asked myself what the reader may want to look for in reading this particular book. While imaging myself in your perspective I have outlined some of the important concepts that are interwoven throughout the various chapters. I hope that my identifying these concepts will provide the stimulus for you to explore, experiment, and develop your own ideas and methods and thereby actively contribute to the future refinement of a developmentally based, relationally focused Integrative Psychotherapy.

Relationship is central: As integrative psychotherapists, we need to maintain and refine our person-centered perspective, which respects the inherent value of each person. This includes a non-pathological attitude about all people, an attitude that is both normative and validating (Erskine, 2021). It is our therapeutic responsibility to find ways to value all clients, even if we do not understand their behavior or what motivates them. We manifest an attitude of *unconditional positive regard* (Rogers, 1951) when we treat all of our clients with kindness, provide them with options and choices, create security, and accept them as they present themselves rather than looking for a possible ulterior agenda.

Psychotherapy is an intersubjective process when based on a foundation of unconditional positive regard or what Martin Buber (1958) called the "I-Thou" relationship. As integrative psychotherapists, we realize that healing of the psychological wounds of neglect and trauma occurs through sustained therapeutic contact. We also recognize the therapeutic effectiveness of consistent phenomenological inquiry as well as the effectiveness of an intersubjective, person-to-person, honest interchange that conveys respect, choice, and integrity. Such therapeutic contact is provided through the therapist's commitment to the client's welfare and attunement with the person's rhythm, affect, cognition, and level of development.

As integrative psychotherapists, we maintain sensitivity to our clients' relational needs throughout each stage of life. We recognize the importance of the person having choice and full, contactful self-expression. With attunement, we can create a relationship that is qualitatively and therapeutically responsive to both the client's relational needs that were unsatisfied earlier in life as well as his or her current relational needs (Erskine et al., 2023).

Developmentally based: The research on child development and the observational writings of child psychologists provide us with a variety of understandings about how children grow and learn, and about how at each developmental age they accommodate themselves to, and compensate for, relational disruptions and the resulting internal distress. If we are to do an in-depth Integrative Psychotherapy, it is essential that we work from a developmental perspective.

I always wonder what childhood story is unconsciously being revealed via my client's body posture and movements, emotional expressions, and repetitive behaviors. I am continually using developmental images that provide me with a glimpse into the person's life as a child. To create a developmental image, I assemble bits and pieces of information about my client's childhood and speculate about the possibility that he or she was once a neglected baby, or a controlled and criticized preschool child, or a school-age child under stress, or a teenager who lacked family support and care.

Developmental images are only hypotheses, but they are valuable in forming our use of both phenomenological and historical inquiry. Such empathic inquiry, in turn, shapes our therapeutic involvement in a unique way with each person. Developmental images provide a powerful form of interpersonal connectedness with our clients' childhood experiences. Yet the potential for non-therapeutic reactive countertransference exists. That is why it is necessary for each of us to have an in-depth psychotherapy of our own so that we can distinguish our own experiences from our clients' childhood experiences.

The present provides a window to the past: As integrative psychotherapists we are always working in the now because unresolved conflicts and losses from the past are continually reenacted in the present. It is crucial that we observe and inquire our client's behaviors in order to decipher what primal dramas of early childhood are possibly being lived out in their transactions with us as well as with other people. The client's behaviors often reveal a story of emotional abandonment, neglect, abuse, or ridicule. Early childhood deprivations of attunement may be revealed in the client's expression of fear, rage, emotional numbness, or despair. The person's manner of escalation of, or immunization to, emotions often reflect the age at which trauma or profound neglect occurred. The past is lived out in our client's current lives.

Continual focus on the client's body: All experience – particularly if it is emotionally or physically overwhelming, or if it occurs early in life – is stored in the amygdala and the limbic system of the brain as both affect and visceral sensations without symbolization and language. Instead of memory being conscious through thought and internal symbolizations, experiences are expressed in the interplay of affect and body as somatic sensations. Our bodies remember the neglects, losses, and traumas of the past even if we cannot visually or verbally recall the events (Cozolino, 2006; Damasio, 1999; Reich, 1945; Van der Kolk, 1994). The past is often embodied in the client's physiology and lived again through current body sensations, gestures, and muscle tension. When we are fully contactful and involved, our client's developmental history becomes embodied in our psychotherapeutic relationship.

It is our task, as psychotherapists, to work sensitively and respectfully with the person's bodily gestures, movements, internal images, and emotional expressions to stimulate and enhance the client's sense of visceral arousal and awareness so that he or she has a new physiological-affective-relational experience. Such sensitivity and respectfulness require us to be attentive to the possibility of overstimulation and retraumatization, and in such cases to take ameliorative action. The narrative of the body is a special language with form, structure, and meaning. Through a body-centered relational psychotherapy we are able to decode the stories entrenched in our client's affect and embodied in their physiology.

Unconscious relational patterns: Early attachment dynamics are expressed in emotional responses, internal thought processes, decision making, and styles of interpersonal communication as well as through script beliefs and attachment styles. Clients' script beliefs reflect early relational patterns that are not only embodied in their physiology and enacted in their behavior but also encoded in stories and metaphors as well as being envisioned in their fantasies, hopes, and dreams. We need to appreciate how script beliefs formed in childhood shape current thoughts, fantasies, and behaviors and how current behaviors, fantasies, and thoughts reinforce script beliefs. These script beliefs are based on implicit experiential conclusions that may have been formed from real experience throughout several developmental stages (Erskine, 2025).

Therapy for the child in the adult: It may be essential for some clients that we create a child-sensitive psychotherapy that is responsive to the physiological, affective, imaginative, and verbal communications of the client's "internal child". Such child-sensitive therapy provides the psychotherapist with empathic and reparative responses to the ways our adult client's internal child is expressing his or her confusion, distress, agony, contentment, or joy. By thinking in a child-centered way, we can create a therapy that goes beyond verbal dialogue, one that makes use of imaginative enactments, play, drawing and art, music, and/or movement and dance.

States of the ego: As integrative psychotherapists, we make use of the concept of ego states because it provides theoretical understandings about how the sense of self can be fragmented into separate identities. Each fragmentation of a sense of self represents a desperate archaic attempt to self-stabilize and self-regulate in order to manage or compensate for previous failures in significant relationships.

Eric Berne's (1961) original model of ego states provides a way to understand both our clients' intrapsychic distress and the nature of their transactions with others. My own model depicts the internal dynamics between a vital and vulnerable self, a social self, introjection, and an internal, self-created critic (Erskine, 2023). This model of ego states helps us to understand how each split in the sense of self epitomizes cumulative neglect or trauma. Each of these ego state models informs our understanding of our clients' internal dynamics and helps us choose our therapeutic interventions.

Paradoxical theory of change: As integrative psychotherapists we appreciate the significance of being fully present and with our clients while we rely on our understanding of the paradoxical theory of change. We use our knowledge that the more change is the focus of our therapeutic practice, the more an individual will unconsciously maintain previously formed modes of behavior, affect, or relational patterns (Beisser, 1971). We facilitate our clients' understanding and appreciation of the psychological functions of their behaviors, repetitive feelings, or obsessions before attending to behavioral change. Change in behavior is often integral to an effective psychotherapy but an emphasis on changing behavior distracts clients from awareness of their phenomenological experiences, the homeostatic functions of their behaviors, and the opportunity to freely choose how to live life.

Presence: Presence refers to our internal sense of being with and for the client, commitment to the client's welfare, and the ability to put our own needs and desires into the background while remaining emotionally responsive to all that occurs in the relationship. Presence expresses an "I-Thou" relationship – a quality of relationship that heals. Presence is a central dynamic in forming a responsive countertransference.

These various concepts represent how I currently practice Integrative Psychotherapy. Each of these concepts becomes meaningful only when we are fully present, when we put our whole self into our practice of psychotherapy, and when we willingly discover the uniqueness of each client. I hope the concepts in this book will provide a blueprint for the future maturation of our theories and methods of a developmentally based, relationally focused Integrative Psychotherapy.

Richard G. Erskine, Vancouver, Canada, December 31, 2024

References

Beisser, A. (1971). The paradoxical theory of change. In J. Fagan & I. L. Shepherd (Eds.), *Gestalt therapy now: Theory, techniques, applications.* (pp. 77–80). Harper & Row.

Berne, E. (1961). *Transactional Analysis in psychotherapy: A systematic individual and social psychiatry.* Grove Press.

Buber, M. (1958). *I and thou*. (R. G. Smith, Trans.). Scribner.

Cozolino, L. (2006). *The neuroscience of human relationships: Attachment and the developing social brain*. W.W. Norton & Company.

Damasio, A. (1999). *The feeling of what happens: Body and emotion in the making of consciousness*. Harcourt Brace.

Erskine, R. G. (2021). *Early affect confusion: Relational psychotherapy for the borderline client*. Science Publishing.

Erskine, R. G. (2023). *Withdrawal silence loneliness: Psychotherapy of the schizoid process*. Phoenix Publishing.

Erskine, R. G. (2025). *Relational patterns, therapeutic presence*. Rutledge Mental Health Classic Editions.

Erskine, R. G., Moursund, J. P., & Trautmann R. L. (2023). *Beyond empathy: A therapy of contact-in-relationship*. Rutledge Mental Health Classic Editions.

Reich, W. (1945). *Character analysis*. Farrar, Strauss & Giroux.

Rogers, C. R. (1951). *Client-centered therapy: It's current practice, implications, and theory*. Houghton Mifflin.

Van der Kolk, B. A. (1994). The body keeps the score: Memory and the evolving psychobiology of posttraumatic stress. *Harvard Review of Psychiatry, 1*, 253–265.

Acknowledgements

I want to express a personal "thank you" to all the psychotherapists with whom I have had the pleasure of teaching and supervising during these past 50+ years. Being with each of you has been a marvelous journey of discoveries. I am honored to use David Forrest's poem "When". David's poem so vividly describes the intersubjective process of relational psychotherapy. Thomas Weil, from Kassel, Germany has beautifully captured the essence of the concept of relational needs in his poem "What I Need from You".

It has been a privilege to work closely with Christine Loyrion in cowriting the chapter entailed "Psychotherapy of Relational Withdrawal: Client's and Therapist's Perspectives". And a very special "thank you" to my long-time friend and coauthor, Janet Moursund, for teaching me how to write from the heart. And for Janet's contribution to our chapter entitled "Contact and Relational Needs in Couple Therapy". I remain grateful to the various journals for granting permission to republish articles in this book.

Chapter 1. Stimulus, Structure, and Relationship: An Integrative Psychotherapy Theory of Motivation

Some of the concepts in this chapter were presented in a workshop entitled "A Therapeutic Relationship: Integrating Object Relations Theory, Self-Psychology and Transactional Analysis" at the Joint International Transactional Analysis Association/European Transactional Analysis Association Conference. Brussels, Belgium, July 22–26, 1990. The concepts were also defined in a chapter entitled "The therapeutic relationship: Integrating motivation and personality theories" published in the 1997 *Theories and Methods of an Integrative Transactional Analysis*. Copyright by the Institute of Integrative Psychotherapy, 1996 and Richard G. Erskine Consulting Inc., 2024. Citation for the original article is: Erskine, R. G. (2025) Stimulus, Structure, and Relationship: An Integrative Psychotherapy Theory of Motivation. *International Journal of Integrative Psychotherapy*, 16:1, 26–33.

Chapter 2. Trauma, Dissociation, and a Reparative Relationship

A grateful "thank you" to Rebecca L. Trautmann, RN, MSW and the members of the Professional Development Seminars of the institute for Integrative Psychotherapy in New York, NY; Kent, CT; Chicago, IL; and Dayton, OH for their valuable suggestions in the development of this chapter. Portions of this paper were presented at the Symposium on the Treatment of Dissociation held at the 29th Annual International Transactional Analysis Association Conference on October 26, 1991 in Stamford, CT, USA. Citation for the original publication is: Erskine, R. G. (1991). The psychotherapy of dissociation: Inquiry, attunement, and involvement. In B. Loria (Ed.), *Stamford papers: Selections from the 29th Annual International Transactional Analysis Association Conference.* Omnipress. It is republished here with permission of the Institute for Integrative Psychotherapy and Richard G. Erskine Consulting Inc., owners of the 1990 and 2010 copyright.

Chapter 3. Wayne: The Emptiness of the Unloved Child

"The Emptiness of the Unloved Child" was prepared as an online seminar on "Writing Psychotherapy Case Studies" for the International Integrative Psychotherapy Association, January 13, 2025. Wayne (pseudonym) said, "Publish my story. There are thousands of people just like me who need to know that they can overcome the abuse of their childhood and stop alcohol forever". Copyright 2020 by Institute for Integrative Psychotherapy and Richard G. Erskine Consulting Inc. Citation for this artice is: Erskine, R. G. (2025). Wayne: The Emptiness of the Unloved Child. *International Journal of Integrative Psychotherapy.* 16:1, 50–56. It is published here with permission from the *International Journal of Integrative Psychotherapy.*

Chapter 4. Child Development in Integrative Psychotherapy: Erik Erikson's First Three Stages

This article describes how child development research and theory provide a basic foundation in the practice of Integrative Psychotherapy. The concepts in this article were first published in: Erskine, R. G. (1971). *The effects of parent-child interaction on the development of a concept of self: An Eriksonian view.* Purdue University, Lafayette, Indiana. This chapter is a modified version of that research report. Copyright 2015 by Institute for Integrative Psychotherapy and Richard G. Erskine Consulting, Inc. Reprint with the approval of the *International Journal of Integrative Psychotherapy* and the International Integrative Psychotherapy Association. The citation for the article that became this chapter is: Erskine, R G. (2019). Child development in Integrative Psychotherapy: Erik Erikson's first three stages. *International Journal of Integrative Psychotherapy, 10,* 11–34. It is published here with the permission of the *International Journal of Integrative Psychotherapy.*

Chapter 5. Contributions of Gestalt Therapy to the Practice of Integrative Psychotherapy

This chapter is based on a keynote address entitled "Contact-in-Relationship: Clinical Applications of Gestalt Therapy" at The Gestalt Therapy Journal Conference. New York, NY, April 24–25, 1998. A special thank you to David Forrest, from GestaltUK, for his valuable suggestions about the organization of this chapter and for his illustrative diagram. David's website is: www.gestaltuk.com. This chapter is copyright in 2023 by the Institute for Integrative Psychotherapy and Richard G. Erskine Consulting, Inc. Reprinted with the permission of the *International Journal of Psychotherapy.* Citation for the original article is: Erskine, R. G. (2025) Contributions of Gestalt therapy to the practice of Integrative Psychotherapy. *International Journal of Psychotherapy, 28*(3) (in press).

Chapter 6. An Integrative Psychotherapy of Obsession: Diverse Concepts and Methods

This chapter entitled "An Integrative Psychotherapy of Obsession: Integrating Diverse Concepts and Methods" was the opening chapter in the 2016 book *Transactional Analysis in Contemporary Psychotherapy.* The book included 12 chapters by 15 authors who described the contemporary applications of the theory and methods of Transactional Analysis in psychotherapy. Copyright 2014 by Institute for Integrative Psychotherapy and Richard G. Erskine Consulting, Inc. Reproduced by permission of Taylor & Francis Group. The citation for the original chapter is: Erskine, R. G. (2016). A Transactional Analysis of obsession: Integrating diverse concepts and methods. In R. G. Erskine (Ed.), *Transactional Analysis in contemporary psychotherapy* (pp. 1–25). Karnac Books.

Chapter 7. Presence and Involvement: Personal Perspectives on Countertransference

Portions of this chapter were presented as a Keynote address entitled "Responsive and Reactive Countertransference" at the 5th International Conference on Supervision in Psychotherapy, Timisoara, Romania. June 9, 2023. Copyright 2020 by Institute for Integrative Psychotherapy and Richard G. Erskine Consulting, Inc. Reprinted with the permission of the *International Journal of Psychotherapy.* The citation for this chapter is: Erskine, R. G. (2024). Countertransference: An Integrative Psychotherapy perspective. *International Journal of Psychotherapy, 28*(1), 47–61.

Chapter 8. Relational Withdrawal, Internal Criticism, Social Façade: Psychotherapy of the Schizoid Process

Concepts in this chapter were originally presented as a keynote address at the Continuing Education Symposium on "The Schizoid Process" held on August 20, 1999 during the International Transactional Analysis Association annual conference in San Francisco. Portions of this article were originally published in 2001 by Richard G. Erskine as "The schizoid process" in the *Transactional Analysis Journal, 31*(1), 4–6. Copyright 2020 by Institute for Integrative Psychotherapy and Richard G. Erskine Consulting, Inc. Reprinted with the permission of the *International Journal of Psychotherapy*. The citation for the original article is: Erskine, R. G. (2022). Relational withdrawal, internal criticism, social façade: Psychotherapy of the schizoid process. *International Journal of Psychotherapy, 26*, 75–93. It is published here with permission from the *International Journal of Psychotherapy*.

Chapter 9. Psychotherapy of Relational Withdrawal: Perspectives from a Client and Therapist

The chapter entitled "Psychotherapy of Relational Withdrawal: Client's and Therapist's Perspectives" was an outgrowth of a series of five-day professional training workshops held at les Fougeres, Mirande, France from 2015 to 2024. The focus of the training series was on exploring "What is effective and what is ineffective in psychotherapy?" A special "Thank You" to coauthor Christine Loyrion, who has courageously told the story about the psychotherapy of her inner turmoil. Copyright 2024 by Institute for Integrative Psychotherapy and Richard G. Erskine Consulting, Inc. Loyrion, C & Erskine, R. G. (2025). Psychotherapy of Relational Withdrawal: Perspectives from a Client and Therapist. *International Journal of Integrative Psychotherapy.* 16:1, 18–25. It is republished here with the permission of the *International Journal of Psychotherapy*.

Chapter 10. The Truth Shall Set You Free: Saying an Honest "Goodbye" Before a Loved-One's Death

"The Truth Shall Set You Free" was presented as a series of lectures in workshops in Italy, Spain, France, and the UK in 2012 and 2013. The citation for this article is: Erskine, R. G. (2014). The truth shall set you free: Saying an honest "goodbye" before a loved-one's death. *International Journal of Psychotherapy, 18*(2), 72–79. Copyright 2011 by Institute for Integrative Psychotherapy and Richard G. Erskine Consulting, Inc. It is published here with permission from the *International Journal of Psychotherapy*.

Chapter 11. Saying an Honest "Goodbye": Three Case Examples

"Saying an Honest 'Goodbye': Three Case Examples" was also presented as part of a series of lectures in workshops in Italy, Spain, France, and the UK in 2012 and 2013. The citation for this article is: Erskine, R. G. (2014). Saying an honest "goodbye": Part 2: Three case examples. *International Journal of Psychotherapy, 18*(3), 52–62. Copyright 2013 by Institute for Integrative Psychotherapy and Richard G. Erskine Consulting, Inc. It is published here with permission from the *International Journal of Psychotherapy.*

Chapter 12. Relational Group Process: Developments in Group Psychotherapy

The chapter entitled "Relational Group Process: Developments in Group Process" was first presented as a three-hour workshop entitled "Developments in Group Psychotherapy: Three Models of Group Psychotherapy" at the 9th Annual Conference, European Transactional Analysis Association, Rome, Italy, July 4–8, 1983. Copyright 1997 and 2011 by Institute for Integrative Psychotherapy and Richard G. Erskine Consulting, Inc. The citation for this article is: Erskine, R. G. (2013). Relational group process: Developments in a Transactional Analysis model of group psychotherapy. *Transactional Analysis Journal, 43*, 262–275. Published here by permission from Taylor & Francis.

Chapter 13. Contact and Relational Needs in Couple Therapy: An Integrative Psychotherapy Perspective

"Contact and Relational Needs in Couple Therapy: An Integrative Psychotherapy Perspective" is coauthored with Janet P. Moursund. Copyright 2018 by Institute for Integrative Psychotherapy and Richard G. Erskine Consulting, Inc. Citation for the original publication is: Erskine, R. G., & Moursund, J. P. (2020). Contact and relational needs in couple therapy: An Integrative Psychotherapy perspective. *International Journal of Psychotherapy, 24*(2), 53–60. Republished here with the permission of the *International Journal of Psychotherapy.*

Chapter 14. Reflections on Supervision in Integrative Psychotherapy

The article on which this chapter is based was first presented at the Seventh Annual Conference of the Society for the Exploration of Psychotherapy Integration (SEPI), London, England, July 11–14, 1991 with the title

"Training and Supervision in Integrative Psychotherapy". The citation for the article is: Erskine, R. G. (2023). Reflections on supervision in Integrative Psychotherapy. *International Journal of Supervision in Psychotherapy, 5*, 7–20. Copyright 2023 by Institute for Integrative Psychotherapy and Richard G. Erskine Consulting, Inc. It is published here with the permission of the *International Journal of Supervision in Psychotherapy.*

Chapter 15. Compassion, Hope, and Forgiveness in the Therapeutic Dialogue

This chapter is based on a Keynote address entitled "Compassion, Hope, and Forgiveness in the Therapeutic Dialogue" at the Manchester Institute for Psychotherapy 7th Biennial Conference, November 15–17, 2019, Manchester, UK. The citation for the original publication is: Erskine, R. G. (2020). Compassion, hope, and forgiveness in the therapeutic dialogue. *International Journal of Integrative Psychotherapy, 11*, 1–13. Copyright 2019 by Institute for Integrative Psychotherapy and Richard G. Erskine Consulting, Inc. It is published here with the permission of the *International Journal of Integrative Psychotherapy.*

Chapter 16. The Psychotherapist's Myths, Dreams, and Realities

This chapter was presented as a keynote address at the Second World Congress for Psychotherapy in Vienna, Austria, July 4, 1999 and published in the *International Journal of Psychotherapy*, with the citation: Erskine, R. G. (2001). The psychotherapist's myths, dreams and realities. *International Journal of Psychotherapy, 6*(2), 133–140. It is republished with the permission of the *International Journal of Psychotherapy.*

What I Need from You

Everyone needs a heart that feels,
A hand that joins us in the game.
An ear that hears what no one says,
A voice that asks and gently stays.
I need arms that carry me,
When fears and doubts won't let me be.
That hold me through the darkest night,
Make me safe till morning light.
I need people full of grace,
Who console without blame's embrace.
Who give me strength when courage wanes,
And help me try, despite the pains.
Everyone needs a heart that feels,
A hand that joins us in the game.
An ear that hears what no one says,
A voice that asks and gently stays.
When I aim too high, too fast,
I need a "stop" to learn at last.
For limits help to find the peace,
That lets my restless mind release.
Sometimes I'm caught in inner strife,
I need someone who shares my life.
A person who believes in me,
And bathes my heart in love's pure sea.
Everyone needs a heart that feels,
A hand that joins us in the game.
An ear that hears what no one says,
A voice that asks and gently stays.
I need people who understand,
That I must walk my path unplanned.
Who value me for who I am,
And say: "It's okay to not blend in".
I need people who will show,
They're here for me, they let me know.

Who think of me with care and cheer,
And simply bring me joy sincere.
Everyone needs a heart that feels,
A hand that joins us in the game.
An ear that hears what no one says,
A voice that asks and gently stays.
I need people who will ask,
What I truly want today, unmasked.
Who listen close and understand,
And never overlook my plans.
People who find joy in me,
In all I give so lovingly.
Who take the gifts I gladly share,
And feel blessed just because I'm there.
Everyone needs a heart that feels,
A hand that joins us in the game.
An ear that hears what no one says,
A voice that asks and gently stays.

       Thomas Weil, 2024, Kassel, Germany

Chapter 1

Stimulus, Structure, nd Relationship

An Integrative Psychotherapy Theory of Motivation

In rereading articles published in the *International Journal of Integrative Psychotherapy*, it is apparent that neither other authors nor I have described the concept of *motivation* and how it interfaces with Integrative Psychotherapy theories of personality development and psychological functioning (Erskine, 2011, 2013c, 2023a; O'Reilly-Knapp & Erskine, 2010). However, the amalgamation of the theories of motivation, personality, and methods are illustrated in detailed case studies of psychotherapy clients who rely on silence and relational withdrawal to self-stabilize (Erskine, 2021b, 2021c) as well as clients who live on the "borderline" between despair and rage (Erskine, 2012, 2013a, 2013b).

The Integrative Psychotherapy theory of motivation includes the concepts of stimulus, structure, and relationship. These three concepts provide a meta-perspective that encompasses and demarcates the various theories of personality such as unconscious relational patterns, ego states, transference, script beliefs, relational needs, and other sub-theories. For a theoretical school of psychotherapy to be coherent and consistent, there must be an interconnection of three distinct theories: the theory of motivation, theories of personality, and a theory of therapeutic methods. A theory of motivation determines which theories of personality can be integrated and which are conceptually inconsistent and do not integrate into a unified, comprehensive theory of human functioning.

In a developmentally based, relationally focused Integrative Psychotherapy, the various understandings of personality include, but are not limited to, the concepts of: relational patterns, relational needs, unconscious process, ego states, splitting of the self, introjection, script beliefs, homeostatic functions, transference, and other sub-theories. The concepts of personality have been defined and elaborated in several publications (Erskine, 2021a, 2021d, 2023a, 2015/2025; Erskine & Moursund, 2022; Erskine et al., 1999/2023).

When theories of motivation and personality have an internal validity and consistency, they work together as a conceptual organization for a unified theory of therapeutic method.

DOI: 10.4324/9781003626718-1

To be coherent, a theory of method must emerge from corresponding theories of human motivation and personality (Erskine, 2015/2025; Erskine & Moursund, 2022; Erskine et al., 1999/2023). A theory of method provides guidelines for how methods may be designed. It provides an orientation to the practice of psychotherapy. In a developmentally based, relationally focused Integrative Psychotherapy, the theory of methods is based on the premise that *the healing of psychological destabilization caused by prolonged neglect, continuous stress, and/or relational abuse occurs through the use of a therapeutic relationship that focuses on enhancing the client's capacity for internal, external, and interpersonal contact.* This theory of method provides both an overall framework from which specific methods are designed and a conceptual beacon that serves as a guide to the therapist in the continual monitoring of observations, hypotheses, and specific interventions (Erskine, 2010, 2011, 2014, 2023b).

An Integrative Theory of Motivation

In my teachings about the theory of motivation, I describe the artist Alexander Calder's mobile constructions as a visual metaphor of the intricacy of stimulus, structure, and relationship. One of Calder's sculptures that is particularly alluring is composed of three diverse shapes: an oval, a square, and a triangle. Each differently colored shape appears to dangle in space, yet at the same time each individual form is delicately balanced by the other two shapes. The slightest movement in one of the forms incites a consequent movement in both of the other shapes. And so it is with people; we are physically and psychologically motivated by a delicate balance of stimulus, structure, and relationship. *These are biological imperatives: we cannot live without internal and external stimulus, we crave structure, and relationships provide a felt sense of identity and belonging.* These biological imperatives provide the concepts for a comprehensive theory of motivation.

Stimulus

Stimulus is necessary for survival. Stimuli operate both internally and externally and provide the informational feedback system that leads to the satisfaction of basic needs. The survival needs for oxygen, water, and food – as well as psychological and relational needs – all begin with internal stimuli that lead to an awareness of a discomfort. As internal biological and psychological processes come to awareness, a person must also become aware of the environment that can supply the resources for survival.

To satisfy that which is needed, a person must make contact not only with their internal sensations and needs, but also with the external environment. Survival and quality of life are ensured through the continual moment-by-moment interplay between internal and external stimuli and the capacity to

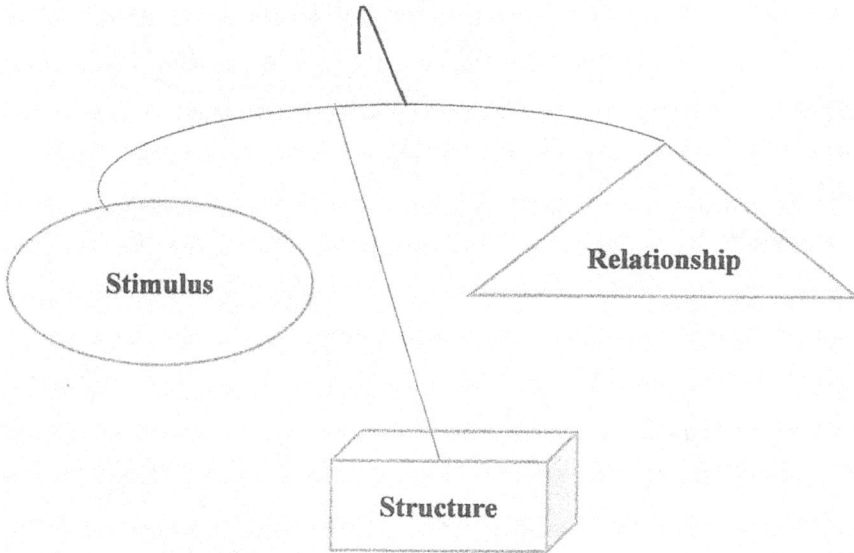

Figure 1.1 Integrative Psychotherapy Theory of Motivation: A Delicate Balance of Stimulus, Structure, and Relationship

make full contact both internally and externally. The biological imperative for stimulus is satisfied through the interaction of the central nervous system and the proprioceptive organs. Our "sensory system provides us with an orientation" (Perls, 1973, p. 17) that makes full external and internal contact possible. Full contact is essential for life – it satisfies the biological imperative for stimuli that influences and regulates the drives for structure and relationship.

While reading the paragraph above, you may have been distracted by a sound in another room (external stimuli). At that moment it may not have been possible to concentrate on these written words. Then you may realize that you are thirsty (internal stimuli), so you get up and pour a glass of water (coordinating several external stimuli) and then have a refreshing drink (internal stimuli). Each of these activities involves the processing of several internal and external stimuli, as well as using various cognitive structures such as chair, glass, and water.

Structure

Structure refers to the human drive to organize experience and to form perceptual configurations – visually, auditorily, tactilely, kinesthetically, and cognitively. The experimental Gestalt psychologists demonstrated that there is an innate drive to form perceptual patterns and configurations (Kohler,

1938; Lewin, 1938). The drive to structure perceptual configurations and the inevitability of figure-ground formation creates and organizes pattern, meaning, and predictability in our lives. This, in turn, makes concept formation, categorization, and language possible. The formation of perceptual configurations refers not only to auditory or visual patterns – such as the recognition of a familiar sound or the meaning in these written words – but also to tactile and kinesthetic patterns such as the habitual tensing of muscles in response to fear or anger and to the creation of beliefs about self, others, and the quality of life.

Stern (1985) referred to the three-day-old infant's capacity to form an olfactory configuration that allows the baby to turn their head toward the smell of breast milk from their own mother rather than in the direction of milk from another woman. This innate tendency to structure configurations that create meaning and predictability and to organize the continuity of experience over time also provides the possibility for perceptual variability and the creation of new organization and meaning. It is only because we form perceptual patterns that it is also possible to perceive novelty, variation, and contrast (Perls et al., 1951).

Both continuity and variability in perception are necessary for the urge for stimulus and relationship to be satisfied. If there is a disruption in the structuring of sensations or perceptions, then there will also be a disruption in the full processing of internal and external stimuli and/or the satisfaction of relational needs. Thus, the drive to organize and generalize patterns of experience (structure hunger) influences the biological imperative of both stimulus and relationship. Human beings continually strive to make meaning of their experiences and observations.

While some of our clients are in conversation with us, they may rely on old beliefs about themselves and others (mental structures) in order to maintain continuity, confirm their identity, or establish predictability. Predictability, identity, and continuity are mental structures that maintain both homeostasis and beliefs about themselves and others (structures about relationship). These mental structures provide meaning about life and emotional regulation (stimulus). Through our empathic involvement and presence, we provide our clients with a different, and perhaps unique, quality of relationship – a relationship that influences a change in both their internal sensations and thoughts about themselves and others.

Relationship

A growing body of literature supports the premise that people are born relationship seeking and continue patterns of bonding and attachment throughout life. Stern's (1985) compilation of research on infant development supports the idea that the infant's and young child's sense of self emerges through interpersonal relationships. In addition, authors writing from a feminist perspective on psychotherapy emphasize the centrality of inter-personal connection and relationship in the formation of a healthy sense of self in both females and males (Bergman, 1991; Miller, 1986; Surrey, 1985). Sullivan's (1953) interpersonal theory also places central importance on establishing and maintaining relationships. Contemporary writings in Gestalt therapy have emphasized the importance of a dialogical, healing relationship (Hycner & Jacobs, 1995; Yontef, 1993). Each of these theorists described a developmental thrust for relationship.

The book *Beyond Empathy: A Therapy of Contact-in-Relationship* (Erskine et al., 1999/2023) details the biological imperative for relationship. It defines eight specific needs inherent in interpersonal relationship throughout every age of our life. These eight needs include: 1) security within a relationship; 2) validation, affirmation, and significance within a relationship; 3) acceptance by a stable, dependable, and protective other person; 4) the confirmation of personal experience; 5) self-definition; 6) to have an impact on the other person; 7) to have the other initiate; and 8) to express love. There may be more than these eight relational needs; these were the needs most prevalent in the qualitative research.

Relationships are built on interpersonal contact that includes the stimulus of physical touch and a valuing recognition by another person of an indivi-dual's being and attributes. Relationships provide the experience from which the configuration of a sense of self, of others, and of the quality of life emerge. Although relationships are built on the stimuli of moment-by-moment verbal and non-verbal transactions, they also reflect the drive to structure pattern and meaning from an individual's whole history of inter-personal experiences. Satisfaction of the biological imperative for relationship depends on the awareness of relational needs (internal stimulus), what the individual believes about self and others in the interpersonal relationships (structure), and the behavior of the other person in the relationship (external stimulus).

The innate urge for relationship is affected by and influences the drives for stimulus and structure. When an individual's needs for relationship are repeatedly not met by a reciprocal response from another person, the indivi-dual may overgeneralize and rigidify the conclusions drawn from this experience. The conclusions and decisions are an attempt to make sense of the cumulative rupture in relationship and thus make it (temporarily) bear-able. From a perspective of a developmentally based, relationally focused Integrative Psychotherapy theory of personality, the compensating structure can be viewed as: maintaining physiological survival reactions, forming implicit experiential conclusions, making explicit script decisions, fantasizing and collecting selective evidence that reinforces script beliefs, or splitting the ego into various states (Erskine, 2015/2025).

If the drive to structure experience does not compensate for a lack of need-fulfilling relationship, the drive for stimulus may be employed in its place.

The compensating drive for stimulus may be manifested as emotional escalation or physical agitation or, conversely, as disavowal of affect, desensitization, or dissociation. Anxious obsessing is one of many examples of psychological phenomena in which stimulus hunger and structure hunger are both used as overcompensation for a lack of fulfillment of relationship hunger.

My client Janice grew up the youngest child in a five-person family. She describes how her family life was "full of loud accusations and constant arguments". Each time she tells me another memory about living in the middle of the family's conflicts, her jaw, neck, and shoulders are tense. As I listen to her, I think about the repeated relational disruption in Janice's young life and realize that she compensated through muscle tension that altered both her internal stimulus and physical structures. As I inquired about the tension in her neck and shoulders, Janice began to weep, "I was never able to cry when my parents and brothers were all fighting". With careful inquiry it became evident that Janice had made sense of her world by believing "I'm insignificant" and "people are only interested in themselves". These beliefs are her cognitive structures that make sense of the child's relational disruptions. Throughout our psychotherapy Janice had difficulty accepting my patience and tender comments. She questioned why I was "kind" and assumed that it was my "professional task". By not accepting my attunement to her affect, she was able to maintain her old mental structure, "I'm insignificant".

Balancing Stimulus, Structure, and Relationship

As already described, the three biological imperatives are in dynamic balance: any disruption in one of the drives causes an overcompensation in at least one of the others. More specifically, the drives for stimulus and for structure, on the one hand, and relationship hunger on the other, are interactive: the satisfaction of one hunger or drive is affected by the satisfaction – or non-satisfaction – of another.

Madeline was a divorced mother of a 9-year-old girl. She came to therapy because she was "despairing" and extremely overweight. In our weekly psychotherapy sessions, I found it difficult to get her to talk about her sense of depression or any internal sensations. She would periodically tell me that my inquiry was "too much to think about". She would bring my inquiry back to her concern about being "fat and unattractive", or she would talk about her daughter's accomplishments at school.

She told me several stories about how she tried to lose weight. I listened with interest and patience. It seemed to me that she was often talking to herself, not to me. Other than a few social friends from church and her activities with her 9-year-old daughter, she had no meaningful relationship. Her time was consumed with her work as a school teacher and caring for her daughter. As I thought about the theories of stimulus, structure, and relationship, it seemed apparent that Madeline's life was marked by an absence of any meaningful relationships. I wondered if her "despairing" was the internal stimuli that reflected the absence of any need-fulfilling adult relationship.

In trying to understand how to provide an effective psychotherapy for Madeline, I thought about the biological imperatives: stimulus, structure, and relationship. Since it was difficult to get Madeline to talk about her feelings or family relationships, my questions were now about how she structured her time. She described how she would finish teaching at 3:30 in the afternoon and then immediately go to a donut shop to purchase a dozen sugarcoated donuts. She talked about feeling a momentary sense of elation when she was buying the donuts. She went on to describe how she did not immediately eat the donuts, but the simple act of taking them home was "jubilant". She would store the donuts in a cupboard out of sight of her daughter; with "delightful thoughts" of eating them later. Madeline explained that once her daughter was asleep, she would consume all the donuts.

I was amazed by how Madeline structured her time and the sense of euphoria in her story. That roused me to ask about her experiences after school when she was 8 or 9 years old. She described coming home to an empty apartment; her mother was at work and would not come home until after 7 pm. She cried for the first time as she talked about being "all alone". Madeline said, "When coming home from school I had only one thing to look forward to; my mother always provided something sweet and delicious. The sweet snack was my companion. I remember how good it felt to eat, but then I would get so sad waiting for my mother to come home". The internal sensation of tasting the sweet was a compensation for the hunger for relationship. I thought about Madeline's oral pleasure in eating the donuts as a form of a baby's oral contact with its mother; the intimate contact with mother provides a soothing stimulus.

Conclusion

The biological imperative for stimulus, structure, and relationship provides the conceptual basis for a theory of motivation in Integrative Psychotherapy. To be coherent the various theories of personality must be consistent with an understanding of these biological imperatives. The theory of methods then emerges from the amalgamation of motivation and personality theories. These interactive theories of motivation, personality, and methods are the core concepts of a developmentally based, relationally focused Integrative Psychotherapy.

Integrative Psychotherapy Theories

Biological Imperatives

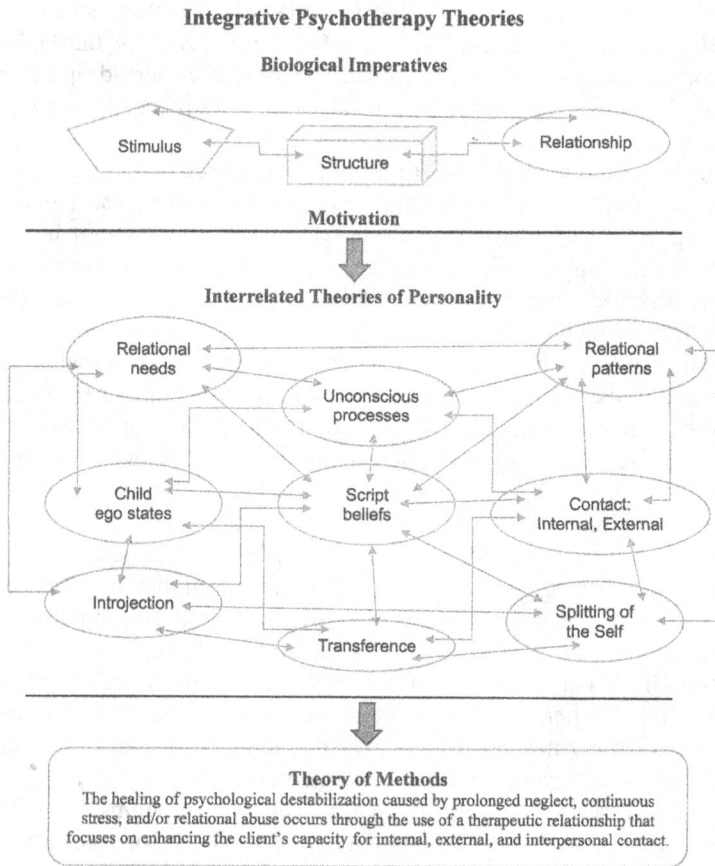

Figure 1.2 Integrative Psychotherapy Theories of Motivation, Personality, and Methods

References

Bergman, S. J. (1991). *Men's psychological development: A relationship perspective.* Works in Progress (No. 48). The Stone Center, Wellesley College.

Erskine, R. G. (2010). Integrating expressive methods in a relational-psychotherapy. *International Journal of Integrative Psychotherapy,* 1(2), 55–80.

Erskine, R. G. (2011). Attachment, relational-needs, and psychotherapeutic presence. *International Journal of Integrative Psychotherapy,* 2(1), 10–18.

Erskine, R. G. (2012). Early affect-confusion: The "borderline" between despair and rage: Part 1 of a case study trilogy. *International Journal of Integrative Psychotherapy,* 3(2), 3–14.

Erskine, R. G. (2013a). Balancing on the "borderline" of early affect-confusion: Part 2 of a case study trilogy. *International Journal of Integrative Psychotherapy,* 4(1), 3–9.

Erskine, R. G. (2013b). Relational healing of early affect-confusion: Part 3 of a case study trilogy. *International Journal of Integrative Psychotherapy,* 4(1), 31–40.

Erskine, R. G. (2013c). Vulnerability, authenticity, and inter-subjective contact: Philosophical principles of Integrative Psychotherapy. *International Journal of Integrative Psychotherapy*, 4(2), 1–9.

Erskine, R. G. (2014). Nonverbal stories: The body in psychotherapy. *International Journal of Integrative Psychotherapy*, 5, 21–33.

Erskine, R. G. (2021a). *A healing relationship: Commentary on therapeutic dialogues.* Phoenix Publishing.

Erskine, R. G. (2021b). Depression or isolated attachment? Part 1 of a 5-part case study of the psychotherapy of the schizoid process. *International Journal of Integrative Psychotherapy*, 11, 28–40.

Erskine, R. G. (2021c). Isolation, loneliness, and need to be loved: Part 3 of a 5-part case study of the schizoid process. *International Journal of Integrative Psychotherapy*, 11, 56–65.

Erskine, R. G. (2021d). *Early affect confusion: Relational psychotherapy for the borderline client.* nScience Publishing.

Erskine, R. G. (2023a). *Withdrawal, silence, loneliness: Psychotherapy of the schizoid process.* Phoenix Publishing.

Erskine, R. G. (2023b). Presence and involvement: Personal perspectives on countertransference. *International Journal of Integrative Psychotherapy*, 14, 1–14.

Erskine, R. G. (2025). *Relational patterns, therapeutic presence: Concepts and practice of Integrative Psychotherapy.* Routledge Mental Health Classic Editions. (Original edition published 2015).

Erskine, R. G., & Moursund, J. P. (2022). *The art and science of relationship: The practice of Integrative Psychotherapy.* Phoenix Publishing.

Erskine, R. G., Moursund, J. P., & Trautmann, R. L. (2023). *Beyond empathy: A therapy of contact-in-relationship.* Routledge Mental Health Classic Editions. (Original edition published 1999).

Hycner, R., & Jacobs, L. (1995). *The healing relationship in Gestalt therapy.* The Gestalt Journal Press.

Kohler, W. (1938). Physical gestalten. In W. Ellis (Ed.), *A source book of Gestalt psychology* (pp. 17–54). Routledge & Kegan Paul.

Lewin, K. (1938). Will and needs. In W. Ellis (Ed.), *A source book of Gestalt psychology* (pp. 283–299). Routledge & Kegan Paul.

Miller, J. B. (1986). *What do we mean by relationships?* Works in Progress (No. 22). The Stone Center, Wellesley College.

O'Reilly-Knapp, M., & Erskine, R. G. (2010). The script system: An unconscious organization of experience. *International Journal of Integrative Psychotherapy*, 1(2), 13–28.

Perls, F. (1973). *The Gestalt approach and eye witness to therapy.* Science & Behavior Books.

Perls, F. S., Hefferline, R. F., & Goodman, P. (1951). *Gestalt therapy: Excitement and growth in the human personality.* Julian Press.

Stern, D. N. (1985). *The interpersonal world of the infant: A view from psychoanalysis and developmental psychology.* Basic Books.

Sullivan, H. S. (1953). *The interpersonal theory of psychiatry.* Norton.

Surrey, J. L. (1985). *The "self-in-relation:" A theory of women's development.* Works in Progress (No. 13). The Stone Center, Wellesley College.

Yontef, G. M. (1993). *Awareness, dialogue and process.* The Gestalt Journal Press.

Chapter 2

Trauma, Dissociation, and a Reparative Relationship

The concept of *contact* – internal, external, and interpersonal – is a central theoretical premise in a developmentally based, relationally focused Integrative Psychotherapy. The basis of the concept of *contact* originated in the writings on Gestalt therapy by Fritz Perls, Ralph Hefferline, and Paul Goodman (1951). In that publication they described "full contact" and the formation of vivid new Gestalten as the foundation of psychological health (From, 1979).

In Fritz Perls' (1944) revision of Freud's theory and methods the client's interruptions to contact became the focus of the psychotherapy. Thus, in Gestalt therapy, as well as in Integrative Psychotherapy, each therapeutic interaction or experiment is designed to increase awareness and to enhance full contact. When Paul Goodman wrote Volume 2 of *Gestalt Therapy: Excitement and Growth in the Human Personality,* he assumed that the readers were familiar with psychoanalytic concepts and Anna Freud's (1937) depiction of defense mechanisms. He defined psychological defenses as interruption to contact, the loss of awareness of id, ego, and personality functions of the self (Perls et al., 1951). In psychoanalytic theory defense mechanisms are the ego's defense against unwanted id impulses. Metaphorically, it is as though the individual's sexual and aggressive impulses are a beast that has to be kept under control (Mitchell, 1988). In a developmentally based, relationally focused Integrative Psychotherapy, the concept of psychological defense or fixated interruptions to contact is the result of an attempt to protect the self from failures in interpersonal relationship (Erskine, 1995a) – a significantly different concept and meaning than that used in Freudian psychoanalysis.

The relational and developmental perspectives of a Gestalt therapy have received welcomed attention in the writings of Gary Yontef (1993), as well as Richard Hycner and Lynn Jacobs (1995). It is through the clinical application of this developmental and relational perspective of Gestalt therapy that psychotherapy is possible for clients who have been traumatized and who use dissociation as a psychological defense. Unfortunately, in some settings, Gestalt therapy has become synonymous with the "hot seat", confrontation

DOI: 10.4324/9781003626718-2

of behavior, a display of aggression, or an overemphasis on self-responsibility (Erskine, 1995b). When relying on these techniques only we as psychotherapists reinforce the use of defenses such as dissociation. We may fail to value the client's sense of vulnerability and perceived need for self-protection; we may fail to respect the client's integrity in constructing his or her system of making meaning; and we may fail to realize how our interventions may increase the client's sense of shame for having his or her experiences or defensive interruptions to contact.

In my experience as a psychotherapist, I have found that "the defense of dissociation results not only from traumatic experience but equally, or even more importantly, from the lack of a protective and reparative relationship" (Erskine, 1993, p. 184). Clients who have been traumatized and use dissociation require a relationship-oriented psychotherapy that emphasizes contact through gentle inquiry into their experience, attunement to their affect and developmental level of functioning, and an interpersonal involvement that provides consistency and dependability through acknowledgment, validation, normalization, and the reliable presence of the therapist.

Dissociation is a complex defensive phenomenon which serves to maintain mental and physical stability. The defense of dissociation during a traumatizing experience allows the person using it to cognitively and/or emotionally remove themselves from the experience and to physically adapt and behaviorally conform to external demands. The continuing use of dissociation after a traumatic event enables the person to disengage from the related needs and emotions and to evade the memory of the traumatic experience and its devastating impact.

Dissociation is the predominant defensive process present in multiple personality disorders, post-traumatic stress disorders, and schizoid disorders and is used in many other less pronounced clinical situations often masked by anxiety or depression. The presence of dissociation as a defensive process provides a highly reliable indication that mental, physical, and/or sexual abuse may have occurred at a previous time in the person s life. In some cases dissociation is a reaction to early abandonment, severe sustained pain, near-death experiences, or prolonged neglect. These overwhelming experiences, usually in childhood, threaten the cognitive and emotional stability and physical security, if not the life, of the individual.

Dissociative Defenses

Defenses are erected as a protection against the discomfort of unmet needs and unexpressed emotions, which includes the pain of overwhelming stimuli. In order to get on with life and adapt as well as possible, many people need to keep these needs, feelings, and traumatic memories continually out of awareness. This results in the fixation of defenses. As these fixated defenses continue over time they interrupt an individual's ability to be in contact, both internally with self and externally with others. It is because of the fixation of contact interrupting defenses that traumatic experiences remain dissociated rather than integrated as ego function of the self.

If the traumatized person also suffered a failure of contact in a caretaking relationship, clinical experience has indicated that they will most likely be unable to integrate the traumatic experience. The needs unmet during the trauma do not get satisfactorily responded to or validated, further compounding the trauma. This begins the process of isolating the experience from awareness, and in more extreme situations may lead to isolating id and ego functions of self from awareness. The person must engage in a complex set of defenses to limit contact and encapsulate the awareness of the traumatizing experience, related feelings, and unmet needs. These needs, feelings, and experiences related to the trauma sit within the self in a separate state of consciousness like an undigested lump, neither contacting nor contactable. The fixated trauma does not become integrated with later experience and learning (Ferenczi, 1932).

Following traumatization, there is an intense need for a reliable other who can respond empathically to the extreme emotional reactions and unmet needs, be attuned to the "unspeakable", offer a realistic understanding of what happened and provide safety through continued involvement and problem solving.

Dissociation is begun because the people in the individual's life failed to provide a necessary restorative and nurturing function. In many incest situations the child was told that she "liked it", or the child's withdrawal and depression were ignored by adults. The absence of attunement, validation, and empathic transactions from a significant other results in the person developing deeply sequestered affects, loss of contact with needs for relationship and a fragmentation of the ego through a complex set of defenses resulting in dissociation.

A relationship-oriented therapy that provides consistent contact, dependability, and safety through inquiry, attunement, and involvement is essential for the successful psychotherapy of dissociative disorders (Erskine, 1995b).

Contact, Inquiry, Attunement, and Involvement

Contact is the medium through which the process of dissociation can be dissolved and the encapsulated traumatic experiences and hidden needs and feelings can be integrated into a cohesive sense of self. Contact is the full awareness of internal sensations, feelings, needs, sensorimotor activity, thoughts, and memories, and the rapid shift to full awareness of external events as registered by each of the sensory organs. With full contact, internally and externally, there is thus a continual integration of experience. Defenses interrupt full contact. They function to impede awareness internally and/or externally. Colloquially, contact also refers to the quality of the transactions between two people: the full awareness of both one's self and the other, as exemplified in an authentic and sensitive encounter.

A guiding principle of a contact-oriented psychotherapy is that of respecting the integrity of the client. Through respect, kindness and compassion an interpersonal relationship can be established that provides affirmation of the client's integrity. This respectfulness may best be described as a consistent invitation to interpersonal contact between client and therapist, with simultaneous support for the client to contact his or her internal experience and receive external recognition of that experience. Withdrawing from contact may often be identified and discussed but the client is never forced, trapped, or tricked into more openness that he or she is ready to handle (Erskine & Moursund, 2011).

The interpersonal contact between client and therapist is the therapeutic context in which the client can explore his or her own feelings, needs, memories, and perceptions. Contact between therapist and client begins to be possible when the therapist is fully present: when he or she is attuned to his or her own inner processes and external behaviors, is continually aware of the boundary between self and client, and is keenly observant of the client's psychodynamics.

Contact within psychotherapy is like the substructure of a building, which cannot be seen, but undergirds and supports all that is above ground. It is contact that provides the safety to drop defenses, to again feel, and to remember.

The psychotherapy often begins with straight conversation and engagement in a contracting process. The ongoing negotiation of therapeutic contracts is an important element in establishing a contactful therapeutic relationship. The traumas that produced the defenses comprising dissociation usually occurred in an environment where the client could not negotiate his or her own needs for physical and mental security. Instead, they were deprived of a sense of impact, valuation, and efficacy. Rather than learning to rely on negotiation as a means to achieve satisfaction for their needs, they anticipate either being completely overwhelmed or having to use strong methods of manipulation or control, including dissociation.

The use of *contracts*, a concept borrowed from Transactional Analysis (Berne, 1966), is an essential part of the initial therapeutic contact for clients who dissociate, perhaps even more important than in the treatment of other psychological problems because their mental and/or physical being has been violated.

Contracts that specifically map out the therapeutic territory in advance of the intervention are increasingly important as the defenses and amnesia dissolve. Such contracts contain clear examples of what the therapist will do and will not do, and how the client may safely stop the procedures. In the process of psychotherapy there can be a number of vividly remembered experiences that may be a surprise to both the client and therapist. These spontaneous remembrances may not be predictable and probably cannot be negotiated beforehand. Nevertheless, procedures should be agreed upon in advance as to how the client can signal that the experience is becoming overwhelming and how the therapist will stop the intervention. One client used a specific word to indicate an entire set of feelings, needs, and impending defenses; others have used gestures or sounds.

Inquiry

Inquiry is a continual focus in a contact-oriented psychotherapy (Erskine, 1995a). It begins with the assumption that the therapist knows nothing about the client's experience and therefore must continually strive to understand the subjective meaning of the client's behavior and intrapsychic process. Through respectful investigation of the client's phenomenological experience the client becomes increasingly aware of both current and archaic needs, feelings, and behavior. It is with full awareness and the absence of internal defenses that needs and feelings, fixated during past traumas, can be integrated into a fully functioning self. A secondary benefit of inquiry is the therapist's increased understanding and attunement with the client's internal process.

It should be stressed that the process of inquiring is as important, if not more so, than the content. The therapist's inquiry must be empathic with the client's subjective experience to be effective in discovering and revealing the internal phenomena (physical sensations, feelings, thoughts, meanings, beliefs, decisions, hopes, and memories) and uncovering the internal and external interruptions to contact used in dissociation.

Inquiry begins with a genuine interest in the client's subjective experiences and construction of meanings. It proceeds with questions from the therapist as to what the client is feeling, how they experience both themselves and others (including the psychotherapist), and what conclusions they make. It may continue with historical questions as to when an experience occurred and who was significant in the person's life. Inquiry includes an investigation of the client's experience of defensive phenomena that may be present and how it interrupts contact.

In the treatment of dissociation, inquiry is used in the preparatory phase of therapy to increase the client's awareness of when and how they dissociate. Inquiry involves the investigation of the client's experiences of the component interruptions to contact that constitute the dissociation. Are they using self-hypnotic activities? How do they do it? Some clients report that they roll their eyes back, get very small inside, or wag a finger.

During the treatment of a client who dissociates it may be important to assess the function of the dissociation relevant to the needs of the whole person. With multiple personalities one might ask each part: "What is your role?" Each "personality" may have a specific function to fulfill, such as expressing a particular feeling (only anger or only sadness), engaging in an isolated defense (compulsive cleaning or amnesia) or coping with life s demands (organizing or producing). Frequently, a personality serves a protective and/or nurturing function that was missing in the past and may still go unfulfilled in current relationships, such as validation, attunement to needs and feelings or providing safety and nurturing. (The film *Denial: Portrait of a Woman with Multiple Personalities* [Verheul, 1991] vividly depicts the psychological function of each personality.)

The therapist could inquire as to who failed in the developmentally necessary functions that should have been provided by a responsible caretaker. How did they fail? Also, inquiring about the client's likely anticipation that others will again fail them in a relationship. This anticipation constitutes one of the dimensions of transference – the dread of retraumatization – and the justification for maintaining defenses to contactful relationships.

It is essential in the psychotherapy of dissociation that the therapist understand each client's unique need for a stabilizing, validating, and reparative other person to take on some of the relationship functions that the client is attempting to manage alone. A contact-oriented relationship therapy requires that the therapist be attuned to these relationship needs and be involved, through empathic validation of feelings and needs and by providing safety and support.

Attunement

Attunement is a two-part process: the sense of being fully aware of the other person's sensations, needs, or feelings and the communication of that awareness to the other person (Stern, 1985). Attunement requires an understanding of the developmentally based needs and related feelings that were fixated in the traumatic experience and are now requiring expression. Yet, more than just understanding, attunement is a kinesthetic and emotional sensing of the other; knowing their experience by metaphorically being in their skin. Effective attunement also requires that the therapist simultaneously remain aware of the boundary between client and therapist. Attunement is enhanced by focusing on the client at the developmental age of the trauma and knowing what a traumatized person of that age is attempting to express, what they require in the way of experiencing needs, and their need for a protective, safe and validating relationship with a caretaker.

The communication of attunement provides a validation of the client's needs and feelings and lays the foundation for repairing the failures of previous relationships. Attunement is demonstrated by what we say, such as "that hurt", "you seemed frightened", or "you needed someone to be there with you". Attunement is more frequently communicated by the therapist's facial or body movements that signal to the client that their affect exists, is perceived by the therapist, that it is significant and that it makes an impact on the therapist.

The defenses which comprise dissociation are connected to traumas involving intense affect. To avoid the painful and often debilitating emotions, both internal and external defenses are used to repress awareness of the trauma and the related needs and feelings. Attunement is often experienced by the client as the therapist gently moving through the defense and making contact with the long-forgotten part of the self. Over time this results in a lessening of external interruptions to contact and a corresponding dissolving of internal defenses.

The communication of attunement by the therapist may be experienced by the client as validating, assuring, and comforting, thereby allowing for an expression of needs and feelings to be met with a suitable response from the therapist. Frequently, the attunement provides a sense of safety and stability to the client which enables the client to dissolve the denial and to endure regressing fully into the traumatic experience, becoming fully aware of the pain of the trauma, the failure of relationship(s), and the disruption of id, ego, or personality functions of the self.

It is not unusual, however, for the communication of attunement by the therapist to be met with a reaction of intense anger, withdrawal, or even further dissociation. The *juxtaposition* of the attunement by the therapist and the memory of the lack of attunement in previous significant relationships produces intense emotional memories of needs not being met. Rather than experience those feelings, the client may react defensively with fear or anger at the interpersonal contact offered by the therapist. The contrast between this interpersonal contact and the lack of interpersonal contact in the original trauma(s) is often more than the client can bear, so they defend against the present contact to avoid the emotional memories.

It is important for the therapist to work sensitively with juxtaposition. The affect and behavior expressed by the client is an attempt to disavow the emotional memories. Therapists who do not account for the defensive reactions may misidentify the juxtaposition reactions as negative transference and/or experience an intense reactive countertransference feeling in response to the client's avoidance of interpersonal contact. The concept of juxtaposition is primarily important for the therapist; it allows for an understanding of the intense difficulty the client has in contrasting the current interpersonal contact offered by the therapist with the awareness that needs for contactful relationship were unfulfilled in the past.

Juxtaposition reactions may be a sign that the therapy is proceeding more rapidly than the client can assimilate. Frequently, it is wise to return to the therapeutic contract and clarify the purpose of the therapy. Explaining the concept of juxtaposition has been beneficial in some situations. Most often a careful inquiry into the phenomenological experience of the current interruption to contact will reveal the emotional memories of disappointment and painful relationships.

With a dissolving of the interruption to contact, the contactful relationship offered by the therapist provides the client with a sense of validation, care, support, and understanding – "someone is there for me". This involvement by the psychotherapist is an essential feature in the total dissolving of the interruptions to contact which constitute dissociation and a resolving of the traumas and unrequited relationships.

Involvement

Involvement is best understood through the client's perception – a sense that the therapist is contactful. It evolves from the therapist's empathic inquiry into the client's experience and is developed through the psychotherapist's attunement with the client's affect and validation of his or her needs. Involvement is the result of the therapist being fully present, with and for the person, in a way that is appropriate to the client's developmental level of functioning. It includes a genuine interest in the client's intrapsychic and interpersonal world and a communication of that interest through attentiveness, inquiry, and patience.

Involvement begins with the therapist's commitment to the clients' welfare and a respect for their phenomenological experiences. Full contact becomes possible when clients experience that the therapist: 1) respects each defense, 2) stays attuned to their affect and needs, 3) is sensitive to the psychological functioning at the developmental age when the trauma(s) occurred, and 4) is interested in understanding their way of constructing meaning of the trauma(s).

The complex set of defenses that constitute dissociation were erected in the absence of a caring and respectful involvement by a reliable and dependable other person. Clients who have relied on dissociation as a protective measure experienced that they alone had to protect and comfort themselves from impinging and overwhelming stimuli. *It is in the lack of reliable and consistent need fulfilling contact by a dependable other that defenses became fixated.*

It is necessary that the therapist be constantly attuned to the client's ability to tolerate the emerging awareness of the traumatic experiences in order not to overwhelm them once again in the therapy as in the original trauma(s). Remembering traumatic and neglectful experiences may be frightening and painful for the client, therefore therapeutic involvement is maintained by the therapist's constant vigilance to providing an environment and relationship of safety and security. When the inquiring of the client's phenomenological experiences and the therapeutic regressions occur in a surround that is calming and containing, the fixated defenses are further relaxed and the needs and feelings of the traumatic experiences can be integrated (Clark & Roth, 1986).

There are times when a client will attempt to elicit attunement and understanding by "acting out" a problem that they cannot talk out or express in any other way. Such expression is simultaneously both a defensive deflection of the emotional memories and also an attempt to communicate their internal conflicts. Confrontations or explanations can intensify the defenses making the awareness of needs and feelings less accessible to awareness. Involvement includes a gentle, respectful inquiring into the internal experience of the "acting out". The psychotherapist's genuine interest in and honoring of the communication, which often may be without language, is an essential aspect of therapeutic involvement.

Involvement may include the therapist being active in facilitating the client's undoing repressive retroflections and activating responses that were inhibited, such as screaming for help or fighting back. The psychotherapist's revealing of their internal reactions or a showing of compassion are further expressions of involvement. Involvement may also include responding to earlier developmental needs in a way that symbolically represents need fulfillment, but the goal of a contact-oriented therapy is not in the satisfaction of archaic needs. That is an unnecessary and impossible task. Rather, the goal is the dissolving of fixated contact interrupting defenses that interfere with the satisfaction of current needs and with full contact with self and others in life today.

A contact-oriented psychotherapy through inquiry, attunement, and involvement responds to the client's current needs for an emotionally nurturing relationship that is reparative and sustaining. The aim of this kind of therapy is the integration of the affect-laden experiences and an intrapsychic reorganization of the client's beliefs about self, others, and the quality of life (Erskine & Moursund, 2011).

Contact facilitates the dissolving of defenses and the integration of the dissociated parts of the personality. Through contact the disowned, unaware, unresolved experiences are made part of a cohesive self. With integration it becomes possible for the person to face each moment with spontaneity and flexibility in solving life's problems and in relating to people without the defense of dissociating.

References

Berne, E. (1966). *Principles of group treatment*. Grove Press.

Clark, N., & Roth, K. (1986). *Shatter: The true story of Kathy Roth's eight separate personalities and her struggle to become whole*. Bantam Books.

Erskine, R. G. (1993). Inquiry, attunement, and involvement in the psychotherapy of dissociation. *Transactional Analysis Journal, 23*, 184–190.

Erskine, R. G. (1995a). A Gestalt therapy approach to shame and self-righteousness: theory and methods. *The British Gestalt Journal, 4*, 107–117.

Erskine, R. G. (1995b). *Inquiry, attunement, and involvement: Methods of Gestalt therapy*. Workshop at the First Annual Conference of the Association for the Advancement of Gestalt Therapy. New Orleans, LA. Available on audiotape, Goodkind of Sound (#SU8 A&B).

Erskine, R. G., & Moursund, J. (2011). *Integrative Psychotherapy in action*. Karnac Books. (Originally published by Sage Publications, 1988 and by The Gestalt Journal Press, 1998).

Ferenczi, S. (1932). *The clinical diary of Sandor Ferenczi*, J. DuPont (Ed). Harvard University Press.

Freud, A. (1937). *The ego and the mechanisms of defense*. The Hogarth Press and the Institute of Psycho-Analysis.

From, I. (1979). *Lecture notes: 1979–1980. Advanced seminar on Gestalt therapy*. (Unpublished).

Hycner, R., & Jacobs, L. (1995). *The healing relationship in Gestalt therapy*. The Gestalt Journal Press.

Mitchell, S. A. (1988). *Relational concepts in psychoanalysis: An integration*. Harvard University Press.

Perls, F. S. (1944). *Ego, hunger and aggression: A revision of Freud's theory, and method*. Knox Publishing.

Perls, F. S., Hefferline, R., & Goodman, P. (1951). *Gestalt therapy: Excitement and growth in the human personality*. Julian Press.

Stern, D. (1985). *The interpersonal world of the infant*. Basic Books.

Verheul, T. (Director) (1991). *Denial: Portrait of a woman with multiple personalities*. Stern's Book Service.

Yontef, G. M. (1993). *Awareness, dialogue, and process: Essays in Gestalt therapy*. The Gestalt Journal Press.

Chapter 3

Wayne

The Emptiness of the Unloved Child

Sandor Ferenczi published an article in 1929 entitled "The unwelcome child and his death instinct" in which he challenged Sigmund Freud's theory of a death instinct. Ferenczi postulated that a person's acts of self-destruction and their fantasies of dying had their origin in having been an "unwelcome guest of the family" (1929, p. 103). He related his clients' tendencies for self-destruction to their having been a child with a complex history of being unloved – a sense of being unloved that stemmed from a combination of disruptions in parental care, such as an unwanted pregnancy, cumulative neglect of a child's developmental needs, physical and/or sexual abuse, and the repeated failure by the parents to ameliorate relational disruptions. The following story of Wayne's psychotherapy illustrates Ferenczi's thesis while it highlights several concepts of a developmentally based, relationally focused Integrative Psychotherapy.

Wayne came to his first therapy session after losing his third job. He said that he wanted to stop using alcohol. He was in his early 50s and had been using alcohol extensively since his early adolescence. He told me how his alcoholism had destroyed two marriages and how he had grown up with parents who were "very social" and "heavy drinkers". He laughed when he told me that his parents gave him his first drink of whisky at age five. He asserted that he came from a good family because his parents were involved in a lot of community and charity activities.

As he told me about his history, his initial transactions with me alternated between two different ways of being in relationship: he was sorrowfully seeking help and he was also conflictual and argumentative. I wondered if I was observing the affect confusion of a young child (Erskine, 2012, 2013a, 2013b), if his conflictual behaviors reflected years of alcoholism (PDM Task Force, 2006, p. 140), or if he was displaying behaviors that reflected post-traumatic reactions (Erskine, 1993). As I allowed myself to emotionally resonate with Wayne's way of transacting with me, my internal reaction was twofold: if he invested in our psychotherapy, he would need me to be direct and firm with him while simultaneously being attentive, respectful, and perhaps tender.

DOI: 10.4324/9781003626718-3

Before the end of this first session, I made a quick assessment. I told Wayne that I would provide psychotherapy only if he went to 90 Alcoholics Anonymous meetings in the next 90 days. Surprisingly, he agreed. I expected Wayne to refuse, and if he had, I knew that I would not continue the psychotherapy. If Wayne was really making a serious commitment to AA, I was willing to make a commitment to his welfare. I knew that I could not provide Wayne with all the relational support that he would require if he were to abstain from using any alcohol. I needed AA to be my co-therapist. I was also leery: I wondered if he agreed to attend the AA sessions to placate me and that he would soon give up on AA. I decided that he was worth the risk. I agreed to see him in individual psychotherapy once a week as long as he immersed himself in the AA program.

Over the next several months, Wayne continued to attend daily AA meetings. In our psychotherapy sessions, Wayne often began our sessions by talking about how he was using AA's 12-Step Program (Wilson, 2002). It seemed important that we spend some time in each session on what was happening in his current life. During these first 10 or 15 minutes he would report on recent activities, difficulties at work, wanting to get "totally drunk", and how he used the AA meetings to avoid drinking. Throughout these conversations I used phenomenological inquiry to bring his attention to his physical sensations, affect, and internal images. My inquiry was aimed at helping him discover and value his body sensations, various affects, and how he made meaning of his experiences. I wanted Wayne to gain awareness of his internal experience.

In addition to my consistent phenomenological inquiry, I began to ask questions about each age of his childhood and the quality of each of his parents' interactions with him. In the first few months Wayne was reluctant to talk about his childhood memories. He was often disdainful when I made empathetic comments. When I inquired about his affect, he periodically made sarcastic remarks about his own needs and feelings. In one session he snapped at me: "Stop talking about my childhood. I don't want to know anything about my past". I talked with Wayne about how our sense of iden-tity is based on conclusions we unconsciously make that shape our life, and how each conclusion was an attempt to manage relational conflicts in child-hood. I emphasize that the psychotherapy could change his life if we gave serious attention to how he, as a child, coped with the conflicts and stress that had occurred in his early life.

Throughout the next year I often focused my inquiry on his affect and physical sensations as well as what actually happened with his parents. I asked about how they responded to his developmental and relational needs at various ages. He described parents who were "more interested in looking good" than in paying any attention to what he wanted. He began to remember examples of their verbal and physical abuse. We talked about the companionship, guidance, and respect that a school-age boy requires from parents in order to grow and prosper.

Throughout our conversations I wanted my transactions with Wayne to model the respect, care, and quality of relationship that he was needing. We identified how, during his adolescence, he "tried to manage with alcohol and sex", but that they always left him "feeling worse the next day". My focus was on reparation as we attended to his affect, relational needs, and his self-esteem – both as an adult today and, importantly, what was essential when he was a child. Wayne reported that our conversations seemed to affect how he acted with other people; he had fewer conflicts at work.

In one session when Wayne was describing his kindergarten years he said in a timid, childlike voice, "I need mama, but mama hurts me. I want Daddy, but Daddy hits me. I have no one. The emptiness feels like I am going to die". As he described the dilemma of his painful experience, I empathetically reflected on the child wanting significant interpersonal contact and at the same time fearing the rejection or punishment – rejection or punishment that is emotionally damaging to the child's sense of self-in-relationship. In response to Wayne, I focused on maintaining relational contact, being responsive to his affect and bodily reaction, and expressing compassion over the painful stories that he was now revealing. I was disturbed and worried when Wayne said, "the emptiness feels like I am going to die". His words put me on alert: I wondered if he was warning me about suicide or if he was telling me about an internal "death" – a death in the emotional bond between a child and parents.

Wayne eventually revealed that many nights after dinner he would have intense urges to "do some heavy drinking". He screamed at me, "I just need to feel the comfort the whisky brings". We made an agreement that he would postpone drinking any alcohol until we could talk together at 10 pm. Over a period of a couple of weeks, I talked to him by phone for 10 minutes almost every night. I listened to his agitation and his urge to get intoxicated. Each evening I used my voice tone and words to calm his agitation and restabilize his affect as we talked about how the alcohol was the way he learned to soothe himself throughout his adolescence.

Wayne began to realize that the after-dinner hours were the times both of his parents would do their "heavy drinking". He told me several stories about "the arguments and physical fights" and how he would be "yelled at and knocked around". Wayne described how he had no comfort in going to bed because "I could hear them fighting". He remembered sneaking out of his room to drink the whisky his parents had left in the bottle. Then he could go to sleep. By talking to him late at night, I wanted to provide, temporarily, a new form of stabilization: I provided our relationship instead of whisky.

He now had clear memories of his parents' physically violent arguments. On several occasions Wayne was the focal point of his parents' verbal fights. He explicitly remembered his mother screaming, "I never wanted him; it was you who made me pregnant". His father yelled back at her, "You tricked me into marrying you. I never wanted this kid. He is yours not mine". As he told me several similar stories of the accusations and arguments between his parents, I remained both concerned and acutely aware of the profound relational neglect of Wayne's childhood and adolescence and his nagging physical sense of "emptiness... going to die".

Midway through the third year of our psychotherapy sessions, Wayne suddenly announced that this was his last session. I was confused and disappointed, at a loss for words. I asked if he was angry at me but he gave no reason for terminating; he just left the session early. I assumed that our therapy had been going well; he had appeared to be more emotionally regulated and present. Over the next few weeks, I agonized over what I had done wrong. After several weeks passed I wrote to Wayne and invited him to return to therapy. When Wayne finally resumed to our sessions he said that "dealing with the trauma of my childhood was too much. I just wanted to drink again. But I didn't. I went to AA instead, sometimes twice a day because I had an urge to drink after every therapy session. It was all too much. I realize now that I have always used booze as a way to stop my memories from taking over".

When Wayne told me this, I had a big sense of physical relief and an important warning – a warning about the pacing and intensity of my historical inquiry. I realized that I had not provided sufficient time and interpersonal contact for Wayne to establish a new sense of affect stabilization before we uncovered more traumatic memory. I was conscious that I had to titrate Wayne's psychotherapy and remain mindful of his internal distress, even though he seldom showed signs of being emotionally overwhelmed. As I took responsibility for the rupture in our relationship, Wayne renewed his commitment to doing an in-depth therapy. Although he was not ready to "talk about other things", he indicated that there was much more abuse than he ever told me.

In our next session, I began with an inquiry about how Wayne experienced our relationship. He reminded me of the late-night phone conversations we had the previous year and how he could feel my commitment to helping him remain sober. He explained how he needed me to anticipate when he would become overwhelmed with emotional memories and to protect him "from the painful and confusing agitation that comes after I remember their abuse". Wayne told me about how differently I interacted with him than his father ever had. He described the contrast as, "You listen to me. You always seem interested in me. You never criticize me. It seems so strange, like something is out of order. I grew up with no one listening to me, no one interested in me. All they both did was slam me down. It is so hard to trust that you are for real. I keep imagining that you will turn on me and be just like them". Wayne concluded this session with, "When I quit the therapy it was because I didn't trust you. I imagined that you were just manipulating me, trying to make me feel good, so that I will keep paying you. You are strangely different than my parents".

During the next phase of Wayne's psychotherapy he called me several times requesting an extra therapy session. On each occasion he said, "You are the only one who can protect me". In each of our additional sessions he would regress to about 6 to 9 years of age and re-experience his father about to beat him with a belt. But each time we reenacted the traumas of his middle childhood, he imagined that I was stopping his father, taking the belt away from the man, and creating safety. What Wayne never knew was that while he was remembering his father's threat of beating him, I was having a fantasy of standing between the father and Wayne, physically stopping the father, and putting an end to the abuse. I imagined demanding that Wayne's father treat him kindly and explaining to the man what a boy needed from a father.

One of the other protective things I did was to advise Wayne to not attend his company's Christmas party. He knew that there would be a lot of alcohol and pressure to drink. He took my advice and arranged to be the main speaker at an AA meeting the same evening as the Christmas party. After, he was thrilled with his speech and the many compliments he received. He said with amazement, "People praised me, they respect me". He described it as one of the best moments of his life.

In one of our sessions, Wayne abruptly walked out of the office 20 minutes before the end of the session, saying, "That's enough for today". In the following session, as I carefully inquired about his experience of our relationship, Wayne slowly revealed a story about the day he rushed out of my office. Wayne said that he saw "a look" on my face that convinced him that I was about to attack him. "I just knew that you were about to pick up that book and smash me in the face just because I was talking. My only hope was to run out the door". I focused our therapeutic conversation on how triumphant it felt to Wayne to be able to "run" and escape the violence he anticipated.

Wayne then wept as he talked about having "no place to run to" when he was a child. He remembered a winter evening when he successfully ran out of the house to escape his father's hitting, but then his father locked the doors and left Wayne "in the freezing cold". At midnight his mother opened the door, said nothing, but "she gave me that horrible look that said I was worthless". We spent the next several sessions exploring his conviction that someday I would physically attack him and how his perception was constructed from a series of memories – memories that became more vivid through our therapeutic dialogue. During this phase of the psychotherapy Wayne had additional vivid memories of neglect and abuse in almost every session.

At the beginning of our fifth year, I learned that Wayne suffered from severe bowel problems. I thought that his retentive bowel problems might be related to his retroflecting his natural protest at his father's physical abuse. Although we talked about his anger, the psychotherapy we did in each of our 50 minute sessions in the office did not provide sufficient time or physical protection for Wayne to express the intense anger that I surmised was contained in his guts. I invited him to attend an intensive weekend therapy group, a group where participants had the time and protection to express intense emotions, and where there was identification and empathy because many of the group members had lived childhoods marked by relational neglect and/or abuse (Erskine, 2010; Erskine & Moursund, 1988/2011).

On the second afternoon of the group Wayne told the group members about his father's emotional and physical abuse. The group members were understanding; they surrounded Wayne with pillows and encouraged him to express what he felt. Wayne began by pushing the pillows with his arms and then he exploded with anger about how his father repeatedly abused him. He repeatedly kicked a mattress and shouted at the internal image of his father. He physically expressed his anger and confronted his father about the painful beatings his father had inflicted on him. He wept about how as a boy he had always been extremely afraid that his father would kill him if he fought back. Following the intensive psychotherapy weekend, and the ongoing work we did each week of acknowledging and normalizing his anger, his bowel functions changed. Wayne said, "I wasn't really alive when that bastard was hitting me. I was on the ceiling looking at that kid being beaten. I had no feelings. I tried to die. But now I have a whole range of new sensations in my body. **I am alive**".

As our weekly psychotherapy sessions continued, Wayne told me of two brutal events occurring at ages 9 and 12, which are good examples of how a specific memory may represent many implicit, never-spoken stories. These two events were fairly easy for him to recall because he could explicitly remember the cruelty in his father's eyes and his mother's refusal to protect him. I assumed that these two explicit stories, although actual, were also metaphors that represented many other implicit memories of even earlier times when his father was physically brutal and his mother failed to provide necessary protection. Throughout the course of our psychotherapy, I periodically brought Wayne's attention to these two stories; each time I inquired further into his subjective experience. Each therapeutic exploration brought to Wayne's awareness fragments of memory, intense body reactions, and childlike self-protective strategies. The two prototypical stories of what occurred at ages 9 and 12 provided further impetus to explore the qualities of Wayne's relationship with his mother when he was an infant and toddler.

When working with Wayne, I often had a couple of *developmental images* that helped me stay attuned to the needs and feelings of a neglected and traumatized boy. I frequently imagined a 10-year-old boy who needed his mother's protection from his father's physical and verbal abuse. Not only did he need her to stop the beatings, he also needed his mother to help him heal the wounds caused by his father's violation of the sacred bond between parent and child. Additionally, I imagined the relational desolation, the emptiness, and intense loneliness that Wayne must have sustained in having a mother who neither protected him from his father's physical and verbal abuse nor comforted him after the abuse. In fostering these developmental images, I had an appreciation of how Wayne tried to compensate through acting out his intense distress by damaging neighbors' properties, scratching cars, and stealing. By early adolescence he compensated for these significant relational disruptions by drinking alcohol to the point of full intoxication.

Wayne often began his sessions by telling me that he had been criticizing himself. When I asked about his criticism, he was vague. As I patiently inquired over several sessions, he described the criticism as a "disgusting sound". He called it "a sound that annihilates me". He demonstrated by making a hawking sound as though he were coughing up phlegm. Over the next few weeks, we worked to translate his "disgusting sound" into actual words. As we proceeded, we had to address his intense shame that accompanied the internal criticism. He was ashamed to let me hear the actual criticizing words: "I'm worthless", "I've destroyed everything", and "I'll never make it".

Each week I inquired about Wayne's self-criticism. I asked him to say the degrading comments aloud and to express the criticism with the same intensity that he felt inside. I wanted him to externalize what had been secretly internal. Each time Wayne reiterated a self-criticism, I wanted him to see my facial and body reactions – reactions indicating that I did not agree with his demeaning self-criticisms. Periodically I said, "I don't believe that description of you".

In several sessions Wayne and I focused on the homeostatic functions of his self-criticism. It became clear to Wayne that his criticism provided a sense of continuity as well as belonging and identity. As we explored the concept of continuity, he could remember the physical beatings and his father's harsh voice saying some version of, "You're worthless", "You'll never amount to anything", and "You're disgusting". We talked about how his self-criticisms were his way to not remember his father's physical cruelty and lethal definition of him. We also explored the concept of identity. His father had defined him, and in order to belong in the family, he assumed the identity his father had cast on him. One day Wayne said, "It's now clear to me that in order to belong I told myself the same shit he told me. But that is not who I am. That was his way to squash me. But I'm NOT worthless and disgusting. I am sober. I am dealing with my feelings and history. And I am doing well at work".

Wayne was often plagued by a deep sense of shame. He admitted that his attempts to disavow shame were one of the reasons he previously drank whisky excessively. The alcohol temporarily drowned his shame until the next day when he was even further ashamed of his drunkenness. Based on several of the stories that Wayne had told me, I introduced the concept of envy. At first he was confused and assumed that I was accusing him of being envious. I explained that in each of his stories, he had described how his father beat him after he had accomplished something important in music, school exams, or boy scouts. Through my use of many historical and phenomenological inquiries, Wayne realized that his father always "belittled and berated everything I accomplished". Wayne also realized that his father was always bragging about his own past accomplishments and that he was probably lying to hide his own failures. It eventually became evident to Wayne that his father was envious of his son's accomplishments.

Wayne summarized a series of sessions with, "Each of my father's criticisms, each beating, was an attempt to 'squash me'. He never wanted me to live". And then he added, "I know now that I was a brighter and more creative child than he ever was. He was cruel because he hated my success. If his hatred was envy, then he was very envious". The concept of envy allowed Wayne to make sense of his internal criticism, his constant shame, and the verbal and physical abuse his father inflicted on him. As a result of this awareness and the quality of our interpersonal connection, Wayne gradually stopped criticizing and blaming himself.

Wayne suffered from severe tension in his neck, shoulders, and upper back. His physical pain was particularly intense after some of our psychotherapy sessions in which he recalled times when his father was physically abusive and his mother ignored his pleas for help. I often managed to titrate the reliving of his parents' cruelty and neglect by slowing down his vivid remembering, focusing on what the experience meant to him, and exploring how these emotionally painful childhood events and their repercussions affected his adult life. Throughout his psychotherapy my primary task was attending to Wayne's uncovering of the long-forgotten stories of the abuse in his childhood so that he could live with internal peace and contentment. However, he still needed much more attention to the intense sensations in his body.

Near my office was a health center where they provided gentle, deep-tissue massages. I asked Wayne to schedule a massage immediately following our sessions. For the next few months following each psychotherapy session he had an hour's massage that significantly relaxed the tensions in his body. After the first few massage sessions, he reported that with the combination of our psychotherapy sessions and the massage, he was able "to have the best sleep ever". On a few occasions the massage triggered intense painful memories, and we arranged as soon as possible for an additional psychotherapy session. The massage therapist provided a valuable service in Wayne's integration of affect, body reactions, and memories.

Wayne has now died from cancer, but after concluding our psychotherapy sessions, he had 18 years in which he enjoyed life. Each year he would phone me on the anniversary of our first therapy session and would tell me, "You insisted that I go to AA. I was reluctant and I was desperate. I knew I had to change or that I was going to drink myself to death. The psychotherapy was painful but now I am content in myself and happy with life".

References

Erskine, R. G. (1993). Inquiry, attunement, and involvement in the psychotherapy of dissociation. *Transactional Analysis Journal*, 23(4), 184–190. doi:10.1177/036215379302300402.

Erskine, R. G. (2010). Relational group psychotherapy: The healing of stress, neglect, and trauma. *International Journal of Integrative Psychotherapy*, 1(1), 1–10.

Erskine, R. G. (2012). Early affect-confusion: The "borderline" between despair and rage: Part 1 of a case study trilogy. *International Journal of Integrative Psychotherapy*, 3(2), 3–14.

Erskine, R. G. (2013a). Balancing on the "borderline" of early affect-confusion: Part 2 of a case study trilogy. *International Journal of Integrative Psychotherapy*, 4(1), 3–9.

Erskine, R. G. (2013b). Relational healing of early affect-confusion: Part 3 of a case study trilogy. *International Journal of Integrative Psychotherapy*, 4(1), 31–40.

Erskine, R. G., & Moursund, J. P. (2011). *Integrative Psychotherapy in action*. Karnac Books. (Original work published 1988).

Ferenczi, S. (1929). The unwelcomed child and his death instinct. *International Journal of Psychoanalysis*, 10, 125–129.

PDM Task Force. (2006). *Psychodynamic diagnostic manual*. Alliance of Psychoanalytic Organizations.

Wilson, B. (2002). *Alcoholics Anonymous: The story of how many thousands of men and women have recovered from alcoholism*. Alcoholics Anonymous World Services.

Chapter 4

Child Development in Integrative Psychotherapy
Erik Erikson's First Three Stages

My client arrives late for our therapy session with his shoe laces untied, his hair uncombed, and his shirt stained with food. He is nervous as he shuffles into the office and plops down on the sofa. I ask him what he is feeling and he shrugs his shoulders. I have learned from past sessions that he quickly agrees with my feedback when I suggest what he may be feeling based on his facial expressions and body gestures. But I am concerned by his compliant answers. This is a pattern I have seen before whenever he is not talking about current difficulties such as his mother's advancing cancer, his financial worries, or his wish for a more interesting job. He reports that he is "used by others" at work and also by his large family. He tells me that he never says "no", certainly not to family members. He describes his boldest form of protest as silently slipping out of an uncomfortable family dinner. It seems to me as though he has no sense of will, agency, or direction in his life.

I notice during our early sessions that he frequently tears pieces of tissue into small fragments and then rolls them into little balls. At first I wonder if he is distracting himself from feeling. I observe his intense facial expressions and body posture and how he plays with the tissue like a toy. In our moments of silence, he seems to be pleased with pulling the tissue into little pieces. I ask what he is experiencing and he says, "I don't know". He immediately puts the tissue down as though being obedient to some unspoken command. A few moments later, he takes another tissue and begins to tears it into fragments.

I wonder what unconscious experience is embodied in his gestures and enacted in the behavior I am observing. At what age would I expect a typical child to retreat into such activity? To engage in repetitive play alone? And to have no words to describe what he or she is sensing? I am raising questions to myself from a developmental perspective. I think about the importance of repetitive and solitary play, the absence of self-reflective words, and the age at which saying "no" is a necessary expression of self-definition. Who is my actual client? Is it this a 38-year-old man or a 2-year-old boy? Or is it both?

DOI: 10.4324/9781003626718-4

Developmentally Based Psychotherapy

Child development theories and various research reports on the social and emotional maturation of children provide the foundations for my therapeutic interventions when I am engaging in psychotherapy with clients. The primary purpose of this article is to describe some of these foundations of a relationally focused Integrative Psychotherapy (Erskine, 2008, 2009, 2015a) in order to provide a guide for therapists providing in-depth psychotherapy. I will articulate some of the ideas and theories that influence the work I do, particularly Erik Erikson's first three stages of child development, which range from birth to about age 6. Erikson delineated these first three of his eight stages as basic trust versus mistrust, autonomy versus shame and doubt, and initiative versus guilt.

Foremost in my understanding of the physical and relational needs and developmental tasks of infants and young children are the observations and hypotheses of many people who have written about child development. They include (but are not limited to) Ainsworth (Ainsworth et al., 1978); Beebe (2005); Bowlby (1969, 1973, 1979, 1980, 1988a, 1988b); Fraiberg (1959); Kagan (1971); Mahler (1968); Mahler, Pine, and Bergman (1975); Main (1995); Piaget (1936/1952, 1954, 1960); Piaget and Inhelder (1969, 1973); Stern (1977, 1985, 1995); and Winnicott (1965, 1971). In addition, the research of several neuropsychologists has validated the way I organize my psychotherapy, including the work of Cozolino (2006), Damasio (1999), LeDoux (1994), Porges (1995, 2009), Schore (2002), and Siegel (1999, 2007). However, it is Erikson's (1959, 1963, 1968) concepts that have been a constant guide in forming my hypotheses about clients' developmental conflicts, what was missing during their early formative years, and how to be in relationship with them.

A developmentally based, relationally focused Integrative Psychotherapy, in theory and methods, emphasizes the therapeutic importance of *developmental attunement*. This presupposes both knowledge of children's emotional and cognitive development and a sensitivity to each client's unique childhood history of relationships. This includes attunement to our clients' various affects, their rhythms and attachment patterns, how they organize experiences, and their variety of needs (Erskine et al., 1999).

Developmental attunement necessitates the therapist's sensitivity and responsiveness to the brief expressions of age regression and the transferential expressions of unresolved relational disruptions that emerge in the process of psychotherapy. Such therapeutic sensitivity requires that we understand the personal and relational crises that young children live, the relational needs that emerge at each developmental stage, the physiological survival reactions and experiential conclusions they may come to, and what constitutes reparative therapeutic involvement.

Sara: Lost and Empty

Sara came to therapy complaining that she was depressed, slept a lot, and would often find herself just staring into space. She entered the office for the first time with a toothpick in her mouth. In the next several sessions, she constantly rubbed her lips with her fingers and often looked at the wall when she talked. Once we had established a comfortable working relationship, I began to make a series of inquiries, first with a variety of questions about her adolescence and middle childhood years and then specifically about her first year of life.

She eventually told me about her mother's breast infection, which occurred at the end of Sara's first month of life. Her mother had been hospitalized for several days, Sara was abruptly placed on bottle feeding, and her mother became depressed. This story helped me to understand Sara's sense of being "lost in space" and her own struggle with depression. I was forming a *developmental image* of a baby longing to nurse and craving her mother's vitality. I wondered if Sara's depression was a reliving of the emotional experience of a depressed baby or if Sara was bearing her mother's depression, or both.

Over the next two years, these hypotheses shaped my interventions. I frequently talked to Sara about what she may have needed as a baby, what well-cared-for babies may experience, and how she may have managed when her mother was depressed during her first year of life. Early in our work, she could not tolerate my looking at her; she was afraid. We spent many sessions with her experimenting with looking at my face and then hiding her face in her hands. Often, she would cry with deep sobs. Later, when I inquired about her crying, she said that she had "no thoughts or words".

As our emotional connection deepened, Sara said that she feared I would disappear. She required reassurance that I was healthy. She suffered when we had a break in our weekly, and sometimes twice weekly, appointments. Eventually, she insisted on holding my hand "just to know you are real". She asked me to sit near her on the couch so that she could feel my presence. On several occasions, she reached out to touch the contours of my face, to rub her fingers over the shape of my nose, forehead, ears, and mouth. Her touching my face was just like a baby exploring its mother's face. She would then close her eyes and touch her own face, back and forth, touching my face and then her own. She repeated this infantile form of exploration several times before she could look into my eyes.

Although our sessions had long periods during which Sara did not speak, when she did talk, she described the deep sense of "emptiness in my stomach", "an emptiness that is never satisfied". Eventually, Sara realized that she was longing for a mother who was alive and happy to be with her. As the therapy continued, I sought occasions for us to share moments of liveliness and exuberance together.

Developmental Image

In the story of Sara, I describe having a developmental image that helped me to remain aware of the relational neglect she experienced as a baby and to respond sensitively to her need for authentic presence. A developmental image is based on a combination of intuition and empathic imagination of what it is like to be in a particular child's experience and to have the quality of relationships that he or she had at a specific age (Erskine, 2008). Creating a developmental image allows us to constantly keep the distressed child in mind, to stay attuned to his or her relational experiences and unrequited needs, and to guide us in forming a reparative relationship.

However, developmental images are formed not only on the basis of empathic imagination and intuition. To be therapeutically effective, developmental images also require a thorough understanding of children's physical, emotional, cognitive, and social development – an understanding based on both informal and professional observations, the findings from child development research, and the theoretical concepts derived from such research. Developmental images remind the therapist to focus on the client's early life, his or her unrequited needs, and the relational crises that may have occurred at various ages. This is especially important in sessions during which the client becomes immersed in current events in his or her life.

Erik Erikson's Developmental Observations

Josef Breuer and Sigmund Freud, in *Studies on Hysteria* (1893–1895/1955), were among the first to report on how early emotionally disruptive childhood experiences shape adult life. Freud (1894/1962, 1915/1957) went on to describe how childhood traumas are defensively "repressed" and thus unconsciously influence an adult's behaviors, attitudes, and emotions. In reflecting the social pressures of Vienna prior to 1900, he defined five psychosexual stages of development: oral, anal, phallic, latent, and genital (Freud, 1905/1953). Although not dominant in my treatment planning, I periodically consider aspects of Freud's psychosexual stages as a broad guide in assessing the psychological age of my clients and in seeking age-appropriate interventions.

Erikson theorized that human development progresses through a life cycle composed of eight developmental stages, ranging from infancy to old age, in which each stage marks a new dimension of personal and social integration. These describe a new dimension in an individual's phenomenological sense of himself or herself as well as how he or she interacts in relationship with others (Erikson, 1959, 1964). This ever-evolving and integrating sense of self is the result of resolving specific personal and relational crises that an individual faces at various developmental ages.

Erikson (1958, 1969) referred to this process of psychological maturation as the *quest for identity*, a term that indicates a process that extends over several developmental stages. Progression toward a healthy personality depends on the successful mastery of personal and relational tasks at each stage of development (Erskine, 1971). Erikson (1968) called each of these personal and relational tasks a *developmental crisis*, a "turning point, a crucial period of increased vulnerability and heightened potential" (p. 96) and, therefore, either a source of internal strength and growth or a source of confusion, maladjustment, and interpersonal conflict.

In infancy, identity is not a mental construct. Rather, it is physiological in that the baby's nervous system may crave, tolerate, or be repulsed by the caretaker's touch. This is reflected in Bowlby's (1969, 1973) descriptions of young children's physical bonding and relational disruptions. The early infancy physiological sense of self, together with the presymbolic experiences of the preschool years and the experiential conclusions and explicit decisions of the school years, are all foundations on which later adolescent identity is formed.

Erikson (1968) said that successful passage through each stage is not an achievement secured once and for all, but rather a sense of accomplishing the developmental task of that age. This sense of accomplishment is not a cognitive or linguistic experience but rather a physically felt experience of security, agency, and/or self-esteem that is consistent with that age. In describing the eight epigenetic developmental stages, Erikson purposefully prefaced each stage's descriptive title with the phrase "a sense of". It is this phenomenological sensation of having achieved or of having been frustrated in accomplishing the stage's task that is important in determining successful development in succeeding stages.

Erikson's (1959) theory is relational in that at each stage the child's mastery of a specific developmental crisis depends on the quality of the parents' presence and involvement; it is epigenetic in that each stage involves both antecedents of previous developmental experiences and the precursors of future stages. For example, trust and mistrust issues will arise repeatedly throughout every stage of development, not just in the first year of life. And, although the formation of identity is at its peak in late adolescence, an aspect of identity begins in infancy when the task of basic trust is predominant. By combining his own insights on child development with Freud's psychosexual stages, Erikson (1946, 1959, 1963, 1968) was able to conceptualize developmental progression as an interaction of biological, psychological, and relational variables that continue throughout the life span, which differed from Freud's static concept of child development. Each of Erikson's stages presents a new form of personal expression and relational engagement that lays the foundation for successive stages. At the same time, future developmental stages have a rudimentary influence on the current developmental stage (Erskine, 1971).

Significant in a child's development are the reciprocal relationships between parents and children (Erskine, 1971). For example, as the infant struggles with issues of trust and mistrust, his or her parents are grappling with issues of generativity, that is, caring for children, negotiating marriage, managing finances, and engaging in employment. The earlier description of Sara's psychotherapy illustrates Erikson's concept of child-parent reciprocity and the effects of the parents' affect and behavior on the child as well as Freud's concept that orality is the essential quality of infancy.

Erikson's (1953, 1959, 1963, 1968, 1971) writings also provide an understanding of the long-term negative effects of childhood relational disruptions and serve as a guide in forming psychotherapy inquiry and shaping a reparative therapeutic relationship. For instance, when an adult client has difficulty with creativity or finishing projects, I often think about the 4- or 5-year-old child's relational need for an adult companion who shares in the child's industrious activity. I may make several historical and phenomenological inquiries about the nature of the child's play time, the creative projects in which he or she engaged, who shared his or her interests, and whether the significant adults were supportive and enthusiastic about the child's play activities or if the child was criticized for or prohibited in exuberant play. Such information allows me to be instrumental in helping the client express appreciation for the need-fulfilling relationships that he or she may have had as a kindergarten-age child – or, alternatively, to therapeutically grieve and/or express anger at the lack of relationship with significant others. A developmentally attuned understanding may then lead me to demonstrate an active interest in the client's projects, hopes, and plans and thereby to create a reparative therapeutic relationship (Erskine & Moursund, 1988/2011; Moursund & Erskine, 2003).

Trust Versus Mistrust

Erikson (1963) placed the foundation for all later development on the first year of life and the corresponding crisis of basic trust versus mistrust. He wrote that even prior to the infant's birth, the mother's attitudes toward her child throughout pregnancy and delivery have an effect on the newborn's responses. Once the child is born, symbiosis with the mother's body is replaced by a mutual activation between mother and infant. Fairbairn (1952), Winnicott (1965, 1971), and Stern (1985) described how an infant is capable of experiencing relationship from the very beginning of life and that the quality of the infant's experiences depends on interpersonal contact with significant others.

The interpersonal contact and reciprocity of giving and receiving permits the mother to respond to the needs and demands of the baby's body and mind. When the infant's needs for nurturing touch, comfort, and security are largely satisfied under this reciprocal relationship, the child learns to trust the mother, himself or herself, and the world. Erikson (1963) emphasized this point by saying that the parents "must be able to represent to the child a deep, almost somatic conviction that there is a meaning to what they are doing" (p. 249). The parents' consistency, reliability, and dependability communicate to the child that he or she is safe and that his or her basic and vital needs will be met, at least most of the time. This intermix of trust and mistrust is echoed by Winnicott's (1965) often quoted idea of the "good-enough mother" (p. 117).

Because the infant still lacks body image and object permanence, his or her sense of trust or distrust is non-specific. It applies to all persons, including the self that is still undifferentiated from the maternal world. A mother who is consistently stabilizing and who regulates the infant's affect and physical needs is experienced as a sense of trust in both self and the external world. An emerging sense of trust leads to the establishment of hope. A mother who is inconsistent or neglectful is experienced by the child with a sense of distrust in himself or herself and in relationships. Distrust of an unreliable mother becomes self-distrust because the infant does not sense his or her mother as separate from himself or herself.

Developmental psychologist Jean Piaget said that during this early "sensory-motor" stage the infant is not aware of cause and effect; self-focused sensations are all that exist (Maier, 1969). Therefore, "the failure of the parent to provide the basis of trust is the infant's failure since he is not 'cognitively' able to perceive his existence as separate from his parents" (Erskine, 1971, p. 39). In my experience, the absence of a secure and trusting relational foundation may result in clients having a physiologically based, indescribable sense of hopelessness. When adult clients talk about a sense of hopelessness – an internal sense of despair that exists even when their life is going well – I am inclined to focus on their first year of life. I begin by inquiring how they receive another person's touch and physical closeness, and I am interested to know if they have a sense of comfort and emotional stabilization through physical closeness or if they feel agitated by such intimacy. I may then inquire about the quality of the infant-mother relationship in significant aspects of baby care: feeding, diaper changing, bathing, play, and sleep time.

If a young child's sense of attachment is infused with a greater degree of mistrust than trust, later in life he or she may react disagreeably to even minor inconsistencies in someone else's behavior and use those inconsistencies as evidence that the person should not be trusted (Erskine, 2015b). If, on the other hand, the child has gained a sense of trust and it has been reinforced over several developmental ages, then in adult life he or she may see such inconsistencies as insignificant and a normal part of life.

I am particularly interested when clients perceive inconsistencies in my behavior or affect that lead them to mistrust me. I want to know how their perception stimulated and influenced this sense of mistrust and devote time to exploring how my behavior may have been an impetus for their lack of trust in our relationship. It is important for me to take responsibility for my inconsistencies and/or therapeutic errors before we investigate any possible early childhood sense of mistrust. It is essential that we work within our current person-to-person relationship to establish (as much as possible) a secure interpersonal connection before investigating the qualities of their early mother-infant relationship.

During the same era that Erikson was working, Bowlby (1969, 1973, 1980) also wrote about early child development. He described the biological imperative of prolonged physical and affective bonding in the creation of a visceral core from which all experiences of self and others emerge. Both Bowlby's and Erikson's writings delineate the unconscious relational patterns that are generalized from experiences in infancy and early childhood (Erskine, 2009). Bowlby proposed that healthy development emerges from the mutuality of a child's and a caretaker's reciprocal enjoyment in their physical connection and affective relationship. Mothers who are attuned to their baby's affect and rhythm, who are sensitive to misattunements and quick to correct their errors of attunement, establish for their infant a *secure base* (Bowlby, 1988b). It is these qualities of interpersonal contact, communication of affect, and reparation that are of utmost importance in forming secure relationships, a sense of mastery, and resilience in later life (Ainsworth et al., 1978).

Bowlby's comments provide an outline of what a relationally focused integrative psychotherapist actually does with clients, that is, we create a secure base. Just as with involved, responsive parents, we attune to our clients' affects and rhythms, are sensitive to and take responsibility for our misattunements, correct our errors, strive to establish and maintain emotional and physical stability, create relational safety, and enjoy who they are (Tronick, 1989).

Bowlby (1973) articulated how the quality of a young child's relationship with his or her parents provides "a sense of how acceptable or unacceptable he himself is in the eyes of attachment figures" (p. 203). These repeated experiences establish *internal working models* that unconsciously determine anticipation, emotional and behavioral responses to others, the nature of fantasy, and the quality of interpersonal transactions. Stern (1995) referred to these same phenomena with the term *schemes of ways of being-with-another*. Both Bowlby and Stern were describing subsymbolic procedural forms of memory – memory that is not available to conscious thought although it is expressed in physiological sensations, affect, and relationships.

Bowlby went on to describe insecure attachments as the psychological result of disruptions in bonding within dependent relationships. Repeated experiences of security or lack of security in the first few months of life are what Erikson (1963) was referring to when he described this period of development as a time of trust versus mistrust.

Although Eric Berne provided no indication that he was aware of Bowlby's early research findings and theoretical ideas, he was well aware of Erikson's emphasis on the formation of trust or mistrust in the first two years of life. Berne (1961) described the relational disruptions in infancy as the "primal dramas of childhood" (p. 116), which resulted in an "extensive unconscious life plan" (p. 123). Berne used the terms *protocol* and *palimpsests* to describe the infant and early childhood interactions between a child and his or her caretakers that are imprinted as presymbolic, subsymbolic, and procedural forms of memory that form "unconscious relational patterns" (Erskine, 2015a) that later in life interfere with health maintenance, problem solving, and relationships with people – the early basis of a life script.

Winnicott referred to this early period in a child's life as a time when body memories are formed even though the infant is non-conscious and does not have a fully formed sense of "me". The infant is only aware of sensation, but body sensations are the neurological substructure of the child's emerging sense of trust and mistrust (Porges, 2009). Winnicott (1965) wrote that the baby is always struggling with the contrast between spontaneously expressing needs and having them fulfilled versus reacting to the demands from outside that interrupt the baby's "continuity of being. ... [W]hen reacting, an infant is not 'being'" (p. 185).

Incidents of relational disruption will undoubtedly occur between children and caretakers. Such reactions denote moments of disruption in the baby's sense of relying on the caretaker. The impediments to trust happen through recurring relational disruptions, wherein the child has an ongoing sense of a lack of security. Such a lack of security, mistrust, and the sense of needs not satisfied is not thought about or cognitive. Such body senses are subsymbolic, procedural forms of memory that are established when the child is preverbal. But these physiological sensations may last a lifetime and are influential in shaping relationships later in life.

Fraiberg's (1982/1983) research showed that behavioral signs of infant and parent relational disruptions are evident in the first few months of life. To paraphrase Fraiberg, these self-stabilizing survival reactions include infants freezing their body movements, flailing in agitation with their arms and legs, turning away from face-to-face contact, and transforming their affect. We may see subtle versions of these same self-stabilizing dynamics in adult clients when they tighten their bodies, agitate, avoid eye contact, or deflect from their feelings. Such behaviors may signal unresolved relational disruptions in early childhood.

Applying Developmental Concepts in Practice

In the first couple of months of psychotherapy, Sheila sat in my office biting her fingernails and constantly shaking her foot. Not only was she physically agitated, she also had great difficulty talking about her internal experience. She could freely tell me about her social interactions with other people during the previous week but usually without any eye contact. If I made more than one or two phenomenological inquiries, she would tighten the muscles in her face, shoulders, and chest and become silent.

Often in the first few months, I thought about Sheila's repetitive body gestures, her tense muscles, and how these behaviors might be an adult's manifestation of an infant's gestures of agitated flailing, physical freezing, and turning away from contact – desperate attempts at self-stabilization when a significant caretaker fails to provide the physical and emotional stabilization necessary for the infant to develop a basic sense of trust (Fraiberg, 1982/1983).

Pacing my developmental investigation with only a few historical questions in each session, we began to slowly construct, over the next nine months, the story of her first two years of life with a mother whom she described (with information provided by her two aunts) as "often high-strung, upset, and distressed". Gradually, Sheila was able to tolerate my inquiries about her body sensations, variety of affects, fantasies, and how she coped, even as a toddler, with what she described as an "uptight mother" who had constant fights with her alcoholic father. She described family stories about how her mother would leave her in a playpen all day until her father came home to change her diaper and eventually feed her. She had a recurring image of being strapped into a high chair, crying to be let out, and "then just giving up".

Sheila said that she did not remember the fights between her parents when she was 2, but she had a number of explicit memories of the verbal fights between them in her preschool and school years. She said, "I know in my body that I lived with constant tension" and "I could not trust anyone". "Even now it seems impossible for me to rely on anyone".

With some clients, I ask what they know about their conception, how their mother felt during pregnancy, and the quality of their parents' relationship with each other both during pregnancy and in the first few months after the birth. The client's rudimentary knowledge is usually based on family stories and fragments of information that he or she has put together over the years. Also, I may ask the client to "imagine" being fed by his or her mother during the first few months of life. I inquire about the client's "internal sense" of mother's touch, the rhythm of the feeding, the mother's sensitivity to the infant's need to be nurtured, and the presence or absence of eye contact. Did mother sing or talk when feeding or was it done in silence? I am curious to know if mother was relaxed or stressed and how my client physically responded to mother's body.

Based on what the person knows of his or her mother's personality, I ask the client to imagine those affectively charged and relationally significant interpersonal interactions (Stern, 1998; Tronick, 1989). Although most clients say that they do not have explicit memories of this period in their life, I am interested in their impressions because those are configured from physiological and emotional experiences that are recorded as subsymbolic memory. Although not based on explicit memory, such prelinguistic, procedural memories are the foundation for unconscious relational patterns that may influence the client's affect, behavior, and relationships later in life (Bowlby, 1969, 1973, 1980; Erskine, 2009). These forms of memory are not conscious in that they are not transposed into thought, concept, language, or narrative, but they are phenomenologically communicated through physiological tensions, undifferentiated affects, longings and repulsions, tone of voice, and interpersonal interactions (Bucci, 2001; Kihlstrom, 1984; Lyons-Ruth, 2000; Schacter & Buckner, 1998).

In helping our clients construct a comprehensive narrative of their life, we are working with *therapeutic inference*, which is made from assembling bits and pieces of information, emotional and body reactions, internal images, family stories, and fantasies (Erskine, 2008, p. 136). These inferences are constructed through intersubjective dialogue between client and psychotherapist about the client's early life and may not be based on verifiable information. They are composed of internal sensations, impressions, physical reactions, and emotions that determine the client's internal processes and perceptions and may shape their behaviors in adult life.

Metaphorically, I think that in a developmentally focused psychotherapy we are constructing the client's narrative in a way that is similar to doing number-to-number drawings where a picture is formed by connecting various dots. For example, just as a child drawing a line between the dots numbered one, two, ... nine, and ten reveals the image of a cat or horse, we help clients construct a narrative that gives meaning to their experience through:

- Affective, rhythmic, and developmental attunement
- Consistent phenomenological and historical inquiry
- Fragments of information
- Developmental images
- Family stories
- Judicious use of child development theory, observation, and research

Autonomy Versus Shame and Doubt

Erikson's (1963, 1968) theory states that the second developmental conflict – autonomy versus shame and doubt – occurs between 18 months and 3 years of age. This period corresponds with Freud's anal stage and is built on the foundations of trust or mistrust established during the oral stage. As the child nears his or her second birthday, a qualitatively new kind of intellectual functioning occurs that Piaget (1951; Piaget & Inhelder, 1969) termed *pre-operational*. The child has become more physically developed (walks and climbs), better coordinated (self-feeds), perceptually aware (observes family interactions), and determined to express his or her own wants (the need for self-definition and to make an impact on another person). This struggle for autonomy starts at age 2 and lasts until about 3-and-a-half years of age, although Piaget describes it as lasting until about age 7.

If the child does not have a basic sense of trust when entering the second stage, Erikson (1959, 1963) theorized that "the child will turn against himself all the urges to discriminate and to manipulate" (p. 70) and will over-manipulate himself or herself, develop a precocious conscience, become obsessive, and, in adult life, subscribe to more authoritarian attitudes.

The dominant behavior of this second stage is manifested in the child's ability to both tightly hold on to items and to willfully throw them away. At the same time, the child is developing physically with "the arrival of a better formed stool and the general coordination of the muscle system which permits the development of voluntary release as well as of physical retention" (Erikson, 1968, p. 107). In writing about this stage, Erikson expanded Freud's concept of the anal period and framed it in terms of the relationship between child and caretakers – a struggle for the child to exercise choice and a growing sense of autonomy. At this age, children are actively exploring, doing what they want, doing things their own way and at their own pace. With ongoing support and a protective environment, they form a sense of autonomy. If a child at this age is repeatedly criticized, if caretakers are demanding, controlling, or impatient, the child may be left with a sense of self-doubt.

Erikson's (1959) discussion of autonomy largely focused on toilet training. But he emphasized that the quality of the relationship between the child and his or her parents at this time is a primary factor in whether or not the child will leave this stage with a sense of self-worth and competency or will feel powerless, ashamed, and inhibited. Erikson (1963) emphasized that it is important that the child not feel that his or her will is being broken. The quality of autonomy that children develop depends on their parents' ability to grant autonomy with dignity and a sense of personal independence.

In addition to the rapid gains in muscular maturation, during this stage the child learns to coordinate a number of highly conflicting action patterns and vocalizations that delineate the world as "I" and "you", "me" and "mine, "no" and "I want". The development of language is a tremendous tool in helping children to expand their world beyond the primary mother-child relationship. Although language at this point is poorly formed and more expressive than communicative, it allows distance between mother and child. Mother can now direct the child verbally without physically having to touch him or her. The child can refuse to obey by saying "no" or ignoring her, thus declaring his or her will, an expression of the emerging sense of autonomy.

Erikson wrote that a child's "sense of self-control, without loss of self-esteem", is the basis for a "lasting sense of autonomy and pride"; it is the ontogenetic source of a sense of free will". He went on to say that "from... a loss of self-control, and of parental over control, comes a lasting sense of doubt and shame" (Erikson, 1959, p. 109). A sense of doubt and shame results from the parents' belittling, teasing, and overcontrol, which robs the child of the sense that he or she is capable of self-control and is able to direct his or her own life successfully.

David: No Will

David came to psychotherapy to resolve his career difficulties as a jazz musician and to address the lack of a permanent partner in his life. In the many months that I worked with him, it was increasingly clear that he became distant each time I was empathetic, such as when I validated his feelings or when we were saying goodbye. David's distancing was subtle, but I could feel the emotional space between us, a vague disquieting sense within me, a desire to emotionally reach out to him and, at the same time, a contradictory sense of respecting the physical space between us. Most likely I was responding to David's recurring patterns of managing emotional closeness and/or to what he may have needed as a boy.

I thought about Erikson's descriptions of how a young child grapples with trust and mistrust. Although David attended his sessions weekly, I wondered if, at some primal level, he did not trust me. In several sessions I asked how he perceived our relationship. He hesitantly talked about how he imagined that I would eventually control him: "I know you won't control me. I've watched you all these times, but I keep waiting for you to manipulate or criticize me". Those transferential transactions prompted me to ask David several questions, first about our current relationship and then about his life as a little boy.

Although he did not have specific memories of his early life, he described his mother as being "strict" and "always in control". I asked him to imagine being 2 or 3 years old and wanting to climb on the furniture. He tightened his shoulder and back muscles and immediately said, "She would hit me if I did that. She would curse at me. She would destroy me". Although David did not have an explicit memory of being hit, he said "I know it to be true". He then went into detail about how he, both as a boy and as a man, feared his mother.

David described several times in his early life when his mother reprimanded, criticized, or hit him for being "willful". He did not want to be physically close to her and never told her what he was feeling or thinking. He realized that with me he was not only enacting an early pattern of mistrust but also that he was afraid of expressing his opinions and aspirations in his intimate relationships and his professional life as a musician. David's sense of will had been stymied. My therapeutic task included creating an emotionally and physically secure interpersonal space, supporting his aspirations, validating his self-definitions, and allowing myself to be impacted by him.

Initiative Versus Guilt

Erikson's (1963) third stage is initiative versus guilt, which begins to develop at approximately 3-and-a-half years and continues until about age 6. However, the time frame may vary for some children. For Piaget, children in this same age range organize cognitive experiences preoperationally, with intuitive thought. They engage in symbolic play and manipulate symbols and toys, but they do not yet use concrete logic or transform, combine, or separate ideas (Piaget, 1951, 1952). This is the beginning of what Fraiberg (1959) called the "magic years", a time of fantasy, egocentrism, and parallel play. What children of this age do not understand in reality they create in fantasy.

This stage encompasses the genital and oedipal stages in Freud's theory. In the previous period of autonomy versus shame and doubt, the driving force behind the child's behaviors was the establishment of self-will and making an impact. The third stage is characterized by the child's capacity to plan and execute playful projects for the pleasure of being active, to self-define, and to satisfy the imagination. It is a time of purpose, direction, and repetitive manipulation of toys. Although children in this stage are full of play, exaggeration, and fantasy, they yearn for companionship, someone to play alongside them, someone who will be used as a toy and will respond to their initiative.

Successful building of children's sense of initiative is based on their increased awareness of their own autonomy, which leads to more self-direction in their behaviors. In the preschool years, children develop a clear notion of goals and how they want to achieve them. If they cannot succeed in reaching their goals, they are able to either modify them or change the method by which they intend to reach those goals.

Erikson (1953) wrote that the dominating behavior of the initiative stage is a variety of repetitive activities and fantasies into which the child intrudes, including into people's ears and minds with loud noises, space by vigorous actions, other people's bodies by jumping and climbing on them, and the unknown with consuming curiosity (Erikson, 1968, p. 116).

At this age, children have developed greater freedom of movement that allows them to move vigorously and to have a wider radius of goals. Language development has progressed so that they can ask about and understand many concrete events, although they may not comprehend diverse human relationships. Their understandings are concrete and egocentric (Maier, 1969).

At the same time, children are expanding their imagination by playing out the roles they imagine are available in life. They model their play on those adults they see as strong and beautiful. It is this imagination of the young child that provides the groundwork for the development of initiative. The selection of goals and the perseverance in accomplishing them have their origin in the child's fantasies about being almost as good as grown-ups.

Because children in this stage may not distinguish clearly between actuality and fantasy, overzealous parents can easily squelch their developing sense of initiative. If many of the child's vigorous and intrusive activities, play projects, or fantasies are forbidden, he or she begins to think of his or her ideas as wrong or bad. A sense of guilt may overshadow the child's playful imagination and resourcefulness (Erikson, 1968, p. 122). The developmental task at this stage is a sense of conviction, without guilt, that "I can be what I imagine myself to be". In my therapeutic experience with adult clients who were repeatedly hindered in their childhood play, expressions of fantasy and a self-defining sense of purpose tend to be inhibited, and they retreat to a passive internal world.

Erikson (1963) agreed with Piaget (1951) that in this stage, between 3-and-a-half and 6 years, play is necessary for a child's development. Play facilitates children's natural progression toward new mastery and new developmental stages; it is their way of reasoning about their world. Erikson (1963) wrote, "The child's play is the infantile form of the human ability to deal with experience by creating model situations and to master reality by experiment and planning" (p. 22). He went on to say that he agreed with Freud that play provides the fantasy needed to rectify anxiety experienced by the young child. It allows the child to free himself or herself of the boundaries of time, space, and reality and provides an acceptable avenue for self-expression. However, a reality orientation is maintained because he or she and others know that it is "just play".

Timothy: Longing for Companionship

After Timothy had been in therapy for 2 years, he embarrassingly described how he frequently masturbated, often more than once a day, from the time he was in kindergarten until today. He said that it was the most pleasurable thing in his life. This stimulated me to think of five developmental dynamics:

- Freud's descriptions of the phallic stage that occurs about 5 years of age
- Erikson's descriptions of the child's budding sense of initiative and play
- The importance of play in Piaget's theory of child development
- Fraiberg's description of how fantasy is a dominant form of mental activity for a kindergarten-age child
- My own observations regarding the 5-year-old child's increased need for a shared experience (Erskine et al., 1999)

These five concepts guided me to inquire about Timothy's family relationships when he was in kindergarten. He described how his mother was always busy, "too busy to be with me". His father was traveling for work. Timothy always played alone because he was not allowed to play outside the house or to invite friends over. His most vivid memory was of being reprimanded for making too much noise. He was prohibited from playing with his toys except in his bedroom. In his telling me this history, I could sense his loneliness and longing for a shared experience, and, at the same time, he was ashamed to tell me about what he was feeling and doing.

As I wove a series of historical and phenomenological inquiries into our sessions over the next several weeks, Timothy became aware of a great sense of emptiness and sadness, a longing for companionship. He recalled at age 5 hiding under the stairs, playing with his penis in order to not feel his loneliness. It dawned on him that as an adult he was still comforting himself with masturbation rather than engaging with people. He remembered how he felt restricted and could not reach out to either parent for comfort. He said, "By age five I was already a loner". This led me to inquire about the earlier years of his life. A year later he joined a men's group that met weekly. After the men's group spent several sessions talking about various aspects of shame in their lives, Timothy told the group about the harsh, cold family in which he had lived and his constant sense of loneliness. He wept in response to compassion and understanding voiced by the other men in the group.

Conclusion

The writings of Erikson and other developmental psychologists mentioned earlier serve as a beacon to guide my phenomenological inquiry and understanding about the relational dynamics of my clients' early lives. Of course, our clients will not have explicit memories of early relational interactions. The symbolic, cognitive, and linguistic areas of the brain are not sufficiently formed during the first few years to allow for explicit memory, but memory consists of so much more. Early childhood memory may be embodied in physiological sensations, entrenched in affect, or unconsciously enacted in relationships (Erskine, 2008). These memories are not available to conscious thought because they are prelinguistic, presymbolic, procedural, and implicit. However, these neurological imprints give rise to "unconscious relational patterns", what Bowlby called internal working models of self-in-relationship (Erskine, 2009, 2015a). When I am with a client, I frequently imagine myself as a curious detective searching for non-obvious clues as to what happened in that person's early life. These clues are encoded in the person's stories, fantasies, hopes, and dreams. Hence, a major psychotherapeutic task includes decoding the clues that may reveal the early childhood ruptures in relationship and thereby help provide a therapeutic relationship that repairs those relational ruptures.

Although sensitively attending to the current crisis and central events in a client's life is essential in a relationally focused psychotherapy, prolonged attention to current events may lessen the time devoted to a developmentally based, in-depth psychotherapy. However, as we know, the client's past relational disruptions are often being relived through current crises. To minimize the amount of time spent on current events in therapy, I make use of consistent phenomenological inquiry. My questions focus on bodily experience and related affect to bring the client's attention to what is occurring internally. I ask about early family dynamics, even though the usual answer early in therapy is, "I have no memories before elementary school".

Nevertheless, I often ask clients to imagine being a specific age, such as a nursing baby, a toddler learning to self-feed, a preschooler having a bath, or a kindergarten-age child playing with toys. I explore with them their feelings and associations when I inquire about bedtime at various ages, what they felt when they observed interactions between their parents, and other emotionally charged happenings in their life. I ask about who was present or absent, what interpersonal involvement happened between the child and grown-ups, and what relational needs were satisfied or ignored (Erskine et al., 1999). I encourage them to interview family members who were either adults or older children when they were between infancy and kindergarten age to gather information that may confirm or disconfirm their own stories.

In much of this work, my clients and I are using therapeutic inference, that is, constructing a story based on clients' internal sensations, impressions, and fragments of information. We are working with early childhood implicit and procedural forms of knowing rather than only with explicit memories. Such phenomenological and historical inquiry stimulates implicit and procedural memory and provides an opportunity to put that memory into thought and language, often for the first time. These are the foundations of a developmentally based, relationally focused Integrative Psychotherapy.

References

Ainsworth, M. D. S., Blehar, M. C., Waters, E., & Wall, S. (1978). *Patterns of attachment: A psychological study of the strange situation*. Erlbaum.

Beebe, B. (2005). Mother-infant research informs mother-infant treatment. *Psychoanalytic Study of the Child*, 60, 7–46. doi:10.1080/00797308.2005.11800745.

Berne, E. (1961). *Transactional Analysis in psychotherapy: A systematic individual and social psychiatry*. Grove Press.

Bowlby, J. (1969). *Attachment. Volume I of attachment and loss*. Basic Books.

Bowlby, J. (1973). *Separation: Anxiety and anger. Volume II of attachment and loss*. Basic Books.

Bowlby, J. (1979). *The making and breaking of affectional bonds*. Tavistock.

Bowlby, J. (1980). *Loss: Sadness and depression. Volume III of attachment and loss*. Basic Books.

Bowlby, J. (1988a). Developmental psychology comes of age. *American Journal of Psychiatry*, 145, 1–10. doi:10.1176/ajp.145.1.1.

Bowlby, J. (1988b). *A secure base*. Basic Books.

Breuer, J., & Freud, S. (1955). Studies on hysteria. In J. Strachey (Ed. & Trans.), *The standard edition of the complete psychological works of Sigmund Freud* (Vol. 2, pp. 1–321). Hogarth Press. (Original work published 1893–1895).

Bucci, W. (2001). Pathways to emotional communication. *Psychoanalytic Inquiry*, 21, 40–70. doi:10.1080/07351692109348923.

Cozolino, L. (2006). *The neuroscience of human relationships: Attachment and the developing social brain.* Norton.

Damasio, A. (1999). *The feeling of what happens: Body and emotion in the making of consciousness.* Harcourt Brace.

Erikson, E. H. (1946). Ego development and historical change. *Psychoanalytic Study of the Child*, 2, 359–396. doi:10.1080/00797308.1946.11823553.

Erikson, E. H. (1953). Growth and crisis of the "healthy personality". In C. Klockhohn & H. Murray (Eds.), *Personality in nature, society and culture* (pp. 185–225). Knopf.

Erikson, E. H. (1958). *Young man Luther: A study in psychoanalysis and history.* Norton.

Erikson, E. H. (1959). Identity and the life cycle. *Psychological Issues*, 1, 18–171.

Erikson, E. H. (1963). *Childhood and society.* Norton.

Erikson, E. H. (1964). *Insight and responsibility.* Norton.

Erikson, E. H. (1968). *Identity: Youth and crisis.* Norton.

Erikson, E. H. (1969). *Gandhi's truth: On the origins of militant nonviolence.* Norton.

Erikson, E. H. (1971). A healthy personality for every child. In R. H. Anderson & H. S. Shane (Eds.), *As the tree is bent: Readings in early childhood education* (pp. 120–137). Houghton Mifflin.

Erskine, R. G. (1971). *The effects of parent-child interaction on the development of a concept of self: An Eriksonian view* [Unpublished research report]. Purdue University, Lafayette, Indiana.

Erskine, R. G. (2008). Psychotherapy of unconscious experience. *Transactional Analysis Journal*, 38, 128–138. doi:10.1177/036215370803800206.

Erskine, R. G. (2009). Life scripts and attachment patterns: Theoretical integration and therapeutic involvement. *Transactional Analysis Journal*, 39, 207–218. doi:10.1177/036215370903900304.

Erskine, R. G. (2015a). *Relational patterns, therapeutic presence: Concepts and practice of Integrative Psychotherapy.* Karnac Books.

Erskine, R. G. (2015b). The script system: An unconscious organization of experience. In R. G. Erskine (Ed.), *Relational patterns, therapeutic presence: Concepts and practice of Integrative Psychotherapy* (pp. 73–89). Karnac Books.

Erskine, R. G., & Moursund, J. P. (2011). *Integrative Psychotherapy in action.* Karnac Books. (Original work published 1988).

Erskine, R. G., Moursund, J. P., & Trautmann, R. L. (1999). *Beyond empathy: A therapy of contact-in-relationship.* Brunner/Mazel.

Fairbairn, W. R. D. (1952). *An object-relations theory of the personality.* Basic Books.

Fraiberg, S. (1959). *The magic years: Understanding and handling the problems of early childhood.* Scribner's.

Fraiberg, S. (1983). Pathological defenses in infancy. *Psychoanalytic Quarterly*, 51, 612–635. doi:10.1080/21674086.1982.11927012. (Original work published 1982).

Freud, S. (1953). Three essays on the theory of sexuality. In J. Strachey (Ed. & Trans.), *The standard edition of the complete psychological works of Sigmund Freud* (Vol. 7, pp. 123–246). Hogarth Press. (Original work published 1905).

Freud, S. (1957). The unconscious. In J. Strachey (Ed. & Trans.), *The standard edition of the complete psychological works of Sigmund Freud* (Vol. 14, pp. 159–215). Hogarth Press. (Original work published 1915).

Freud, S. (1962). The neuro-psychoses of defence. In J. Strachey (Ed. & Trans.), *The standard edition of the complete psychological works of Sigmund Freud* (Volume 3, pp. 41–61). Hogarth Press. (Original work published 1894).

Kagan, J. (1971). *Understanding children: Behavior, motives, and thought.* Harcourt Brace Jovanovich.

Kihlstrom, J. F. (1984). Conscious, subconscious, unconscious: A cognitive perspective. In K. S. Bowers & D. Meichenbaum (Eds.), *The unconscious reconsidered* (pp. 149–210). Wiley.

LeDoux, J. E. (1994). Emotion, memory and the brain. *Scientific American, 270,* 50–57. doi:10.1038/scientificamerican0694-50.

Lyons-Ruth, K. (2000). "I sense that you sense that I sense …": Sander's recognition process and the specificity of relational moves in the psychotherapeutic setting. *Infant Mental Health Journal, 21,* 85–98. doi:10.1002/(SICI)1097-0355(200001/04)21:1/2-85:AID-IMHJ10-3.0.CO;2-F.

Mahler, M. S. (1968). *On human symbiosis and the vicissitudes of individuation.* International Universities Press.

Mahler, M. S., Pine, F., & Bergman, A. (1975). *The psychological birth of the human infant: Symbiosis and individuation.* Basic Books.

Maier, H. W. (1969). *Three theories of child development.* Harper & Row.

Main, M. (1995). Recent studies in attachment: Overview with selected implications for clinical work. In S. Goldberg, R. Muir, & J. Kerr (Eds.), *Attachment theory: Social, developmental and clinical perspectives* (pp. 407–474). The Analytic Press.

Moursund, J. P., & Erskine, R. G. (2003). *Integrative Psychotherapy: The art and science of relationship.* Brooks/Cole-Thomson Learning.

Piaget, J. (1951). *Play, dreams and imitation in childhood.* Heinemann.

Piaget, J. (1952). *The origins of intelligence in children.* (M. Cook, Trans.). International Universities Press. (Original French edition published 1936).

Piaget, J. (1954). *The construction of reality in the child.* Basic Books.

Piaget, J. (1960). The general problems of the psychobiological development of the child. In U. M. Tanner & B. Inhelder (Eds.), *Discussions on child development: Proceedings of the World Health Organization study group on the psychobiological development of the child, 4,* 3–27.

Piaget, J., & Inhelder, B. (1969). *The psychology of the child.* Basic Books.

Piaget, J., & Inhelder, B. (1973). *Memory and intelligence.* Routledge and Kegan Paul.

Porges, S. W. (1995). Orienting in a defensive world: Mammalian modifications of our evolutionary heritage. *Psychophysiology, 32,* 301–318. doi:10.1111/j.1469-8986.1995.tb01213.x.

Porges, S. W. (2009). The polyvagal theory: New insights into adaptive reactions of the autonomic nervous system. *Cleveland Clinic Journal of Medicine, 76* (Suppl. 2), S86–S90. doi:10.3949/ccjm.76.s2.17.

Schacter, D. L., & Buckner, R. L. (1998). Priming and the brain. *Neuron, 20,* 185–195.

Schore, A. N. (2002). Advances in neuropsychoanalysis, attachment theory, and trauma research: Implications for self-psychology. *Psychoanalytic Inquiry, 22,* 433–484. doi:10.1080/07351692209348996.

Siegel, D. (1999). *The developing mind: Toward a neurobiology of interpersonal experience.* Guilford.

Siegel, D. J. (2007). *The mindful brain: Reflection and attunement in the cultivation of well-being.* Norton.

Stern, D. N. (1977). *The first relationship: Infant and mother.* Harvard University Press.

Stern, D. N. (1985). *The interpersonal world of the infant: A view from psychoanalysis and developmental psychology.* Basic Books.

Stern, D. N. (1995). *The motherhood constellation: A unified view of parent-infant psychotherapy.* Basic Books.

Stern, D. N. (1998). The process of therapeutic change involving implicit knowledge: Some implications of developmental observations for adult psychotherapy. *Infant Mental Health Journal*, 19(3), 300–308. doi:10.1002/(SICI)1097-0355(199823)19:3-300:AID-IMHJ5-3.0.CO;2-P.

Tronick, E. Z. (1989). Emotions and emotional communication in infants. *American Psychologist*, 44, 112–119. doi:10.1037/0003-066X.44.2.112.

Winnicott, D. W. (1965). *The maturational processes and the facilitating environment: Studies in the theory of emotional development.* International Universities Press.

Winnicott, D. W. (1971). *Therapeutic consultations in child psychiatry.* Basic Books.

Chapter 5

Contributions of Gestalt Therapy to the Practice of Integrative Psychotherapy

The premier issue of the *Gestalt Review* featured an editorial by Joseph Melnik that outlined six "underlying assumptions and organizing principles" of Gestalt therapy (1997, p. 4). Included in that editorial were the concepts of field theory, phenomenology, dialogue, figure/ground, resistance as creative adjustment, and the therapeutic use of the Gestalt experiment. I agree with Melnik's statement that it is a "difficult and challenging task to try to convey the breadth and scope of Gestalt therapy in a brief editorial" (1997, p. 7). Yet, I was surprised that he gave the theory of *internal* and *external contact* only a passing reference.

In my training with both Fritz and Laura Perls, as well as with Isidor From, they each emphasized "contact" as the central organizing principle of Gestalt therapy. Metaphorically, the concept of contact is like the hub of a wagon wheel around which the other theoretical concepts radiate. Our psychotherapy methods, awareness-enhancing experiments, and therapeutic dialogue are represented by the wheel's outer rim, and similar to a wheel, the spokes support and connect the hub to the rim. Field theory, phenomenological experience, presence in the moment, figure/ground formation, interruptions to contact, and resistance as creative adjustment are the supportive spokes. These theoretical concepts and assumptions are the significant constructs of Gestalt therapy. In a 1967 lecture in Chicago entitled "Gestalt Therapy: Now and How", Fritz Perls emphasized that "Contact is the central organizing principal of Gestalt therapy".

In Laura Perls's teaching of Gestalt therapy, she referred to both her theoretical foundation and practice of psychotherapy as "applied existential philosophy" (L. Perls, 1977). Laura's philosophical perspective was influenced by the work of several existential philosophers: Martin Heidegger's (1976) concept of presence; Soren Kierkegaard's (1936, 1941) emphasis on the centrality of subjectivity (Schacht, 1973); the significance of Edmund Husserl's (1931) views on phenomenological experience; Paul Tillich's (1952) descriptions of the discovery of being; and Martin Buber's (1958) commitment to establishing an I-Thou relationship. Each of these existential philosophers was describing some aspect of either personal or

DOI: 10.4324/9781003626718-5

interpersonal contact. Laura Perls demonstrated these intricate philosophy concepts in her therapeutic work through her continual respect for the client's integrity and an invitation to meet in dialogue at the contact boundary between Self and Other. She focused on the therapist identifying and appreciating the client's various attempts at making creative adjustment to the demands and losses in their life. Her therapeutic work emphasized the client's experiencing environmental support through an interpersonal therapeutic relationship, as well as gaining a visceral sense of self-support. To enhance self-support, Laura often drew attention to the restrictions in her client's breathing and posture as she stressed the importance of physical movement.

In watching Fritz Perls work, I was impressed by the variety of ways in which he used, what he called, the "Gestalt experiment" – the client's active discovery of both their self-imposed limitations and their exploration of new ways of being. Fritz's use of the "empty-chair" experiment and the creation of "top dog – under dog" dialogues are two examples of his dynamic "here-and-now" therapeutic encounter that revealed to the client their interruptions to internal and external contact. Fritz's use of the Gestalt psychology concept of figure-ground formation was evident when he invited clients to enact each part of a dream in a "first-person" voice. Although Fritz often described individuals' reluctance to change as "creative adjustment", he was not patient with the amount of relational support and preparation time that some clients require. Fritz's therapeutic work was exciting and growth-producing for many of us, but his style of conducting psychotherapy was neither dialogical nor relational.

Isidor From, as the principal in the faculty of the New York Institute for Gestalt therapy, focused his teaching on the significance of internal and external contact, the various interruptions to contact (retroflection, confluence, introjection, projection, and egotism) and the cycles of contact (fore-contact, contact, full-contact, post-contact). From's teaching about the practice of Gestalt therapy emphasized the use of a contactful interpersonal relationship that facilitated the client's full awareness and integration of three primary functions of the self: id-function (physiological sensations); ego-function

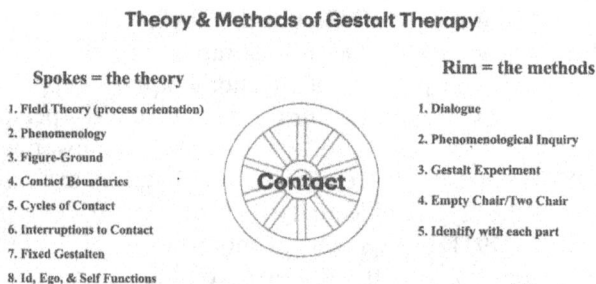

Theory & Methods of Gestalt Therapy

Spokes = the theory

1. Field Theory (process orientation)
2. Phenomenology
3. Figure-Ground
4. Contact Boundaries
5. Cycles of Contact
6. Interruptions to Contact
7. Fixed Gestalten
8. Id, Ego, & Self Functions

Rim = the methods

1. Dialogue
2. Phenomenological Inquiry
3. Gestalt Experiment
4. Empty Chair/Two Chair
5. Identify with each part

Contact

Figure 5.1 Theory and Methods of Gestalt Therapy

(identifying me and not me); and personality-function (social presentation). In his practice of Gestalt therapy, Isidor From emphasized the significance of the client's phenomenological experience and the growth producing aspects of interpersonal dialogue.

The Gestalt therapy concepts of phenomenological experience, figure-ground formation, mutual influence (field theory), and functions of the self are all facets of contact-making. Both habitual interruptions to contact (such as retroflection, introjection, or projection), and fixed Gestalten (rigidly held patterns of behavior and beliefs about self, others, and the quality of life) each represent a lack of full internal contact, and as a result, a disruption in external contact. These interruptions to contact impede awareness internally, externally, and interpersonally. These concepts provide the theoretical foundation for a contact-orientated Gestalt therapy. They also provide some of the core concepts in a relationally focused Integrative Psychotherapy.

Contact: Internal, External, Interpersonal

In Gestalt therapy, the concept of "contact" is defined as the means whereby a person's bodily and emotional sensations, physical and relational needs, and phenomenological experiences are integrated into a full sense of Self. Contact involves the full awareness of internal sensations, affect, needs, sensory-motor activity, thoughts, and memories with a rapid shift to full awareness of external events as registered by each of the sensory organs. With full contact, both internally and externally, there is a continual integration of sensations, experiences, and perception. It is through full contact that people have a sense of being alive, an awareness of both con-tinuity and novelty of experience, and a clarity of self-in-relationship with others. The coalescing of internal, external, and interpersonal contact is the medium through which archaic self-stabilizing patterns and fixed Gestalten can be dissolved; whereby disallowed affect, previously unacknowledged needs, and emotionally disruptive experiences can be integrated into a cohesive and lively sense of self-in-relationship.

Contact is the touchstone of relationship; it is what makes relationship possible. The essence of our being human is inextricably tied up in the ways we relate to others. We are conceived and born within a matrix of relation-ships, and we live our lives in the world that is inevitably and consequently populated by other humans, both externally and internally via fantasies, expectations, introjections, and memories.

The philosophical concept of "contact" is not only about awareness of internal sensations and external stimuli; the term "contact" also refers to the interpersonal meeting of people – it constitutes the building blocks of relationship. Although the term is not used in the book *Gestalt Therapy: Excitement and Growth of the Human Personality* (Perls et al., 1951), the colloquial use of the words "interpersonal contact" describes a quality of transaction between two individuals: the full awareness of both one's self and the others, as exemplified in an authentic and sensitive encounter – a meeting of the Other with both presence and an I-Thou perspective (Buber, 1958; Hychner & Jacobes, 1995; Yontef, 1993). Interpersonal contact is what Laura Peals meant when she described her practice of Gestalt therapy as "applied existential philosophy" (1977).

The existential philosophical foundation of Gestalt therapy also provides guiding principles for a relationally focused Integrative Psychotherapy – a psychotherapy that fosters respect for the client's integrity through attending to and valuing the psychological function of the client's archaic patterns of self-support, attempts at creative adjustment, and the homeostatic functions of their fixated beliefs about Self, Others, and their quality of life. Each of these fixated beliefs, these interruptions to contact, was originally an attempt to solve ruptures in relationships (disruptions at the contact boundary) and to gain self-support in situations where the relationship with others was devoid of interpersonal contact (Erskine, 2021; Erskine & Moursund, 2011; Erskine et al., 2023).

Interpersonal dialogue between client and therapist provides the therapeutic context in which the client can explore his or her own feelings, needs, memories, and perceptions. Interpersonal contact between client and therapist begins to be possible when the therapist is fully present: when the therapist is continually aware of their own inner processes and external behaviors, is cognizant of the boundary between self and client, and is keenly observant of the client's psychodynamics (Erskine, 2024). Interpersonal contact is enhanced through respectful phenomenological inquiry about the client's thoughts, feelings, memories, behaviors, and physiological reactions; it fosters the client's sense of awareness of their moment-by-moment inner experience. The client's capacity for internal contact is increased through the therapist's responses that acknowledge and validate the client's phenomenological experience.

A Relationally Focused Integrative Psychotherapy

The *integrative* aspect of Integrative Psychotherapy has two distinct meanings. Primarily, it refers to the *process of making whole* through facilitating each client's capacity to re-own disavowed affects, identifying previously desensitized body sensations, relaxing archaic ways of self-stabilization and self-protection, relinquishing script-beliefs (fixed Gestalten), and re-engaging with the world and relationships with full contact. The therapeutic focus of Integrative Psychotherapy is on the internal integration of the client's personality: helping the client to assimilate and harmonize internal fragmentations of their sense of Self and to establish meaningful relationships. Through internal integration, it becomes possible for people to have the capacity to face each moment openly and freshly, without the protection of preformed opinion position, attitude, or expectation.

The term *integrative* also refers to the integration of theory, the melding of affective, cognitive, behavioral, physiological, and systemic approaches to psychotherapy. Integrative Psychotherapy makes use of many theoretical perspectives: Gestalt therapy, client-centered therapy, Transactional Analysis (particularly ego-state and script theory), breathing and body-oriented therapies, family systems therapy, as well as psychoanalytic self-psychology, and object relations theory. The concepts and various methods of these theoretical perspectives are utilized within the realm of human development, in which each phase of life presents heightened developmental tasks, need sensitivities, crises, and opportunities for new learnings (Erskine, 2019). The guiding principle as to whether a theoretical construct or therapeutic methods is "integratable" is that of *relationship.*

If a theory or method is integratable in a relationally focused Integrative Psychotherapy depends on whether or not it incorporates the concept that *interpersonal relationships are central to life* (Erskine & Moursund, 2022). Ronald Fairbairn (1954) instituted a significant change in the theory and practice of psychoanalysis when he declared that people are born relationship seeking from the beginning of and throughout their lives. He described how the need for relationship (contact with another) constitutes the primary motivating experience of human behavior. Relationships are the source of that which gives meaning and validation to the Self.

John Bowlby (1969, 1973, 1980) expanded this concept with the idea that the quality of relationship with significant others in early childhood forms unconscious patterns from which all experiences of Self-with-Others emerge. Bowlby proposed that healthy psychological development emerged from the mutuality of both the child's and caregiver's reciprocal enjoyment in their physical connection and affective relationship.

Relationships are established and maintained through contact. These concepts about the significance of interpersonal relationship are central to the practice of psychotherapy because "an effective healing of psychological distress and relational neglect occurs through a contactful therapeutic relationship – a relationship in which the psychotherapist values and supports vulnerability, authenticity, and interpersonal contact" (Erskine, 2021, p. 212).

Contact

A person cannot have full contact with internal sensations, feelings, needs, thoughts, and memories, while at the same time pushing some of those internal events out of awareness. As a result, contact with the external world, with other people, becomes impaired because meeting another person authentically requires a full acknowledgement of one's own self. Since relationships between people are based on internal and external awareness, prolonged contact disturbance causes a disruption in the person's ability to form and maintain relationships. The result is an ever-increasing fragmentation and a growing inability to integrate new experiences.

Gestalt therapy has given us a useful way to understand how our needs shift and change in normal life. It uses the concept of "figure-ground" relationships: a vast complex of potential needs that lie in the background of our experiencing. And at any given moment, one of those needs is "figure" (Perls, 1947; Perls et al., 1951). We move ahead, not so much propelled by instinctive drives (as Freud believed), but by acting purposely to satisfy the shifting patterns of our own needs. Those needs include what will allow us to survive physically; but, they also include the psychological needs for stimulation, for contact with Self, and with Others, for creating meaning and predictability, and for relationship.

When working with the client's interruptions to contact the therapist's continual self-monitoring is essential. Drawing from the philosophical influence of Heidegger (1976), Tillich (1952), and Buber (1958), a question that I frequently ask myself is: "What is the effect of my inner affect and behavior on the client?" When I take at least partial responsibility for my client's interruptions to contact, I create an atmosphere that enhances contact-in-relationship. My ongoing inquiry about the client's experience of the effect of my feelings, behavior, value system, or orientation toward the psychotherapy provides a relationship-oriented basis for both Gestalt therapy and relationally focused Integrative Psychotherapy. When contact-in-relationship is the focus of our psychotherapy, the client can make ever-increasing internal contact with memories, needs, desires, feelings, fantasies, and the process of meaning-making. With full internal contact, the client can communicate their internal awareness to another who is involved and fully present. An interpersonally contactful therapeutic relationship provides an opportunity for healing, integration, and wholeness (Erskine et al., 2023, p. ix).

Phenomenological Inquiry and Acknowledgement

The client's increasing awareness of the existence of their interruptions to contact is the initial focus of a contact-oriented psychotherapy. Some clients begin psychotherapy with a lack of awareness of their needs and desires, with disavowed affect, inconsistent memory of their history, a desensitization of physiological sensations, and/or an insensitivity to the effect of their behavior on others. The psychotherapist's use of a respectful phenomenological inquiry is intended to enhance the client's awareness of their internal processing of affect, physical sensations, fantasy, meaning-making, and perceptions. The possibility of internal contact is enhanced through the therapist's use of phenomenological inquiry. Some examples are:

- "What's happening in your body at this moment?"
- "What are you remembering?"

- "How do you make sense of that experience?"
- "What are you imagining?"

In each of these phenomenological inquiries, the effectiveness of the inquiring is in the client's discovering and contacting an internal aspect of Self – such as feelings, memory, fantasy, or relational needs.

Phenomenological inquiry is not just about gathering facts of the client's life, but rather, inquiring about his or her subjective experience, and providing the opportunity to have that experience acknowledged and validated by an interested other. With such an effective inquiry, the client gains an ever-increasing awareness of their internal processes. Inquiry is usually 90% for the client's self-discovery and 10% as a guide to the psychotherapist.

When we genuinely listen and empathetically respond to what the client says, we provide a valuable form of acknowledgment. Acknowledgement may be a simple nod of the head that signals to the client, "I am with you: I'm attentive to what you're saying". Acknowledgement is often in the form of our next inquiry, where we reflect back to the client what they have just said as we form the next phenomenological inquiry. Acknowledgement may also include respectful confrontations that bring to the client's awareness discrepancies between affect and behavior: what is said now, and what was previously said (i.e., "You say that you yearn to talk to your father, yet you describe avoiding each opportunity to talk to him"). Such acknowledgement, if done in a non-shaming way, often leads to the client's increasing self-discovery. Acknowledgement is often followed by further phenomenological inquiry ("Do you experience any discrepancy?"). Or an inquiry regarding the client's perception of the therapist's involvement ("What do you experience happening within you when I point out what appears to me to be a discrepancy?").

Historical Inquiry and Validation

Just as phenomenological inquiry reveals the existence of internal and external interruptions to contact, the origins of contact disturbances are often revealed through historical inquiry. Historical inquiry involves questions about: *what* happened to the client; the developmental age *when* a disturbance in relationship may have occurred; and *who* was involved. A sensitively constructed historical inquiry will often provide information about the nature of previous relationships, the client's vulnerability, and the relational needs that were unmet. When we empathically respond to our client's discovering their psychological history, we provide validation of their internal experience. Historical inquiry often involves factual questions whereas phenomenological inquiry is about the client's internal, subjective experience. As we shuttle between phenomenological and historical inquiry, the client will often reveal the absence of need-fulfilling relationships, as well as the hope that "someone will be responsive to my needs".

Although we cannot verify what we have not observed, the therapist can validate that the client's attempts at affect stabilization, fantasy, or "weird" behaviors have significant psychological functions, such as predictability, identity, continuity, and affect stabilization. These homeostatic functions are attempts at managing disruptions in relationship while also serving as an unconscious request for a reparative relationship.

Coping Inquiry and Normalization

An important dimension of inquiry is through the psychotherapist's respectful exploration into the client's style of coping and how they have managed stress, interpersonal conflict, loss, or abuse. The intent of inquiry into the client's style of coping is to facilitate the client's awareness of the physiological survival reactions, implicit conclusions, and explicit decisions that they may have made when living with stress, neglect, or in relational conflicts. In such an inquiry, the psychotherapist facilities the client in being cognizant of how these old patterns of coping may continue to affect their current life by inhibiting their spontaneity and limiting their flexibility in problem solving, health maintenance, and in their relationships with people.

Normalization is composed of transactions that provide an alternative view to the client's childhood ways of understanding stressful situations. For example, one client continually berated himself with "It's my fault that my parents were always fighting". Another client talked about how she never protested against her father's constant criticism and physical punishment of her brother. With the first client I responded with, "It is common for a child to blame themselves for conflicts between their parents in order to maintain a good image of their parents". With the second client I said, "Of course you would remain quiet to avoid further criticism and possible punishment. That was a smart thing to do". Both of these responses to the client help to normalize their thoughts and behavior and pave the way for them to discover what they needed in the relationship with their parents. Normalization of the client's old patterns of coping opens the possibility for the client to change behavior.

Inquiry about the client's coping style illuminates – for both the client and therapist – the stabilizing, regulating, and reparative functions that the client has been managing alone. Our phenomenological inquiry and acknowledgement, historical inquiry and validation, as well as our inquiry into the client's patterns of copying and normalization all provide an interpersonally contactful relationship where the various relational functions can be identified and explored within the therapeutic relationship. In a relationally focused psychotherapy, we provide both the validation and normalization that fosters the client's full awareness of how they have managed the difficult situations in their life.

Therapeutic Involvement

Involvement is an essential component of an authentic, person-to-person therapeutic relationship. Therapeutic involvement is the expression of the philosophical principles reflected in Marin Heidegger's concept of presence, in Paul Tillich's focus on the continuous discovery of being, and in Martin Buber's compassionate perspective on the sacred uniqueness of the other. To paraphrase Laura Perls, *therapeutic involvement* is the manifestation of existential philosophy.

Therapeutic involvement emerges from the psychotherapist having a genuine interest in the client's intrapsychic and interpersonal worlds and then communicating that interest through attentiveness, patience, and respectful inquiry. Our involvement is reflected in our acknowledgment, validation, and normalization of what the client presents, as well as our willingness to be known. When we are fully involved in the therapeutic process, we allow ourselves to be emotionally aroused and to share judiciously our internal experience with the client because therapeutic involvement has more to do with being than doing.

Therapeutic involvement begins with the psychotherapist's commitment to the client's well-being, an unwavering awareness that the client, and what they need in a therapeutic relationship, is most important. This commitment is the bedrock that makes an authentic involvement possible. The involved psychotherapist is with and for the client, fully contactful, honest and willing to put energy and effort into helping clients achieve their goals. When we are fully committed to the client's welfare, our involvement enriches the client's vitality and helps them form a secure sense of self. Involvement is what makes relationship vibrant: two people exchanging ideas and feelings, each challenging and enhancing the authenticity of the other.

Therapeutic involvement is also about the intersubjective interplay between us, the dance of interpersonal contact. The important aspects of psychotherapy are embedded in the distinctiveness of each interpersonal relationship, not in what we consciously do as a psychotherapist, but in the quality of how we are when in relationship with the other person. Our attitudes and demeanor, the qualities of our interpersonal relationship, and the authenticity of our intersubjective connections are central in creating an effective psychotherapy. A central premise of a relationally focused Integrative Psychotherapy is that effective healing of our clients' psychological distress and relational neglect occurs through a contactful therapeutic relationship – a relationship in which the psychotherapist values and supports vulnerability, authenticity, and interpersonal contact (Erskine, 2015).

Conclusion

As we integrate the various therapeutic concepts of Integrative Psychotherapy, such as phenomenological inquiry, acknowledgement, validation, and therapeutic involvement, we rely on the philosophical principles expressed in the writings of several authors who have also influenced Gestalt therapy. Martin Buber has provided a compassionate perspective on the sacred uniqueness of the other person. Martin Heidegger's concept of presence lays the foundation for full contact in our therapeutic involvement with clients. Paul Tillich and Soren Kierkegaard's focus on the continuous discovery of being emphasizes the importance of both subjectivity and intersubjective dialogue, while Edmund Husserl's views on the significance of subjective experience provide the impetus for engaging in phenomenological inquiry. These existential philosophical foundations of Gestalt therapy provide the foundation on which relationally focused Integrative Psychotherapy is based.

Appreciation

"Thank you" to David Forrest, from Gestalt UK, for the illustrative diagram of the theory and methods of Gestalt therapy. David's website is: www.gestaltuk.com.

References

Bowlby, J. (1969). *Attachment. Volume I of attachment and loss.* Basic Books.
Bowlby, J. (1973). *Separation: Anxiety and anger. Volume II of attachment and loss.* Basic Books.
Bowlby, J. (1980). *Loss: Sadness and depression. Volume III of attachment and loss.* Basic Books.
Buber, M. (1958). *I and thou.* (Trans. R. G. Smith). Scribner.
Erskine, R. G. (2015). *Relational patterns, therapeutic presence: Concepts and practice of Integrative Psychotherapy.* Karnac Books.
Erskine, R. G. (2019). Child development in Integrative Psychotherapy: Erik Erikson's first three stages. *International Journal of Integrative Psychotherapy*, 10, 11–34.
Erskine, R. G. (2021). *Early affect confusion: Relational psychotherapy for the borderline client.* nScience Publishers.
Erskine, R. G. (2024). Countertransference: An Integrative Psychotherapy perspective. *International Journal of Psychotherapy*, 28(1), 47–61.
Erskine, R. G., & Moursund, J. P. (2011). *Integrative Psychotherapy in action.* Karnac Books. (Originally published by Sage Publications, 1988 and by The Gestalt Journal Press, 1998).
Erskine, R. G., & Moursund, J. P. (2022). *The art and science of relationship: The practice of Integrative Psychotherapy.* Phoenix Publishing.
Erskine, R. G., Moursund, J. P., & Trautmann, R. L. (2023). *Beyond empathy: A therapy of contact-in-relationship.* Routledge Mental Health Classic Editions. (Original work published 1999).
Fairbairn, W. R. D. (1954). *Psychoanalytic studies of the personality.* Basic Books.
Heidegger, M. (1976). *Basic writings from Being and Time (1927) to The Task of Thinking (1964).* Harper & Row.
Husserl, E. (1931). *Ideas pertaining to a pure phenomenology and to a phenomenological philosophy.* (Trans. F. Kersten). Kluwer Academic Publishers.

Hychner, R., & Jacobes, L. (1995). *The healing relationship in Gestalt therapy.* The Gestalt Journal Press.

Kierkegaard, S. (1936). *Philosophical fragments or a fragment of philosophy.* (Trans. D. F. Swenson). Princeton University Press.

Kierkegaard, S. (1941). *Concluding unscientific postscript.* (Trans. D. F. Swenson and W. Lowrie). Princeton University Press.

Melnik, J. (1997). Welcome to Gestalt Review: An editorial. *Gestalt Review,* 1, 1–8.

Perls, F. S. (1947). *Ego, huner, and aggression.* George Allen & Unwin.

Perls, F. S. (1967). Gestalt therapy: Now and how. Lecture, Chicago City College, Chicago, Illinois, September 28.

Perls, F. S., Hefferline, R. F., & Goodman, P. (1951). *Gestalt therapy: Excitement and growth in the human personality.* Julian Press.

Perls, L. (1977). *Theory and practice of Gestalt therapy.* Keynote address, European Association of Transactional Analysis, July 8, Seefeld, Austria.

Schacht, R. (1973). Kierkegaard on "truth is subjectivity" and "the leap of faith". *Canadian Journal of Philosophy,* 2(3), 297–313.

Tillich, P. (1952). *The courage to be.* Yale University Press.

Yontef, G. M. (1993). *Awareness, dialogue, and process.* Gestalt Journal Press.

Chapter 6

An Integrative Psychotherapy of Obsession

Diverse Concepts and Methods

"Worry, worry, worry. That's all I do", despaired my first client on Monday morning. She had been worrying for most of her life and was convinced that she would never stop worrying. Like many of the clients I was scheduled to work with that week, habitual worrying and repetitive fantasizing absorbed much of their mental activity and interfered with their capacity for spontaneity, intimacy, and living joyfully in the present. I knew that I would be attending, at least some of the time, to aspects of obsession with several of my clients throughout the week no matter what other issues we may be addressing.

Psychological problems such as repetitive fantasizing, habitual worrying, and obsessing appear to be on the rise the last few years among people seeking psychotherapy. These types of problems seem to cut across many psychological diagnoses and include some clients who would not necessarily receive a confirmed DSM-IV or DSM-V diagnosis (American Psychiatric Association, 2000, 2013). Obsessing and habitual worrying may be among the major treatment issues of our time, reflective of the lifestyle and career pressures, developmental experiences, deficits in interpersonal relationships, and issues of life script (McAdams & Pals, 2006). Obsessing, repetitive fantasizing, and habitual worrying are so common, and often so private, that these issues may go on unreported in therapy. When addressed in psychotherapy such rumination may receive only cursory attention or may not seem pertinent.

This chapter is the outcome of a qualitative multiple case study that has identified six major facets of psychotherapy that integrate both an under-standing of the psychological dynamics of obsessing, repetitive fantasizing, and habitual worrying and an integration of psychotherapy methods that are effective in maintaining permanent change to such dynamics (Erskine et al., 2001). In describing human personality characteristics, such as obsessing and worrying, Kluckholm and Murray (1953) wrote that every person is like all other persons, like some other persons, and like no other person, therefore we can often take clinical data from a few individuals and effectively generalize our knowledge to a larger population provided that we constantly monitor and also inquire into the unique, phenomenological experience of

DOI: 10.4324/9781003626718-6

each client. This chapter is a compilation of the psychotherapy methods that were significantly effective with some clients, and suggests that these methods may be equally effective with a wide variety of clients seeking psychotherapy.

The *Psychodynamic Diagnostic Manual* describes obsessions as relatively common symptoms which are an attempt to disavow affect and engage in intellectualization rather than to feel emotions, especially among more cerebral and perfectionistic individuals. Obsessing, habitual worrying, and repetitive fantasizing often indicate a person's reluctance to feel emotions associated with either being "overwhelmed" or "out of control" (PDM Task Force, 2006, p. 58).

Freud (1913/1958b) described obsession and worry as originating in early child-parent dyadic struggles. He related the stubborn, punctilious, and hoarding tendencies of the adult with obsessional neurosis to childhood battles over toilet training. However, current client narratives indicate the significance of power struggles between child and parents around rigid standards of behavior, eating, school work, sexuality, and general obedience as the childhood conflicts that underlie many obsessions and repetitive worries. In essence, growing up with relational discord is central for people who engage in habitual worrying, repetitive fantasies, and obsession.

Many such clients report that their childhood attempts at expressions of subjectivity and affect were labeled as bad or immature or not rational. As a result, many clients are absorbed with repetitive fantasies or reoccurring obsessions; they are out of touch with their emotions and are more pre-occupied with self-definition or making an impact than interpersonal relationships. They appear to be internally compelled by their rumination and often fear their own feelings and thoughts, especially if they are aggressive. "Living Machines" was the term used by William Reich in *Character Analysis* (1933) to describe such obsessive people. Obsessive thoughts are an attempt to counteract phenomenological experience that is feared to be overwhelming. As a result, such clients have trouble relaxing, joking, being intimate, and living in the now. Obsessive people are chronically "in their heads": thinking, reasoning, judging, doubting (Fisher & Greenberg, 1985; Salzman, 1980; Shapiro, 1965, as cited in PDM Task Force, 2006).

The treatments identified as empirically supported therapies are behavioral or cognitive-behavioral in nature, reflecting the greater formal or empirical research activity of psychotherapy outcome researchers of that orientation (Chambless, 2005). However, addressing and resolving the client's underlying loneliness, resolving unconscious longing for meaningful relationship, appreciating and reorienting the homeostatic functions of obsessing, dissolving archaic script beliefs and introjections, and enriching their emotional lives requires considerable time – time with an involved psychotherapist who is willing to help them explore emotional memories and express phenomenological experiences that they otherwise spend an inordinate amount of time and energy to avoid. An in-depth psychotherapy of this nature is a profoundly cocreative process that does not lend itself to empirical research. Yet clinical discussions among experienced colleagues have clarified several therapeutic facets that seem to be effective with a number of clients.

As an overview I want to briefly describe how I organize the psychotherapy of obsession along six distinct facets. I use the word "facets" rather than "stages" because the psychotherapy is not linear. Our therapeutic dialogues cycle from one facet to another in response to what is emerging in the inter-subjective process. The client and I may address one or two of these facets in a particular session or series of sessions, then move on to another facet for a while, eventually returning to a previous facet. In due course we interweave all six facets to form a comprehensive psychotherapy.

Relationship: The therapeutic relationship is central no matter what methods or other perspectives we may use. My clinical experience has shown that clients who are habitually worrying are unconsciously longing for a meaningful rela-tionship. They are lonely, yet they often carry a fear of repeating the disruptions and failures of past relationships. As a result they avoid full interpersonal contact and fill the emptiness with internal dialogue, fantasy, or anticipations.

In this first facet the therapeutic focus is on establishing and maintaining the client's sense of relational security, self-definition, and interpersonal agency and efficacy (Erskine, 2003a). This is accomplished, in part, by the psychotherapist's transactions of respect, acceptance, kindness, clarity, and patience. At the same time, the therapeutic focus is on inquiring about the client's current relational needs, his or her unrequited archaic needs, how he or she coped with previous relational disruptions, and the unconscious story encoded in the emotional transference of previous relational experiences – transference both with the psychotherapist and with others (Erskine, 1991, 2010a; Little, 2011; Moiso, 1985; Novellino, 1984).

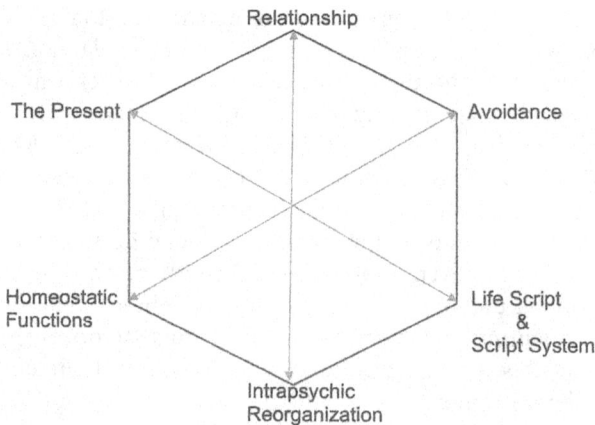

Figure 6.1 Integration of Six Therapeutic Facets

Avoidance: The second facet involves discovering what is being avoided through the repetitive fantasizing or obsessing. The anxiety associated with obsessing or fantasizing is often about avoiding one's feelings, thoughts, and/ or memories (Erskine, 2001, 2003a, 2008). People who are obsessing may focus on a specific feeling such as fear, anger, or helplessness as a distraction from what they may be authentically experiencing, such as shame, despair, or loneliness (Berne, 1972; English, 1971, 1972).

I may ask, "What would you be feeling if you were not feeling the fear in your fantasy?" or "What would you be experiencing right now if you were not distracted by what you are saying?" Some clients are clear in answering these questions and others are initially confused by them. These are the types of questions to which I often return throughout the psychotherapy. The client's answers are often surprising and lead us to other facets of the psychotherapy, to new levels of discovery and awareness.

Life script and the script system: The third facet requires uncovering and dissolving the client's life script. Life scripts are a creative and accommodating strategy to manage the psychological stress, or even the shock, of repetitive, problematic relationships (Erskine, 2010b). I usually work with the script system to help the client identify his or her accommodating strategies – the core beliefs about self, others, and the quality of life. Script system work often begins with identifying the behaviors or fantasies that generate reinforcing memories that, in turn, maintain the script beliefs (Erskine & Zalcman, 1979; O'Reilly-Knapp & Erskine, 2010). Life scripts keep people within a closed system composed of archaic feelings and needs, childhood conclusions and decisions, egocentric fantasies, and related body-tensions. This closed system interrupts both internal sensitivity to current relational needs and the capacity for full interpersonal contact (Erskine, 2010b). The therapeutic resolution of a life script involves an affective/cognitive

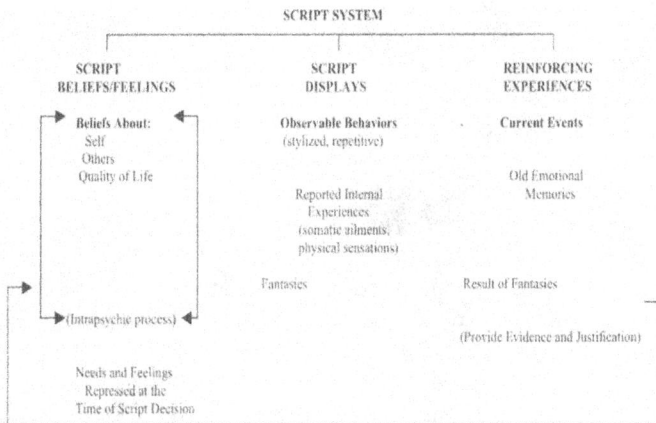

Figure 6.2 The Script System

reorganization of core beliefs about self-in-relationship. Such an intrapsychic reorganization both precedes and maintains changes in behavior and fantasy.

Intrapsychic reorganization: The fourth facet of the psychotherapy encompasses working with the client's archaic experiences via a developmental perspective, therapeutic inference, and a secure relationship that allows the client to have a supported and restorative regression. The therapeutic focus is on the client's processes of archaic self-stabilization and self-protection, his or her restrictions in physiology and affect, as well as decoding the client's enactments of implicit and procedural memories. This is where the therapy is concentrated on the feelings, needs, and reactions of a young child and the qualities of a reparative relationship that the client requires. This work may include:

- Deconfusion of the client's childhood view of self and others
- Deep emotional/physiological expression and intrapsychic reorganization
- Psychotherapy of introjection
- Working with the retroflections and inhibitions in the body

The aim of such intrapsychic work is to provide a reorganization of subsymbolic experience and archaic homeostatic functions that interfere with the client's current life. In-depth psychotherapy, when done according to the client's needs and rhythm, facilitates a physiological/affective reorganization that involves a neurological realignment of the amygdala-hippocampus-adrenal system of a nuclear sense of self (Cozolino, 2006; Damasio, 1999).

Homeostatic functions: The fifth facet, homeostatic functions, contributes an understanding and appreciation of affect and physiological equilibrium – a homeostasis that maintains both external behaviors as well as internal processes such as script beliefs, habitual worrying or repetitive fantasies, and emotionally laden habits. Obsessing, habitual worrying, and repetitive fantasizing are each creative strategies to maintain an emotional balance and to manage the psychological stress, or even the shock, of repetitive, problematic relationships. These accommodating strategies are a desperate attempt at either self-stabilization, self-regulation, self-reparation, or self-enhancement.

There are several possible psychological functions. Some other examples include *compensation, self-protection, orientation,* and *insurance against shock* of further disruptions in relationship. The repetitive behavioral patterns and internal rumination may also function to maintain *a sense of integrity* – a continuity of the struggle to define and value one's self within a variety of relationships. These examples of psychological functions reflect the person's outmoded attempts to generate and maintain a sense of psychological equilibrium following affectively overwhelming disruptions in significant relationships. They are homeostatic strategies that provide predictability, identity, consistency, and stability (Erskine, 2015; Erskine et al., 1999).

A frequently used way to stop obsessing and worrying is to say to one's self, "Stop!" Such an exhortation may work temporarily; however, a more effective way to permanently stop obsessing is to identify and maintain awareness of the archaic homeostatic functions that perpetuate the obsession and to transform those archaic functions into mature functions. Underpinning any emotional or behavioral change, I find it essential to work collaboratively with clients in uncovering the various archaic functions of obsessing and habitual worrying and then to transpose those archaic functions to mature forms of self-regulation and self-enhancement (Kohut, 1977; Wolf, 1988).

The present: The sixth facet focuses on helping the obsessing client live in the present moment rather than ruminating about the past or fearfully anticipating the future. Habitual worries and fantasies or repetitive uncomfortable memories are each an attempt to influence either the past or the future; they serve as a distraction from living in the now. Paradoxically these habitual worries and fantasies are a sign of hopefulness in that they serve as an insurance against emotional shock if something were to go wrong.

Awareness of what is currently occurring both internally and externally is a central point in the psychotherapy of obsessing. I often have the client look back over time and examine the wasted energy and lost opportunities for enjoyment, spontaneity, creativity, or adventure that may have occurred if he or she were not obsessing. In this facet of therapy we focus on fostering the client's sense of OKness through discovering and maintaining self-awareness, accepting the uncertainties of life, living in the "now", and perhaps developing a sense of universal connectedness or spirituality. As an alternative to habitual worrying I may work with the client to develop a motto such as, "No matter what the outcome, I will learn and grow from the experience" (Erskine, 1980). A principal focus in the psychotherapy of obsession is helping the client to develop present centered mindfulness (Allen, 2011; Trautmann, 2003; Verney, 2009; Žvelc et al., 2011).

An Elaborative Case

Bobby's wife had insisted that he seek psychotherapy because his obsessive worries and behaviors were interfering with both their marriage and the relationship with his two young children. He was not certain that he "needed psychotherapy" or that he even had "a problem". "I only worry a bit", he said. His body squirmed and tensed as he complained about his wife not understanding him, how hard he worked, and how some of the other men at work were "not taking responsibility". Although he expressed some concern about his marriage he was primarily worried about his firm's success and his future career. My reaction in this first meeting, and during the next few sessions, was to relax and listen – to listen with a sensitive ear, not only to his current distress, but to the stories he was unconsciously telling, to the interpersonal conflicts he had endured, to how he had coped, and for his unarticulated developmental and relational needs.

Bobby at age 36 was an executive in a growing firm and proud of his responsible position. In the first few sessions he described how he had a reputation for being "on top of things", always anticipating that "something will go wrong". He proudly described how the phrase, "something will go wrong" had become his motto for success both as a university student and on the job. The other men at work, his only male companions, teased him about being "Mr. Doom and Gloom". Yet they also expressed their appreciation for how he anticipated problems in securing materials and production.

Although I customarily inquire about each client's subjective experience, I sensed that Bobby needed me, in these first several weeks, to simply listen attentively to what he was telling me, even though he was repetitive. I concentrated on acknowledging each thing he was saying, sometimes with words and most often with my body language. I wanted Bobby to feel secure with me. It seemed crucial that he be the one to set both the rhythm and interpersonal stage for our work together. I had the impression that Bobby, like most clients who engage in obsessing and habitual worrying, was deeply lonely – a loneliness that had been with him so long that he did not distinguish that sensation from other affects.

A relational perspective and the use of phenomenological and historical inquiry, validation, and normalization would become central in our therapeutic dialogue (Erskine et al., 2023). For now it was apparent that he needed my undivided attention on, and acknowledgment of, the little nuances of emotion and patterns of attachment, or non-attachment, encoded in his stories (Erskine, 2009).

In our individual psychotherapy sessions over the next month Bobby described in detail how he had received several promotions because he could anticipate what would go wrong in his firm. What the men at work did not know was that Bobby could not sleep at night. He hesitantly told me how he would lay awake and worry about the various aspects of his job. Sleeping pills did not work to ease worrying. Slowly he came around to telling me that his obsessing propelled him to get up during the night to work on his computer or to stay late at the office. He was reluctant to tell his wife about the full extent of his constant worries and his feeling of exhaustion. The tentative way in which he was beginning to reveal his personal story prompted me to inquire about his sense of shame.

Talking about shame, even thinking about it, was painful for Bobby. He repeatedly avoided my initial attempts to bring his possible experience of shame into our therapeutic dialogue. For the next couple of months I took some time in each session to address his avoidance and to inquire about possible sadness at not having been accepted as he was or fear of being rejected for who he is (Erskine, 1994). For the first time in our therapy relationship he began having fragments of memory about feeling ashamed of his family when other kids at school were talking about their family activities. This provided us with several opportunities to talk about how habitual worry was an attempt to avoid emotionally laden memory. Throughout the three years of our work together we often returned to investigating what feelings, memories, or thoughts he was possibly avoiding, particularly when he wanted to tell me about current events or the happenings at work.

I knew from experience with clients who habitually worry that they not only avoid their feelings and memories but that they are often lonely; they fill the relational gap with mental activity. I wondered about his possible loneliness. I speculated about the nature of the relationships and qualities of life for the little boy and adolescent that he once was. I hypothesized about how he had managed, and how the relational experiences of that child affected his life today. I could see that his chest was concave; he described the tension in his shoulders and upper back. I wondered if these muscle constrictions were a "script signal" (Berne, 1972, p. 315) reflecting very early physiological and subsymbolic survival reactions, the "protocol" and "palimpsests" of a life script (Berne, 1961, pp. 116–126).

I was reminded of Eric Berne's descriptions of how Child ego states are formed from early relational traumas that are mentally registered as internal confusions, restrictions, and fears. I could feel an internal pull to be fully present with Bobby, to remain sensitive to his slightest affect, to follow his body movements, to be completely with him. I searched internally to ascertain if my feeling sorry for him and desiring contact with him was a *reactive* or *responsive countertransference*. My introspective sense was that my feelings were an emotional response to what he needed in a therapeutic relationship and that my sensations would become central in our work together.

Over the next few months it became increasingly clear that Bobby was deeply lonely. As a young boy, Bobby sat in the window most Sundays waiting for his father to pick him up for their one day a week together. His father would often be hours late or on occasion he would not show up at all; he would not even telephone. Bobby began to anticipate disappointment.

He protected himself from the emotional pain of his father's broken promises by predicting that "something will go wrong". He grew up being a "loner"; he had no close friends in school. As a child Bobby never told his mother or the kids at school about his deep disappointment in his father. He kept all the disappointments to himself, "held back the tears", and imagined various ways to avoid further disappointment.

Bobby's mother never inquired about his feelings or what he experienced on the many Sundays when his father would be hours late or not show up. He could not remember any conversations with his mother; it seemed to him that they had never talked together. Bobby's only memory of conversation with his mother was about school work or her complaints about her ex-husband's "irresponsibility" in their marriage. Bobby said that he would "tune her out" when his mother would complain about his father or criticize him for being like his father. At an early age Bobby figured out that he could not rely on any parental relationship for emotional stabilization or regulation. He learned to stabilize and regulate himself through fantasy.

At this point in the psychotherapy it was time for me to increase the use of phenomenological inquiry – a respectful inquiry aimed at increasing his awareness of internal processes of affect, body sensations, associations, fantasy, and memory. Phenomenological inquiry is particularly effective in stimulating the retrieval of implicit and procedural memories, converting those subsymbolic memories from affect and body sensations to narrative, and encouraging personal introspection (Erskine, 1993).

Loneliness and the absence of a meaningful relationship is a core issue for clients who engage in obsessing, habitual worrying, and repetitive fantasizing. The worries and fantasies divert the awareness of the need for relationship. Berne stated that "a hunger for human contact" was one of the three motivations for all human behavior (1970, p. 208). When *relationship hunger* is repeatedly not satisfied the person may overcompensate through increased absorption in the biological imperatives for *stimulus* and/or *structure*. I based my therapy with Bobby on the premise that obsessing is a response to increased internal stimulus and a compensating reliance on structure – a displacement of the "sensations that can only be supplied by another human being" (Berne, 1972, p. 21). One result of this displacement is the intense anxiety and rumination associated with obsessing and habitual worrying, what Winnicott called "overactivity of mental functioning" (2004, p. 246).

Based on this theoretical premise and many clinical observations, I approached this first year of therapy with a relational perspective (Erskine & Moursund, 2022; Trautmann & Erskine, 1999). I emphasized our mutual dialogue, although he often did much of the talking. I maintained an attitude of acceptance, respect, kindness, and patience. As the therapy progressed I used more and more phenomenological inquiry, coupled with an increased historical inquiry into his relationship with his mother and father, as well as an inquiry about his various strategies of coping with conflict, stress, and disappointment. These inquiries were paired with my active acknowledgement, my validation of his affect, and my normalization of his reactions and ways of coping with relational neglect (Erskine & Trautmann, 1996).

From time to time I worked with Bobby's transference on other people (such as the men at work) and within the transference/countertransference interchanges of our emerging relationship. Space in this chapter does not allow me to describe the many subtle transferential enactments that ensued throughout our work. Briefly, there were many occasions wherein Bobby assumed that I was not listening to him, that I would not be in the office when he arrived, or that I would belittle him. He periodically anticipated that I would "outright reject" him.

Bobby and I examined our interpersonal communication transaction by transaction to uncover what he and I both brought to our interpersonal encounter (Stolorow et al., 1987). These occasions required me to soul search and make an internal evaluation of my relational style, attitudes, and feeling. I was continually mindful that my various affects and behavior may have an adverse as well as beneficial impact on him so I often inquired about how he experienced both my behavior and our relationship. We compared and contrasted our mutual transactions with the qualities of the relationships he previously had with his father, mother, and others.

I made several therapeutic errors in my work with Bobby. He never commented on or complained about my various misattunements but he would turn his eyes away, change the subject, or launch into one of his catastrophic fantasies. At these crucial moments I surmised that I had been the first to disrupt our interpersonal contact. It was up to me to take responsibility by acknowledging that I had missed him in some important way, to identify my error, and to find a way to correct my error.

These important error-correcting transactions were significant in the ongoing development of a secure therapeutic relationship. Near the end of Bobby's psychotherapy, he talked about a few of the occasions when I took responsibility for "misunderstanding" or "pushing" him. He said that each event was significant in that "no one", neither of his parents nor any teacher, had ever "owned-up" to their errors and that when I made it my "fault", "something happened inside"; he felt "honored and cared for in a new way".

On several occasions he described what Freud termed the "transference of everyday life": he feared that the men at work would laugh at him if they ever knew about his worries, fears, or family history (Freud, 1912/1958a). Each of these transferential stories provided an opportunity for us to explore together both the current and historical context of his relationships with his fellow workers and with family members. The Transactional Analysis of our conversations and an analysis of his enactments with family members and coworkers provided the stimulus to recall both explicit memories as well as sensations and emotions that I assumed were significant memories, albeit implicit and procedural. This approach to understanding transferential enactments is based on the biological, developmental, and existential dynamics of interpersonal relating, what Berne referred to as "advantages" of games (Bary & Hufford, 1990; Berne, 1964, pp. 56–58).

When Eric Berne wrote about the script protocol (1972) and the "primal dramas of childhood" he was writing about unconscious infantile attachment patterns that formed an "extensive unconscious life plan" (1961, p. 123), a concept similar to Bowlby's "internal working models" (Bowlby, 1969, 1973, 1980). Through our transference/countertransference work it became increasingly evident that Bobby dismissed the significance of relationship and avoided intimacy; he inhibited his emotional expression, he insisted on the importance of self-reliance, and he was not conscious of his needs for interpersonal connection. Bobby avoided vulnerability. I concluded that his life script was based on an *avoidant attachment pattern* (Erskine, 2009; Horowitz et al., 1993; Kobak & Sceery, 1988; Main, 1990, 1995). It was clear to me that Bobby needed my investment in him, my involvement and presence – a responsive countertransference – if he were to heal from his avoidant attachment pattern, obsessive coping style, and lifelong feelings of loneliness.

A relational psychotherapy was essential throughout Bobby's psychotherapy, not only in this first year of therapy, but as the foundation to which we returned in every session, even when our attention was on cognitive understanding, behavioral change, or deep emotional work. I was always mindful of the little boy's loneliness and his need for a healing relationship. The contactful quality of the relationship between us provided the secure foundation on which all the other facets of therapy relied.

In the second half of this first year I increased my use of three other therapeutic operations: explanation, confrontation, and illustration (Berne, 1966, pp. 233–247). Over the years I have modified how and when I use these three therapeutic operations: Berne used them to decontaminate and strengthen the Adult ego state; I use these methods to stimulate the client's awareness of implicit and procedural memories of early family dynamics, childhood vulnerabilities, sensitivities, and developmental needs. I am always thinking developmentally and my explanations and illustrations are based on an understanding of child development. I frequently ask myself questions such as: What is the psychological age(s) of my client? How does a child of that age achieve validation, influence others, and define him or herself? What does a child of that age need in a healing relationship? How will a young child make sense of what I am saying?

I kept in mind that confrontation is only effective when done respectfully and when the client has the conviction that "this therapist is invested in my welfare". By this point in our work together I assessed that our therapeutic relationship was sufficiently secure that I could periodically confront Bobby's obsessions. My aim was to bring his attention to how he was avoiding uncomfortable sensations and memories. I accompanied these confrontations with extensive use of phenomenological and historical inquiry to activate his internal contact with feeling, needs, associations, and memories. I also focused on how he managed the relational disruptions of his early life and how he still relied on old patterns of coping with neglect and disappointment. He responded with ever increasing memories of his father's neglect, his mother's ridicule and coldness, his constant childhood loneliness, and how he tried to restore and stabilize himself with fantasy.

He was beginning to differentiate sadness from loneliness, withdrawal from anger, and how he often disavowed the fear underlying his script belief, "no one is there for me". These were the very sensations and memories that he avoided through obsessive fantasy.

In many sessions I used explanation or illustration to communicate to Bobby that every child needs validation, companionship, and someone steady to rely on; his stories revealed that his normal relational needs for security, self-definition, and agency seemed to be ignored by his parents (Erskine & Trautmann, 1996). Bobby's range of emotions and detail of memories increased with our sessions and his obsessions lessoned. The building of a secure therapeutic relationship and our attentions to his avoidance of affect, body sensation, and memory had the effect of lessening his obsessing. It was now time to concentrate on his script system and how it reinforced his life script.

Although we had addressed his script system in previous sessions, during this second year we again returned to examining his script system in finer detail (Erskine, 2015; O'Reilly-Knapp & Erskine, 2010). Interwoven with our relational psychotherapy and our focus on the avoidance of feelings and memories in Bobby's obsessions, we spent several sessions writing a description of his overt behaviors and how they were linked to other people's behavior which Bobby in turn used as a reinforcing experience to confirm his script beliefs. We paid particular attention to how each fantasy also became another reinforcing experience, the imagined evidence to support the script conclusions he had made in childhood: "I don't need anything from anyone"; "I'm the only responsible one"; "No one is there for me"; "People are only interested in themselves"; and "Life is full of disappointments".

Throughout this period of time in our therapy I used a combination of phenomenological inquiry, explanation, confrontation, and illustration as the impetus for a "systematic experiential disconfirmation" of Bobby's script beliefs (Widdowson, 2014, p. 202). As part of the overall therapy these cognitively and behaviorally focused sessions had several purposes:

- To stimulate Bobby's awareness of how his childhood reactions, fantasies, and conclusions continued to affect him as an adult
- To gather additional information about how Bobby's life script was being lived out day-by-day
- To help him understand and transform the homeostatic functions of his script system
- To assess his willingness or reluctance to relinquish his old script beliefs
- To set a more secure base for doing any reparative age-regression therapy that may be necessary

There were occasions when Bobby talked about his intense hurt as a result of the criticisms from the men at work or his anger at his wife's "demands" for more pleasurable time together. Although his description of these events had many of the elements that Eric Berne (1964) described as constituting a "game", I found it more effective to address his experience as an emotional enactment of his primary relationships as a child. Rather than confront his playing a game we sensitively explored how his experience fit the "con" and "gimmick" of Berne's game formula (Berne, 1972, pp. 23–25).

We defined the con as his unrequited developmental and relational needs and the gimmick as his archaic self-stabilizing and self-protective facade. The "cross-up" in the game occurred when other people did not display a suitable empathy and understanding that he was needing in the relationship. We investigated how his hurt or angry feelings (Berne's "game pay-off") were a replay of what he felt as a boy with his mother's criticism, neglect, and demands, and his father's disregard of what he needed. We clarified how these enactments became a reinforcing experience that once again confirmed his script beliefs.

In the midst of working with the script system Bobby told me that his mother would often tell him that his father "lacked any true emotion", that he was "irresponsible", "without morals". Bobby remembered promising himself that he would have his mother's love if he were responsible and moral. I could see the tension in his body so I asked him to close his eyes and imagine his mother sitting in front of him. I encouraged him to move his tight shoulders and say whatever came to him.

He began to shout at the internal image of his mother and tell her about his anger at her degrading comments about his father. He went on to express his anger at her "coldness" and "control". Then he shouted "You were never there for me". He repeated these words a few times and then added "and that is how I live, mom, believing that no one will ever be there for me". At this moment he burst into tears and sobbed for a few minutes. At several points in this work I encouraged him to keep talking to her, to tell her his truth, to tell her what he had never said. He then softly cried, "I am always so afraid... I'm afraid, mom, that I won't be responsible and then you will never love me".

I encouraged him to repeat what he was saying and to do it louder. He shouted it again and then said, "I have lived my whole life in fear that you would not love me if I weren't the responsible one. You are always cold, mom. You were never there for me. You are always interested only in yourself. I have lived my whole life believing that no one was there for me and that I had to be the responsible one. Martha and Robie and Sheila [his wife and children] are there for me, mom, not you. I am loved by them and I need them. With you I learned to never need... but I do need them. I am changing that, mom. I don't have to always be the responsible one. I need my family". With these final words he took several deep breaths. Bobby was disconnecting the emotional "rubberband" and making a "redecision" (Erskine, 1974, 2011; Erskine & Moursund, 2011; Goulding & Goulding, 1979). This therapy session generated a physiological and affective reorganization leading to a new sense of self.

In our weekly individual psychotherapy sessions, over the next year and a half, I often addressed the relationally neglected boy – a child of several different ages – who lacked the opportunities to express himself, who unconsciously yearned for validation and companionship, and who needed someone to help him put his emotional experiences into words. I talked to the boy that Bobby once was. If someone were to analyze our transactions during this phase of the therapy it would often appear as though I was a benevolent father helping a vulnerable and bewildered child to understand and articulate his feelings, needs, and aspirations (Clark, 1991). On many occasions I could feel the fatherliness of my relationship with Bobby. I acquired a love for him and he was slowly allowing himself to be emotionally attached to me. This new style of attachment was evident in his "longing to talk" to me when there were holiday breaks in our scheduled appointments or when I was traveling.

Early in our therapy together I invited Bobby to join a weekly therapy group. I assumed that the relational group process of the ongoing therapy group would augment our individual sessions and help to address and resolve his shame and loneliness (Erskine, 2013). He repeatedly refused. However, after the deep emotional work with the internal image of his mother, he agreed to attend a weekend marathon therapy session. These sessions, which met from Friday evening until Sunday afternoon, were a combination of relational group psychotherapy, supported regression, and some body psychotherapy (Erskine, 2014; Erskine & Moursund, 2011).

In his first therapy marathon Bobby did another piece of emotional reorganization therapy similar to what he had spontaneously done in his individual session. This time we focused on his mother's criticism of him. He was angry at her self-centeredness which he connected to his script conclusion that all "people are only interested in themselves". As he expressed his anger, he had several insights about his relationship with his mother and how he reenacted that relationship with his wife. This intensive session involved an affect/cognitive reorganization leading to an important awareness about how he avoided intimate involvement with people and operated as a "loner". The group was caring and supportive of Bobby's experimenting with new ways of being in relationship. Bobby was able to talk to the group members about his shame and loneliness. In addition to our weekly therapy sessions, Bobby eventually attended a series of three more weekend therapy marathons.

In the second marathon he focused on the absence of his father. He cried deeply, calling for his father while his body spasmed with emotion. He was reliving being a little boy and crying out, "Daddy where are you? Daddy you are not there for me". He reached out, grabbed my shirt, and pulled himself into my arms and continued to weep for many minutes. He then nestled his head onto my chest and put his ear to my heart. The latter part of this therapy was without words; it was a mixture of sounds, movement, and tender touch – an affect/physiological reorganization. In our debriefing later that day Bobby said that "something had shifted inside", that he felt "much more present and adult". "My chest is much more open".

Several months later, in his individual psychotherapy Bobby talked at length about his self-criticism, as though it was his own voice chastising him with "I'm not being good enough". We used a two-chair method (Perls, 1969) to create a dialogue between his own voice as the "criticizer" and his felt sense of being "criticized". Bobby realized that he had learned to criticize himself to make sure that no one else would ever criticize him. This therapy work had some positive effect in reducing the intensity of the internal criticism.

Weeks later, at his third marathon therapy group he talked about the internal criticism that remained. I again began with a two-chair dialogue (Erskine & Moursund, 2011; Goulding & Goulding, 1979; Moursund & Erskine, 2003) but soon discovered that the "criticizer" was no longer talking in a first-person voice, "I am...", but was now talking in a second person voice, such as, "You are useless". I began a dialogue with Bobby's critical voice; after a couple of minutes it was as though Bobby was talking in his mother's voice.

I continued the conversation and inquired about her life, the kind of family in which she had grown up, her marriage and divorce, and the stresses and fears she felt as a single parent. Our therapeutic dialogue focused first on the neglect and criticism that she received as a child from her mother. Then I turned the discussion to how she had neglected Bobby's relational needs when he was a young boy. My inquiry was guided in part by Noriega's description of transgenerational scripts (Noriega, 2004, 2009). She talked about her disappointment in her marriage, how she never wanted to have a child, and her anger at her former husband. She then confessed that she criticized Bobby because she was angry at his father, whom she described as "useless". She cried when she talked about how she had "mistreated" Bobby. In response to my inquiring and empathically responding, just as though she was my own client, Bobby's introjected mother (his Parent ego sate) was expressing the emotionally charged story of her own life script.

Near the end of our hour-long session, she told Bobby that he was a "fine son", "never any trouble", and that she was proud of him. I then asked Bobby to change chairs and respond to his internal image of his mother. He told her about his "emptiness" and "loneliness" and how she was never there for him in the ways he needed her. He cried. His body relaxed. Several hours after, Bobby said, "I feel as though there is a giant load off my back". Weeks later he reported that he had several weeks of living without any internal criticism. The absence of any internal criticism reflects the affect/cognitive/physiological reorganization that therapy with the image of an introjected other can provide for a client (Erskine, 2003b; Erskine & Trautmann, 2003).

An investigation of possible archaic homeostatic functions was woven throughout many of our sessions. From our early sessions onward, I was often silently hypothesizing about the various functions underlying Bobby's habitual worrying. Periodically I used these hypotheses to form some of my inquiries. From clinical experience I was fairly certain that Bobby would not totally stop his obsessing as long as his fantasies and related script beliefs

Script Beliefs >>>	Script Manifestations >>>	Reinforcing Experiences
Self: I don't need anything from anyone.	**Overt Behavior:** No meaningful relationships. Self-protective facade. No talk about emotions. No close friends, a loner. Silenced by shame	**Current:** Others don't inquire. Others tease. People show no personal interest. Hurt by criticism.
I'm the only responsible one.	Takes all the responsibility. Complains about others not taking responsibility.	Notices others not taking responsibility. Appreciation from men at work. Promotions.
Others: No one is there for me.	Awake at night, on computer.	Wife complains about his getting up at night and not coming home in evenings. Wife withdraws.
People are only interested in themselves.	Reacts to wife as though she were his mother.	
	Physiological: Chest concave, tension in shoulders & back. Sense of "emptiness".	Body & sub-symbolic memories.
Quality of Life: Life is full of disappointments.		**Old Memories:** Waiting for father. Absent father.
Something will go wrong.	**Fantasy:** Worry about work and career. Catastrophic fantasies of something going wrong. Richard will belittle me or not listen. Richard will not be there for me. Richard will reject me. "I will get mother's love if I'm Responsible". Mother will never love me as I am.	Mother is cold. Mother's; neglect. criticism, demands, self-centeredness, & lack of validation. Mother never asks about feelings. Mother says father has no morals, irresponsible. Mother says "You are useless".

Repressed Feelings & Needs
Loneliness, anger, emotional pain.
Need for security-in-relationship, validation, someone to rely on, companionship, to define self, to make an impact, to give and receive intimacy.

Figure 6.3 Bobby's Script System

served archaic homeostatic functions such as predictability, identity, continuity, or stability (Erskine et al., 1999).

I periodically inquired about Bobby's subjective experiences with the realization that he would eventually discover and appreciate his internal urge for a familiar sense of equilibrium – the homeostatic stabilization – that maintained his habits of worrying and obsessing. Fairly early in the psychotherapy I asked Bobby if he could describe the purpose of his fantasies about "something will go wrong". He immediately exclaimed, "To know what will happen!" This led us into several memories where he described his internal urge for predictability and his intense fear when he could not predict the outcome of events. We further explored how his fantasies served to reinforce his script beliefs and, at the same time, functioned to provide insurance against the shock of disappointments.

Through my consistent phenomenological inquiry Bobby became aware of three other homeostatic functions:

- That his script belief "I don't need anything from anyone" and his related fantasies of being "totally independent of anyone" were a childhood form of identity
- That many of his fantasies and their accompanying script belief "no one is there for me" served as an orientation in his relationships with others
- That his habitual worrying provided a sense of continuity throughout his life

Each of these homeostatic functions was a child-like attempt at self-reparation and provided a synthetic stabilization of his intense affect – a self-stabilization necessary to reduce the strong emotional reactions that occurred as a result of the absence of need fulfilling contact with significant others, either in actuality in his current life, as fantasy, or as traces of implicit memory (Kohut, 1977; Wolf, 1988).

However, to relinquish archaic insecure attachment patterns and the homeostatic functions that both constitute and maintain a life script, clients such as Bobby have to shift the archaic functions to mature functions. This shift often involves experimenting with and temporarily allowing the therapeutic relationship to provide such psychological functions as stabilization, predictability, or a new identity-in-relationship. Over the three years of his psychotherapy Bobby did a lot of experimenting and testing of my honesty, consistency, reliability, and dependability.

During this phase of the psychotherapy I repeatedly used the method of *relational inquiry* to ascertain how Bobby experienced me, to define our intersubjective processes, and to contrast the difference in the qualities of our relationship with the various other relationships in his life. When doing this sort of relational inquiry we were cycling back to the relational phase of our work together and simultaneously relying on what we had discovered about Bobby's life script and his script system. Each phase of our psychotherapy became interfaced with the other phases. I periodically had the perception that we were working in a hologram of therapeutic concepts and methods.

Gradually throughout his psychotherapy I fostered the transferring of Bobby's archaic homeostatic functions into a reliance on the consistency and dependability of our therapeutic relationship. My aim was to provide a secure relational base as an alternative to his previous avoidant attachment patterns and to provide a transitional phase in the establishment of mature homeostatic functions. Gradually Bobby's out-of-date identity was replaced with a new sense of identity, an identity based in the current contexts of his life – a mature identity that included an intimate relationship with his wife and children and a more open and contactful relationship with the men at work. Through our psychotherapy together he was developing new and mature forms of affect stabilization and intersubjective regulation.

During the second and third year we periodically focused on the sixth facet of our psychotherapy, the concept of "living in the now". A year earlier in our therapy Bobby disregarded my attempts to introduce awareness exercises. He did not like the concept of living in the present and argued with me that "worrying about the future was good insurance". I talked about how his worrying was a sign of hopefulness – hopeful that he could protect himself from the surprise and shock of "something will go wrong". In a number of sessions I reiterated the stories he had told me about various hurts and disappointments and explained how it would be normal in those situations to emotionally stabilize and regulate himself by predicting the worst. In several sessions we talked about his struggle to control the future. Hope and control was a theme to which we returned for some minutes during several sessions.

During our psychotherapy sessions, while I continued to make use of phenomenological inquiry and our intersubjective experiences, I began to introduce some awareness and grounding exercises and requested that he practice them at home. Over time we created two new mottos, "I don't know yet" and "What I am now worried about will pass", to replace his script belief, "Something will go wrong". During the second year I suggested that he attend a meditation weekend. At first he was uncomfortable with the experience but I was pleasantly surprised when he continued in an ongoing meditation program.

In the final year of the therapy I suggested that he join a twice a week yoga class, which he did. After a few weeks Bobby was pleased with how his body was changing. He was committed to continuing the yoga and meditation; they were both providing mature forms of self-stabilization and self-regulation. His reliance on me was now much less than in the previous year. He involved himself in family activities as he had never done before. And he was delighted that he was no longer obsessing and was enjoying a full night's sleep. When things were uncertain he focused on what he was experiencing within his body in the present moment.

Bobby was out of the city when one of his children had a severe accident; he stabilized his anxiety with "I do not have enough information to be worried". When his wife was having complications with a new pregnancy he taught her to use the motto, "I don't know yet. We will solve the problem if it ever happens". He was living spontaneously in the present: in touch with his vulnerability, aware of the functions of his previous obsessions, and intimate in his relationships. When we terminated our psychotherapy sessions he planned to continue with both his meditation and yoga.

Conclusion

The story of Bobby's psychotherapy provides a collection of concepts, therapeutic facets, and methods that merge together to inform you, the reader, about the use of the concepts in psychotherapy. I have chosen to present a case involving the psychotherapy of obsessing, habitual worrying and repetitive fantasizing because the psychotherapy of such clients illustrates the use of several aspects of a developmentally based, relationally focused Integrative Psychotherapy:

- Psychotherapy from a developmental framework, informed by current knowledge of neurobiology and the developmental and relational needs of children
- The significance of reenactments and transference as the communication of unconscious experience and the interplay between a reactive and responsive countertransference
- The affect/physiological/cognitive reorganization that can result from the deconfusion of child-like understandings and fantasies, a therapeutically supportive regression, and the decommissioning of introjections
- The identification of the script system and the interchange between script beliefs, behavior and fantasy, and script reinforcing experience
- The homeostatic functions of behavior, repetitive fantasies, and script beliefs and the importance of shifting the client's habitual use of archaic functions to mature functions
- The mature stabilization and regulation of living in the present moment

An Integrative Psychotherapy of obsessing, habitual worrying and repetitive fantasizing is complex and requires a multifaceted approach that addresses and resolves the client's underlying loneliness and unconscious longing for meaningful relationship, thereby reorienting the client's archaic homeostatic functions of obsessing to mature function, dissolving archaic script beliefs and introjections, facilitating a physiological/affective/cognitive reorganization, and enriching the client's emotional life via intimacy and living in the present moment.

This article has outlined a six-faceted approach that associates of the Institute for Integrative Psychotherapy and I found effective in our work with clients who are immersed in obsessing, repetitive fantasying, and habitual worrying. More exploration and clinical research may reveal other therapeutic facets effective in the psychotherapy of obsession. For now these six facets (relationship, avoidance, script and script system, intrapsychic reorganization, homeostatic functions, and living in the present) each form a useful orientation in the practice of Integrative Psychotherapy.

References

Allen, J. R. (2011). The experienced self as a developmental line and its use in script work. *Transactional Analysis Journal*, 41, 58–68.

American Psychiatric Association. (2000). *Diagnostic and statistical manual of mental disorders* (4th ed., text rev.). Author.

American Psychiatric Association. (2013). *Diagnostic and statistical manual of mental disorders* (5th ed.). Author.

Bary, B. B., & Hufford, F. M. (1990). The six advantages to games and their use in treatment. *Transactional Analysis Journal*, 20, 214–220.

Berne, E. (1961). *Transactional analysis in psychotherapy: A systematic individual and social psychiatry.* Grove Press.

Berne, E. (1964). *Games people play.* Grove Press.

Berne, E. (1966). *Principles of group treatment.* Oxford University Press.

Berne, E. (1970). *Sex in human loving.* Simon & Schuster.

Berne, E. (1972). *What do you say after you say hello? The psychology of human estiny.* Grove Press.

Bowlby, J. (1969). *Attachment. Volume I of attachment and loss.* Basic Books.

Bowlby, J. (1973). *Separation: Anxiety and Anger. Volume II of attachment and loss.* Basic Books.

Bowlby, J. (1980). *Loss: Sadness and Depression. Volume III of attachment and loss.* Basic Books.

Chambless, D. L. (2005). Compendium of empirically supported therapies. In G. P. Koocher, J. C. Norcross, & S. S. Hill (Eds.), *Psychologists' desk reference* (pp. 183–192). Oxford University Press.

Clark, B. D.(1991). Empathetic transactions in the deconfusing of Child ego states. *Transactional Analysis Journal*, 21, 92–98.

Cozolino, L. (2006). *The neuroscience of human relationships: Attachment and the developing social brain.* Norton.

Damasio, A. (1999). *The feeling of what happens: Body and emotion in the making of consciousness.* Harcourt Brace.

English, F. (1971). The substitution factor: Rackets and real feelings: Part 1. *Transactional Analysis Journal*, 1, 27–32.

English, F. (1972). Rackets and real feelings: Part 2. *Transactional Analysis Journal*, 2, 23–25.

Erskine, R. G. (1974). Therapeutic intervention: Disconnecting rubberbands. *Transactional Analysis Journal*, 4, 7–8. Republished 1997 in: R. G. Erskine, *Theories and methods of an integrative Transactional Analysis: A volume of selected articles* (pp. 172–173). TA Press.

Erskine, R. G. (1980). Script cure: Behavioral, intrapsychic, and physiological. *Transactional Analysis Journal*, 10, 102–106. Republished 1997 in: R. G. Erskine, *Theories and methods of an integrative Transactional Analysis: A volume of selected articles* (pp. 151–155). TA Press.

Erskine, R. G. (1991). Transference and transactions: Critique from an intrapsychic and integrative perspective. *Transactional Analysis Journal*, 21, 63–76. Republished 1997 in: R. G. Erskine, *Theories and methods of an integrative Transactional Analysis: A volume of selected articles* (pp. 129–146). TA Press.

Erskine, R. G. (1993). Inquiry, attunement, and involvement in the psychotherapy of dissociation. *Transactional Analysis Journal*, 23, 184–190. Republished 1997 in: R. G. Erskine, *Theories and methods of an integrative Transactional Analysis: A volume of selected articles* (pp. 37–45). TA Press.

Erskine, R. G. (1994). Shame and self-righteousness: Transactional Analysis perspectives and clinical interventions. *Transactional Analysis Journal*, 24, 86–102. Republished 1997 in: R. G. Erskine, *Theories and methods of an integrative Transactional Analysis: A volume of selected articles* (pp. 46–67). TA Press.

Erskine, R. G. (2001). Psychological function, relational needs and transferential resolution: Psychotherapy of an obsession. *Transactional Analysis Journal*, 31, 220–226.

Erskine, R. G. (2003a). Bonding in relationship: A solution to violence? *Transactional Analysis Journal*, 32, 256–260.

Erskine, R. G. (2003b). Introjection, psychic presence and Parent ego states: Considerations for psychotherapy. In C. Sills & H. Hargaden (Eds.), *Ego states: Key concepts in Transactional Analysis, contemporary views* (pp. 83–108). Worth Publishing.

Erskine, R. G. (2008). Psychotherapy of unconscious experience. *Transactional Analysis Journal*, 38(2), 128–138.

Erskine, R. G. (2009). Life scripts and attachment patterns: Theoretical integration and therapeutic involvement. *Transactional Analysis Journal*, 39, 207–218.

Erskine, R. G. (2010a). Integrating expressive methods in a relational psychotherapy. *International Journal of Integrative Psychotherapy*, 1, 55–80.

Erskine, R. G. (2010b). Life scripts: Unconscious relational patterns and psychotherapeutic involvement. In R. G. Erskine (Ed.), *Life scripts: A Transactional Analysis of unconscious relational patterns* (pp. 1–28). Karnac Books.

Erskine, R. G. (2011). Therapeutic involvement. In H. Fowlie and C. Sills (Eds.), *Relational Transactional Analysis: Principles in practice* (pp. 29–45). Karnac Books.

Erskine, R. G. (2013). Relational group process: Developments in a Transactional Analysis model of group psychotherapy. *Transactional Analysis Journal*, 43, 262–275.

Erskine, R. G. (2014). Nonverbal stories: The body in psychotherapy. *International Journal of Integrative Psychotherapy*, 5, 21–33.

Erskine, R. G. (2015). *Relational patterns – Therapeutic presence: Concepts and practice of Integrative Psychotherapy*. Karnac Books.

Erskine, R. G., D'Amico, J., King, E., Markevitch, J., Nack, C., & and Reiser, I. (2001). *[Investigation of effective methods in the psychotherapy of obsession]*. Unpublished raw data. Institute for Integrative Psychotherapy, New York.

Erskine, R. G., & Moursund, J. P. (2011). *Integrative Psychotherapy in action*. Karnac Books. (Originally published by Sage Publications, 1988 and by The Gestalt Journal Press, 1998).

Erskine, R. G., & Moursund, J. P. (2022). *The art and science of relationship: The practice of integrative psychotherapy*. Phoenix Publishing.

Erskine, R. G., & Trautmann, R. L. (1996). Methods of an Integrative Psychotherapy. *Transactional Analysis Journal*, 26, 316–328.

Erskine, R. G., & Trautmann, R. L. (2003). Resolving intrapsychic conflict: Psychotherapy of Parent ego states. In C. Sills & H. Hargaden (Eds.), *Ego states: Key concepts in Transactional Analysis, contemporary views* (pp. 109–134). Worth Publishing.

Erskine, R. G., Moursund, J. P., & Trautmann, R. L. (1999). *Beyond empathy: A therapy of contact-in-relationship*. Brunner/Mazel.

Erskine, R. G., & Zalcman, M. J. (1979). The racket system: A model for racket analysis. *Transactional Analysis Journal*, 9, 51–59.

Eusden, S. (2011). Relational Transactional Analysis and ethics – Minding the gap. In H. Fowlie & C. Sills (Eds.), *Relational Transactional Analysis: Principles in practice* (pp. 269–277). Karnac Books.

Fisher, S., & Greenberg, R. P. (1985). *The scientific credibility of Freud's theory and therapy*. Columbia University Press.

Freud, S. (1958a). The dynamics of transference. In J. Starchey (Ed. & Trans.), *The standard edition of the complete psychological works of Sigmund Freud*, Vol. 12 (pp. 97–108). Hogarth Press. (Original work published 1912).

Freud, S. (1958b). The disposition to obsessional neurosis. In J. Starchey (Ed. &Trans.), *The standard edition of the complete psychological works of Sigmund Freud*, Vol. 12, (pp. 311–326). Hogarth Press. (Original works published 1913).

Goulding, M., & Goulding, R. (1979). *Changing lives through redecision therapy.* Bruner/Mazel.

Horowitz, L. M., Rosenberg, S. E., & Bartholomew, K. (1993). Interpersonal problems, attachment styles and outcome in brief dynamic psychotherapy. *Journal of Consulting and Clinical Psychology*, 61, 549–560.

Kluckholm, C., & Murray, H. A. (1953). Personality formation: The determinants. In C. Kluckholm, H. A. Murray, & D. M. Schneider (Eds.), *Personality in nature, society, and culture* (pp. 53–67). Knopf.

Kobak, R. R., & Sceery, A. (1988). Attachment in late adolescence: Working models, affect regulation, and representation of self and others. *Child Development*, 59, 135–146.

Kohut, H. (1977). *The restoration of the self: A systematic approach to the psychoanalytic treatment of narcissistic personality disorder.* International Universities Press.

Little, R. (2011). Impasse clarification within the transference-countertransference matrix. *Transactional Analysis Journal*, 41, 23–38.

Main, M. (1990). Cross-cultural studies of attachment organization: Recent studies, changing methodologies, and the concept of conditional strategies. *Human Development*, 33, 48–61.

Main, M. (1995). Recent studies in attachment: Overview with selected implications for clinical work. In S. Goldberg, R. Muir, & J. Kerr (Eds.), *Attachment theory: Social, developmental and clinical perspectives* (pp. 407–474). The Analytic Press.

McAdams, D. P., & Pals, J. L. (2006). Fundamental principles for an integrative science of personality. *American Psychologist*, 61, 204–217.

Moiso, C. (1985). Ego states and transference. *Transactional Analysis Journal*, 15, 194–201.

Moursund, J. P., & Erskine, R. G. (2003). *Integrative Psychotherapy: The art and science of relationship.* Brooks/Cole-Thomson Learning.

Noriega, G. (2004). Codependence: A transgenerational script. *Transactional Analysis Journal*, 34, 312–322.

Noriega, G. (2009). On receiving the 2008 Eric Berne Memorial Award for Mechanisms of Transgenerational Script Transmission. *Transactional Analysis Journal*, 39, 8–13.

Novellino, M. (1984). Self-analysis of countertransference in integrative Transactional Analysis. *Transactional Analysis Journal*, 14, 63–67.

O'Reilly-Knapp, M., & Erskine, R. G. (2010). The script system: An unconscious organization of experience. In R. G. Erskine (Ed.), *Life scripts: A Transactional Analysis of unconscious relational patterns* (pp. 291–308). Karnac Books.

PDM Task Force. (2006). *Psychodynamic diagnostic manual.* Alliance of Psychoanalytic Organizations.

Perls, F. S. (1969). *Gestalt therapy verbatim.* Real People Press.

Reich, W. (1933). *Character analysis.* Farrar, Straus, & Giroux.

Salzman, L. (1980). *Treatment of the obsessive personality.* Jason Aronson.

Shapiro, D. (1965). *Neurotic styles.* Basic Books.

Stolorow, R., Brandschaft, B., & Atwood, G. (1987). *Psychoanalytic treatment: An intersubjective approach.* The Analytic Press.

Stuthridge, J. (2012). Traversing the fault lines: Trauma and enactment. *Transactional Analysis Journal, 42,* 238–251.

Trautmann, R. L. (2003). Psychotherapy and spirituality. *Transactional Analysis Journal, 33,* 32–36.

Trautmann, R. L., & Erskine, R. G. (1999). A matrix of relationships: Acceptance speech for the 1998 Eric Berne Memorial Award. *Transactional Analysis Journal, 29,* 14–17.

Verney, J. (2009). Mindfulness and the Adult ego state. *Transactional Analysis Journal, 39,* 247–255.

Widdowson, M. (2014). Avoidance, vicious cycles, and experiential disconfirmation of script: Two new theoretical concepts and one mechanism of change in the psychotherapy of depression and anxiety. *Transactional Analysis Journal, 44,* 194–207.

Winnicott, D. W. (2004). Mind and its relation to the psyche-soma. In D. W. Winnicott, *Through pediatrics to psycho-analysis: Collected papers* (pp. 243–254). Kanac Books. (Original work published 1949).

Wolf, E. S. (1988). *Treating the self: Elements of clinical self psychology.* Guilford Press.

Žvelc, G., Černetič, M., & Košak, M. (2011). Mindfulness-based Transactional Analysis. *Transactional Analysis Journal, 41,* 241–254.

Chapter 7

Presence and Involvement

Personal Perspectives on Countertransference

"Countertransference"! In my early years as a psychotherapist, I suffered whenever someone alluded to my having any countertransference with my clients. I believed that countertransference was irrefutable evidence that something was wrong with me as a psychotherapist. I reacted with intense shame – shame for being keenly interested in my client's private life, in worrying about them when they were in crisis, for feeling irritated by them, for wanting to protect them, for being bored by them, or for loving them. If my emotions were influenced by my clients, that was proof that something was wrong with me. I thought that I should be emotionally neutral – free of any countertransference.

I did not talk about my emotions and fantasies, either in supervision or with colleagues, because I was ashamed. In those early years, I had only a superficial understanding of countertransference. I believed that if I had an emotional reaction in response to my clients, it meant that I was unconsciously reliving some unfinished aspect of my own life and enacting it within the psychotherapy. It was convenient to disavow my feelings and focus on being "neutral". Without realizing it, my superficial understanding of the theory of countertransference, and the resulting sense of shame for having my emotions, was interfering with how I practiced psychotherapy.

Neither my supervision in client-centered therapy nor my training in Gestalt therapy addressed countertransference. My Transactional Analysis supervision only focused on the clients' personality dynamics and how I could identify their games and life scripts. However, I was influenced by a cursory understanding of psychoanalytic concepts. I was aware that Sigmund Freud and other psychoanalysts postulated that countertransference is the analyst's transference of old emotional reactions onto the client, which is a hindrance in the psychoanalysis. Freud (1910/1957) said that countertransference was the "result of a patient's influence on his [the psychotherapist's] unconscious feelings" (p. 144).

Eric Berne (1972) echoed this idea when he warned that psychotherapists often play out their life script in response to the client's script. As I understood it, countertransference meant that I was possibly reliving my own

DOI: 10.4324/9781003626718-7

unsettled story through unconscious interactions with clients. I was troubled by this idea and repeatedly questioned myself:

- If I enjoy my interactions with one client more than another, does that mean I am reliving some unfinished business from my childhood?
- If I feel angry when I hear about the physical abuse that my client received as a child, does that mean I have a neurotic parental transference to my client?
- If I feel irritated with the client's frequent bragging about their successes, does that mean I am envious?
- If I repeatedly look at my female client's revealing cleavage, does that indicate that I have an erotic countertransference, or is her behavior unconsciously revealing something about her life?
- If I dislike a client, is that an indication that I have an unresolved relational problem, or am I responding to something within the client?

I was relieved of my worry when, early in my psychoanalytic training, I read Donald Winnicott's article entitled "Hate in the counter-transference" (1959), in which he depicted countertransference as having two dimensions. Winnicott referred to one as *personal countertransference*: the therapist's reactions that are based on their own unresolved issues. The other he termed *objective countertransference*: the tender, understanding response by the therapist that may be needed by a client who was consistently criticized as a child. Winnicott saw objective countertransference as normal, understandable responses "to the actual personality and behaviour of the patient" (1959, p. 60).

I spent hours in my own psychoanalysis talking about my emotional and behavioral reactions to my clients, feeling ashamed of how I had failed to be empathic, and wondering what I could have done differently. I searched the psychoanalytic literature for more understanding and discovered that Paula Heimann (1950) elaborated on Winnicott's idea. She said that the psychoanalyst's total emotional reactions to the client were often an indicator of what was happening within the client's unconscious. This idea, along with my psychoanalytic supervision group's discussions of our personal reactions to our clients, shifted my understanding of countertransference. I no longer viewed it as solely my personal failure. Countertransference was also a way to understand the client's unconscious experience.

Heinrich Racker (1957) furthered Heimann's ideas and delineated two distinct types of countertransference identifications: *concordant* and *complementary*. In a concordant identification, the psychotherapist is stimulated by the client and responds to them with empathy. In a complementary countertransference, the analyst identifies with the client's internal "other" and responds with indifference, boredom, distain, superiority, or merely a lack of empathy. Otto Kernberg (1976) reiterated Racker's ideas when he described countertransference as being present in any therapy situation because of two factors: the therapist's history of relationships and the feelings induced by the client. Heinz Kohut (1971) defined the concept of *self-object transference* as an unconscious portrayal of significant others onto the psychotherapist and how such a portrayal mobilized countertransference in the psychotherapist. Kohut proposed that in order to understand the client's intrapsychic process, it is essential that the psychotherapist be introspective about their own feelings and fantasies – and to then use their phenomenological experience to empathically respond to the client's subjective experience.

Earlier, Kurt Lewin (1935), writing from the perspective of Gestalt psychology, saw countertransference as a dynamic field, the interplay of both the client and therapist as though they were cocreating a story together. Although the psychotherapist's countertransference is part of the client's unresolved emotional conflicts, it may also reflect what is unresolved in the psychotherapist and therefore warrants psychotherapy for the psychotherapist. In their discussion of contemporary psychoanalytic theory, Greenberg and Mitchell (1983) defined the interpersonal field this way: "Countertransference is an inevitable product of the interaction between the patient and the analyst rather than a simple interference stemming from the analyst's own infantile drive-related conflicts" (p. 389). This is what Stolorow et al. (1987) described as *intersubjective* – the melding together of two unique perspectives.

Sandor Ferenczi (1932, 1949) was the first psychoanalyst to propose that countertransference was the psychotherapist's identification with the client's unconscious communication, and therefore, countertransference constituted an essential component in understanding the client's relational history and inner life. Ferenczi declared that the psychotherapist's feelings of tenderness, patience, and concern were the core of the relationship between therapist and client. However, classical psychoanalysis continued to characterize counter-transference as the analyst's transference onto the client (Greenson, 1967).

Ronald Fairbairn (1952) elaborated on Ferenczi's ideas when he called for "genuine emotional contact" (p. 16) in the practice of psychotherapy – a form of intimacy from the psychotherapist to the client that provides the client with a new, transformative relationship. Harry Guntrip underscored Fairbairn's relational perspective when he wrote, "It is the psychotherapist's responsibility to discover what kind of parental relationship the patient needs in order to get better... If the psychiatrist cannot love his clients in that way, he had better give up psychotherapy" (Guntrip, as cited in Hazell, 1994, pp. 401–402).

Transference or Countertransference?

The 16th-century Spanish author Miguel de Cervantes (1605/1992) wrote a novel entitled *The Ingenious Gentleman Don Quixote of La Mancha*. His entire book is about transference. His main characters, Don Quixote, Sancho Panza, and Dulcinea, are all in transference with each other. The intriguing plot of the book lies in the various characters' reenactment of their life story via their illusions about each other. There are many examples in classical literature and modern novels that depict the transferential illusions of everyday life. In the psychotherapy profession, Sigmund Freud was the first to describe such illusions; he called these aroused psychological experiences "transference", wherein a person is inappropriately reacted to as though they were a person in the other's past (Freud, 1905/1955, p. 116).

As a starting point in understanding transference and countertransference, it may be helpful if we use the same definition of transference. Therefore, let us keep the following definition in mind while we think about the concept of transference from a couple of coinciding perspectives. Transference is:

> the expression of the universal psychological striving to organize experience and create meaning; as well as the means whereby the patient can demonstrate his or her past, the developmental needs which have been thwarted, and the defenses which were erected to compensate.
>
> (Erskine, 1991, p. 73)

Therefore, transference is an unaware enactment of an old story that may include three additional impulses:

1   A reluctance to feel the discomfort of fully remembering
2   An unaware enactment of earlier relationally disruptive experiences
3   The desire to achieve resolutions in relationships

If we emphasize the first part of this definition, then we are all in transference all the time. We cannot escape our own way of organizing a lifetime of experiences. Transference is our distinct way of creating meaning; it is simply the idiosyncratic way we express ourselves. We transfer our unique predisposition into every situation.

When we emphasize the second part of this definition, we focus on the relational disruptions, unrequited relational needs, and how the person has managed to stabilize and regulate themselves. These stories are revealed, often without awareness, through physical gestures, unaware enactments, snippets of memory, or metaphors (Erskine, 2009). Consequently, the transferences that occur in the process of psychotherapy may be the client's unaware attempt to reveal and heal. This definition asserts that transference is a normal and universal experience.

Clarifying Countertransference

Is countertransference transference? Yes, according to the definitions of transference that I am suggesting, we cannot escape our own internal organization of life experiences: physically, affectively, cognitively, and behaviorally. Heimann (1950) defined countertransference as "all the feelings which the analyst experiences towards his patient" (p. 81), whereas Winnicott distinguished between a personal reaction to the client and an objective response – what Racker called complementary and concordant counter-transference. I prefer to use the terms "reactive" and "responsive" to describe the psychotherapist's various interactions with their client. The term "reactive countertransference" describes the psychotherapist's emotional expressions and behaviors that are an expression of their own internal conflicts in reaction to their client. This is what has been traditionally thought of as countertransference.

Here are some examples of the type of questions I ask myself to help distinguish between a reactive countertransference and a responsive countertransference:

- Am I in a responsive countertransference when I am fully present, in contact with my own affect and motivation, while at the same time being committed to the client's welfare? Or does this describe an intimate person-to-person involvement?
- Am I in a reactive countertransference or am I genuinely engaged with my client when I worry about them at night, when I feel irritated by their mannerisms, or when I feel love for them like I do for my children?
- Are my feelings – such as affection, boredom, or disregard – a reactive expression of my own experiences, or am I responding with something intrinsic in the client's history?

Perhaps it is beneficial if we think of countertransference as everything the psychotherapist brings into the therapeutic situation – their internal organization of experience and their unique way of creating meaning. Our professional training, the theories on which we rely, the style of how we transact with our clients, our childhood and school experiences, the joys and sorrows of our love life, the quality of our current family relationships, what we read and the music we enjoy, the things we dislike or avoid – all of these individual proclivities form the unique substance of what we bring to each therapeutic encounter. When we consider this perspective, every moment of the psychotherapy involves the interplay between two people, a coconstructive process.

We provide a responsive countertransference when we are in attunement with our client's affect, rhythm, and developmental level of making meaning; when we are compassionate with their sadness; when we are angry at the person who abused them; when we are patient and sensitive to their needs; and when we communicate with respect and choice. In each of these circumstances, we may be engaging in a responsive countertransference, that is, attunement to what the client requires in a healing relationship (Erskine, 2021b).

We are in a reactive countertransference when our transactions with our clients are unconsciously tinged with unresolved anger at someone in our own life, if we are inhibited by our own grief and fears, when we disavow our own emotional history, when we are constrained by remnants of loss or trauma, or when we are confined to a specific theory. When there is a reactive countertransference in play, the client-therapist dialogue becomes a manifestation of the psychotherapist's truncated needs, and their communication is no longer in the service of the client. Reactive countertransference is countertherapeutic, whereas responsive countertransference can promote the client's healing and growth.

However, not all that transpires from the psychotherapist to the client should be called countertransference. Each psychotherapist has their own natural inclinations and demeanor; some tend to be quiet while others are more exuberant, some are sensitive to the client's affect while others attend to how the client is reasoning. It is essential that we psychotherapists remain aware of our own relational needs and cognizant of how our needs influence our therapeutic dialogue (Stewart, 2010).

Each psychotherapist, even if using the same theories and concepts as others, will conduct their interactions with their clients in a different manner. The central challenge for each psychotherapist is how to make use of our natural proclivities in providing for our client's welfare. This requires acceptance and appreciation of our own natural inclinations and vigilance about how our affect and behavior may influence our clients.

Theory-Induced Countertransference

Often overlooked in training programs, supervision, and professional publications is a distinctive countertransference that is induced by psychotherapy theory. Psychotherapists often form allegiances to specific psychotherapy schools, each of which emphasizes certain theories of personality and preferred therapeutic methods. When we as psychotherapists repeatedly rely on a particular concept or therapeutic technique, we increase the possibility that we will not understand what is occurring within the client or in the therapeutic interchange.

I remember the days when I was actively involved in attending Gestalt therapy and Transactional Analysis training workshops. I watched well-known psychotherapists who valued short, 20–30 minute therapy sessions. These therapist-client encounters often gave prominence to the psychotherapist stimulating immediate and dramatic change. For a while I tried to follow this model of a short, intense piece of therapy. I was captivated by the concept; it was evident that for some clients the fervent work was effective. I was following the theory, but my reliance on the concept interfered with the therapeutic involvement that some of my clients needed.

It took me a few years to realize that this rapid, dramatic therapy approach did not work for those clients whose distress and agony were masked by their compliance with my expectations and fast-track pace. My clients might have achieved a very different outcome if I had understood that some individuals find greater benefit when the therapist is patient and gracious, focused on their inchoate affect, and engaged in a person-to-person dialogue.

Throughout the 1970s, it was the trend in both Transactional Analysis and Gestalt therapy to make frequent use of confrontation. Although my original background underscored the importance of respect and empathy, I joined this trend and used confrontation often with my clients. It was only after I observed the distress and shame my confrontations caused that I realized that confrontation was a powerful intervention and should only be used with full awareness of its impact on the relationship between therapist and client. I still use confrontation but now much like I use hot pepper in cooking: sparingly, in order to not overpower the food. When I relied on the concept of confrontation, I created a situation in which my transactions were countertherapeutic.

I have a concern about the future of our developmentally based, relationally focused Integrative Psychotherapy. We have a unique set of theories and methods. I do not want our theoretical ideas – attunement, phenomenological and historical inquiry, relational needs, involvement, or any other concepts – to become static, where the psychotherapist using these ideas slides into a theory-induced countertransference. We all need to evaluate in an ongoing manner our reliance on a specific concept or method. Our task is to have a substantial repertoire of concepts and the flexibility to relate to each client according to who they are and what they need in a therapeutic relationship.

My Inner Conflict: Reactive or Responsive?

When Loraine came for her first psychotherapy session, I was repulsed by her. Over the phone she was pleasant, but when she arrived, I discovered that she was slovenly dressed, with unwashed hair that smelled like mold. Her teeth were obviously in need of dental repair. I wished that she had not come to my office. Yet, in our initial session, I sensed that she was serious about improving her life. That stimulated me to commit myself to being fully present with her.

During the next several weeks, I became fascinated by Lorraine's intellectual brilliance, her articulate language, and her frequent quotations of literature, but, at the same time, I could not escape my sense of repulsion. Listening to her was interesting if I did not look at her. I did not want her to sit close to me. I wished that I could hold my breath for an hour. I certainly did not want her to ask me for a goodbye hug. Disgust may be too strong a word to describe my feelings, but I certainly had a strong urge to turn away from her. Staying in contact with Loraine was a constant struggle. I was committed to doing effective psychotherapy with her, but I was perturbed. Repulsion and tender concern were my conflicting sentiments.

We were many months into the psychotherapy before Loraine allowed me to inquire about her childhood relationship with her mother. When she talked about her childhood, she reported stories of perpetual neglect, such as wearing the same clothes for a few weeks at a time and eating the same rice soup every day because her mother "didn't like to cook". She described how notes were sent home from both kindergarten and elementary school asking that she be bathed and her hair washed before returning to school. I wondered if my sense of repulsion was only my own proclivity, a reactive countertransference (what Winnicott called "personal countertransference"), or was I sensing and identifying with her mother's emotional reactions to her (what Racker called a "complementary countertransference")?

In subsequent sessions, Lorraine talked about the absence of any conversation with her mother: "She always watched TV. She never attended any of my school activities. There was never any affection". Loraine said that her mother never wanted to touch her and certainly did not want to give her a bath. The few times she had a bath, her mother screamed and told her she was making a mess. When Lorraine was an adolescent, her mother admitted, "I wish you had never been born". I was impacted by how Lorraine recounted the relationship with her mother, and I had two primary responses: I felt an intense tenderness for the neglected child and anger at her mother's disregard for her daughter's welfare.

As Lorraine continued to tell me stories of how she was uncared for, I thoughtfully examined my sense of "repulsion". Although at first I assumed that my feeling of repulsion was my own, I began to wonder if I was picking up on some unconscious communication encoded within her stories. One day I inquired, "I wonder if your mother was disgusted by you". She immediately responded with, "That's it. That's the word... DISGUSTED, that describes my mother... she was always repulsed by me".

My sense of repulsion and my subsequent inquiry revealed an integral part of Loraine's childhood experience. My reaction had provided me with a window into the disdain Loraine's mother felt about her and allowed me to come up with the word "disgust". For almost a year I was non-consciously identifying with Loraine's mother's attitude of "disgust" and assumed that it was mine. Yes, Lorraine's musty smell remained, but what was now most important was my anger at her mother's neglect of her and my desire to be protective and gracious to the child she once was. Our therapy eventually addressed how Loraine replicated her mother's behavior by neglecting her own appearance, cleanliness, and health.

Identifying with the Client

Over the years I have explored my own countertransference as well as the countertransferential experiences of many supervisees. It is apparent that countertransference begins with our identifying with our client. In facilitating an in-depth psychotherapy, it is essential that the psychotherapist attune to the unintegrated and unaware aspects of the client, such as their physical sensations, affects, stabilizing fantasies, or unrequited needs. We may also identify with some features of an internalized significant other, such as a father's criticism, a mother's lack of tenderness, or a grandmother's harsh expectations. At first, we may mistakenly identify these aspects of the client as our own. The story of Loraine's psychotherapy provides an example of how I was influenced by her unconscious communication of her mother's "disgust". I used this unaware identification – what I experienced as my "repulsion" – to eventually shape my inquiry about her mother's attitude toward Loraine. This changed both the direction and depth of our psychotherapy.

Henry also influenced me, but in a different way than Loraine had. Henry was a successful actor who in our first session described himself with "something is missing within me". As I listened to Henry's constant sadness, I resonated with his lament. He touched my heart. I had the sense that his sad expressions were those of a 5-year-old boy who longed for the playful companionship of his father. Perhaps I was particularly sensitive to Henry's developmental needs because I too had lived without a father's caring involvement. I envisioned Henry being alone with no emotional support and guidance. I used my internal image to form several inquiries about his life and the quality of his relationship with his parents when he was in his early school years.

Henry held back his tears as he told me about never being sure if his father would visit him or not on weekends. "Sometimes he would take me to meet his friends in a bar, but I hated that; I just wanted him to teach me how to play ball". Later on, he talked about his "absent-minded mother": "She was always too busy or too tired to play with me or even help me with school work". He cried, "I was in a lot of school plays but neither of them ever seemed interested". Throughout our psychotherapy, I expressed interest not only in his history but in many of the activities of his life. I inquired about the TV scripts he was reading and how he made the characters he played come alive. I focused on his relational need for a shared experience, the companionship that had been missing during his young life. With my consistent involvement, Henry's persistent sadness dissipated.

Developmental Image

A significant feature of a responsive countertransference is the psychotherapist's capacity to have a developmental perspective and to use that knowledge to cultivate a developmental image. As I attune to my client's affect, rhythm, and manner of thinking, I imagine them as a child, usually at a specific age. I form an impression about the interpersonal crisis in their life, the relational needs that may have been unrequited, and what a child of that specific age needed in a stabilizing and regulating relationship. I keep in mind that my developmental images are only mere impressions, but they are impressions that guide my phenomenological and historical inquiry.

In accordance with my image of the child's age, I inquire about the emotionally vulnerable moments in the child's day: breakfast time, bathing activities, going to and coming home from school, play time, and bedtime rituals. I ask my clients to describe their parents and any other significant adult with whom they interacted during their childhood. I also inquire about who was at the dinner table and particularly about the nature and quality of the communication between the child and other family members.

The details of my inquiry shift as I focus on different ages. The kinds of questions I ask if I am inquiring about the interpersonal relationships of a 9-year-old are very different from those I might ask if I imagine my client at age 2. Most clients will initially answer with "I don't remember". I remind them that they know their parents' personalities and to just imagine how they would have responded to the child's needs at that particular age. Although their responses may not be an accurate representation, like a photograph might, their answering provides an important outlook on what may have occurred, much like an impressionistic painting. It is through consistent inquiry about the client's developmental experiences that their various affects, nascent understandings, and physiological sensations are shaped into a narrative.

Resonating with the Vibes

As Melissa walked into my office for the first time, I was shocked by how skinny she was. She walked with her head slumped forward and her chest curved inward. I wondered if she was hiding her breasts. She sat on the sofa and pulled her knees up to her belly as she told me how she needed psychotherapy because of her constant body tension. I was concerned that she was anorexic. Although I did not address her appearance directly, in the first several sessions I made many inquiries about her nutrition, level of exercising, and general health care. As we had those conversations, I began feeling sexually excited. I was both surprised and disconcerted that my body was feeling aroused. I did not find her attractive. She looked more like an emaciated 12-year-old girl than a 28-year-old school teacher.

Over the next several sessions I continued to be aroused and considered terminating the therapy on the basis of my having an erotic counter-transference. I was worried. Ethically I was committed to my client's welfare, but my body was reacting to something that I did not understand. I talked about my sexual arousal with a colleague who previously had served as the chairperson of her association's ethics committee. She suggested the possibility that I was picking up some "vibrations" and misidentifying them as emanating from within me.

Based on Melissa's waifish appearance and apparent body tension, I formed a developmental image of a preadolescent under stress. I decided to ask about her life when she was 12 years old. Over the next several sessions she painstakingly told me about her father's sexual abuse of her, which began when she was 11 years old and continued until she had her first menstruation at age 14. As soon as she told me about her father's sexual abuse, my sexual arousal stopped. I was then able to attune to and concentrate on her frightening and painful experiences. In hindsight, it became clear that my sexual arousal was in resonance with Melissa's yet untold experience of sexual abuse.

Responsive Countertransference

Ronald was encouraged to come to therapy by his sponsor in Alcoholics Anonymous. He had lost two jobs because of his alcoholism before he seriously joined the 12-step program. From the beginning of the work with Ronald I felt protective of him. I could sense a fragile boy-in-the-man. My protectiveness seemed right even though I did not know why. My phenomenological inquiry appeared to be too intrusive for Ronald, so I let our work together flow its natural course rather than setting a direction by inquiring. Instead, I quietly listened to him and responded with tenderness and compassion. Eventually, Ronald revealed stories of the physical abuse his father had inflicted on him. On one occasion he was shaking with fear as he vividly remembered being 9 years old; his father was demanding that he fetch a leather belt that his father then used to whip him.

As Ronald relived this memory, I imagined myself standing between him and his father, blocking his father from hitting him. I said nothing to Ronald about my protective imagery; I just focused on it. Suddenly Ronald looked up at me and said, "I feel so safe with you". Then he angrily shouted at his image of his father and fantasized running out of the house. Although I never said anything to Ronald about my sensitivity to the boy-in-the-man and my desire to protect him, he could feel my involvement. One day he said, "I've never told anybody about the beatings, not even my wife". When I inquired about why he was telling me, he said, "I feel safe in your presence. Until I went to AA, whenever I would have any memory of my father, I would get drunk. But when I'm here with you, I feel protected. I can let myself feel the terror I felt when he beat me. And I can now feel my anger at his cruelty".

A therapeutic relationship based on the psychotherapist's responsive countertransference creates a relational environment in which the client can depend on the psychotherapist's consistent and reliable presence, their capacity to provide affective attunement and stabilization, and their sensitivity to the client's developmental needs.

Reactive Countertransference

For many years I have been ashamed of my strong reactive countertransference and how I acted when I told a group member that I wanted him to leave the Tuesday evening men's group because I was no longer willing to work with him. Matthew was a mental health counselor and the business manager of a large private clinic. He was in group therapy to fulfill the therapy requirements for his training as a professional counselor. In the early months of the group, Matthew was an active participant, appreciated by most of the men for his lively contributions.

After the group had met for several months, Matthew began to boast about the lies he perpetuated at work and how no one was wise enough to realize what he was doing. He bragged about the famous people he knew as well as his academic and sports accomplishments. Soon it became evident that he did not have the university degrees that he pretended to have. I wondered if his telling us these stories was an exhibition of narcissistic grandiosity. The confrontations that various group members made seem to have no impact on Matthew. He remained jovial and impervious to the group's feedback. All this while I curiously listened to his exploits. I was apprehensive. I was waiting to see what more might be revealed.

As I observed the group's dynamics, it was evident that each week the men in the group were steadily more silent after Matthew told us some story. It seemed that the group members no longer knew what to say to him. And I did not know what was true and what was not; he certainly was embellishing his accomplishments. My discomfort with Matthew had been building for several weeks. I had been unsuccessful in addressing his dishonesty because he always seemed to deflect from taking any responsibility. One evening he was excited as he told us how he had embezzled money from his employer. Suddenly I was furiously angry at him for his constant lying and now for his stealing. I jumped up from my seat, opened the door, and told him to never come back. As the group resumed, it was evident that some members were relieved and a couple were shocked by my impetuous behavior.

I certainly had experienced a reactive countertransference. I was frustrated in my attempts to get Matthew to be aware of how his behavior affected other people. The emotional tension that I felt inside had been building for several weeks. In response to Matthew's dishonesty, I had lost my capacity to be sensitive and empathetic. In hindsight, I realize that I could have invited Matthew into individual psychotherapy where I would have had the time and opportunity to explore with him the various psychological functions underlying his lying and stealing. I regret how I reacted to Matthew; my behavior was not therapeutic. The shame about how I treated Matthew was significant enough that I sought more training in how to provide an effective psychotherapy with narcissistic clients.

Bernard was another client with whom I had a reactive, and therefore nontherapeutic, countertransference. Even though we had a weekly session for several months, I doubt if I was ever therapeutically helpful to him. From the beginning of our work together, Bernard bragged about his affluent lifestyle. I was impressed by his detailed descriptions of lavish vacations, the championship sporting events he attended, and the important people he had met at various parties.

When we were not in session, I thought about his narcissistically inclined self-aggrandizement and how I could therapeutically address him. However, when we were in session I was often dazzled by his stories. Several times in our first months together I attempted to develop a therapeutic contract with him, but Bernard always seemed to move the subject of our conversation to some dramatic event. I tried unsuccessfully to inquire about his phenomenological experiences, something at which I am usually quite good. My attempts at inquiry about Bernard's subjective sensations only brought about more stories of impressive social events. His answers to my questions about his childhood were superficial. I was able to learn that his father was a "full-time gambler" who had taught him how to gamble and that Bernard had lived most of his childhood in casino hotels.

In my own psychoanalysis, I explored the possibility that both my lack of empathy and my floundering therapeutic skill with Bernard were the result of my being envious of his affluence or resentful that I had no influence on him. It was clear that Bernard's impressive stories continued to distract me from making any therapeutic impact. During this time, when I was evaluating my possible contribution to our therapeutic impasse, Bernard began to challenge me with, "You are not really interested in me" and "You are only tolerating me because of the money you make". I was dumfounded. Internally, I wanted to both defend myself and confront him about his self-centeredness. Instead, I tried, unsuccessfully, to inquire about the relationship between us. I was frustrated that I could not find a way to have an authentic person-to-person dialogue with him.

I had been listening carefully for a possible metaphor encoded in the story that Bernard was telling me when he surprised me with, "I am wasting my time with you. You never clicked with me". He walked out of my office. Often with other clients who have abruptly terminated, I have reached out to them with a note or phone call to invite them to discuss their ending of the psychotherapy. With Bernard I did not reach out and contact him. I was relieved that he had terminated. He was correct; we just did not "click".

I indeed had reactive countertransferences with both Bernard and Matthew. When we have a reactive countertransference, we are self-absorbed in our own internal story. With both Bernard and Matthew, I lost my sense of presence – a personal and ethical commitment to be with and for the client. I was not able to respond to what either man needed within a restorative therapeutic relationship. As a result of my reactive countertransference, the psychotherapy for both Bernard and Matthew was damaged.

Presence: Fostering a Healing Relationship

Earlier I described how Donald Winnicott used the term "objective countertransference" to describe the psychotherapist's tender, understanding responses that may be needed by a client. Most likely he was delineating the concept of *presence*: a form of countertransference that is in resonance with the client. Presence is fundamental to the process of relationship-focused Integrative Psychotherapy. It is provided through our sustained attunement to the client's verbal and non-verbal communication and through our constant respect for and enhancement of our client's integrity.

Presence is an expression of our full internal and external contactfulness, and it communicates our dependability and willingness to take responsibility for our part in whatever happens in the therapeutic relationship. It includes receptivity to our client's affect, that is, our willingness to be impacted by our client's emotions, to be deeply moved while not becoming anxious, depressed, or angry. At times my eyes have filled with tears or I have felt a protective anger when I hear about the neglect or abuse my clients suffered in their young lives. Presence occurs when our behavior and communication, at all times, respects and enhances the client's integrity.

There is a duality to presence that entails our simultaneous attention to our client and to ourselves. Presence flourishes when we temporarily decenter from our own needs, feelings, fantasies, or desires and make the client's process our primary focus. But, paradoxically, we must not lose awareness of our own internal process, resonance, and reactions. Our personal history, relational needs, sensitivities, theories, professional experience, own psychotherapy, and reading interests all shape our unique reactions to every one of our clients. These are the essential parts of therapeutic presence.

Each psychotherapist has a unique set of past experiences, current interests, needs, and wants. We have our preferred theories, concepts, and methods, and we use our experience as a kind of reference library that helps us attune to our clients and to understand how they function. Importantly, presence includes our willingness to be transparent in our uniqueness, to let our clients see who we are and what we are experiencing, to be impacted by that which is significant to our client, and for that impact to be seen.

Presence provides a container for our therapeutic involvement, an interpersonal safety net that supports without constraining and protects without demeaning the client (Schneider, 1998). More than just verbal communication, presence describes a communion between us and our clients. It is the basis of a healing relationship. The respectful interplay between our self-awareness and decentering opens the way for what Buber (1958) called an "I-Thou" relationship, a relationship between two connected, contactful, self-and-other-aware individuals. The I-Thou relationship, in turn, is the primary source of the transformative potential of relationship-focused Integrative Psychotherapy.

Involvement: With and for the Client

Does the term "involvement" imply countertransference? From a classical psychoanalytic perspective, involvement violates the principal of therapeutic neutrality. For several decades, the task of the psychoanalyst was to remain a blank screen, with evenly hovering attention (Freud, 1912/1958; Greenberg, 1986). For the psychoanalyst to provide the client with more than a reflecting mirror was considered to be a therapeutically disruptive countertransference (Poland, 1984).

In Integrative Psychotherapy, we consider involvement to be one of the essential dimensions of an authentic, person-to-person relationship. A central premise of a relationally focused Integrative Psychotherapy is that "effective healing of psychological distress and relational neglect occurs through a contactful therapeutic relationship – a relationship in which the psychotherapist values and supports vulnerability, authenticity, and inter-subjective contact" (Erskine, 2021a, p. 212).

Therapeutic involvement begins with the psychotherapist's commitment to the client's well-being, an unwavering awareness that the client, and what they need in a therapeutic relationship, is most important. This commitment is the bedrock that makes an authentic involvement possible. The involved psychotherapist is with and for the client, fully contactful, honest, and willing to put energy and effort into helping clients achieve their goals. When we are fully committed to the client's welfare, our involvement enriches the client's vitality and helps them form a secure sense of self. Involvement is what makes relationship vibrant: two people exchanging ideas and feelings, each challenging and enhancing the authenticity of the other.

Involvement emerges from the psychotherapist having a genuine interest in the client's intrapsychic and interpersonal worlds and then communicating that interest through attentiveness, patience, and respectful inquiry. When I am fully involved, I am vulnerable; I allow myself to be emotionally touched. I strive to let my caring for the client show by being curious, tender, and respectful. My involvement has to do with my commitment to being an active, caring, vulnerable, and authentic participant in the therapeutic process. Our involvement is reflected in our acknowledgment, validation, and normalization of what the client presents as well our willingness to be known. Involvement has more to do with being than doing.

Involvement is about the therapist-client interchange. It is about us as psychotherapists: how we feel, think, and respond to the client. And involvement is about the client: how they perceive our investment in them and how we are impacted by what happens in the relationship. Involvement is about the intersubjective interplay between us, the dance of interpersonal contact. Involvement is best understood in terms of the client's perception: their sense that the therapist is attending to their relational needs and truly committed to their welfare.

When we psychotherapists identify and resonate with our clients – when we are fully aware of our reactive countertransference and make therapeutic use our responsive countertransference – we create an intersubjective process of two people sharing an intimate experience together. The important aspects of psychotherapy are embedded in the distinctiveness of each interpersonal relationship, not in what we consciously do as a psychotherapist but in the quality of how we are in relationship with the other person. Our attitudes and demeanor, the qualities of our interpersonal relationship, and the authenticity of our intersubjective connections are central in creating an effective psychotherapy. Presence and involvement are the essential ingredients of a healing relationship.

References

Berne, E. (1972). *What do you say after you say hello? The psychology of human destiny*. Grove Press.

Buber, M. (1958). *I and thou* (R. G. Smith, Trans.). Scribner.

de Cervantes, M. (1992). *Don Quixote* (P. A. Motteaux, Trans.). Wordsworth. (Original work published 1605).

Erskine, R. G. (1991). Transference and transactions: Critique from an intrapsychic and integrative perspective. *Transactional Analysis Journal*, 21(2), 63–76. doi:10.1177/036215379102100202.

Erskine, R. G. (2009). Life scripts and attachment patterns: Theoretical integration and therapeutic involvement. *Transactional Analysis Journal*, 39(3), 207–218. doi:10.1177/036215370903900304.

Erskine, R. G. (2021a). *Early affect confusion: Relational psychotherapy for the borderline client*. nScience Publishing.

Erskine, R. G. (2021b). *A healing relationship: Commentary on therapeutic dialogues*. Phoenix Publishing.

Fairbairn, W. R. D. (1952). *An object relations theory of the personality*. Basic Books.

Ferenczi, S. (1932). *The clinical diary of Sándor Ferenczi* (M. Balint, Trans.). Harvard University Press.

Ferenczi, S. (1949). Confusion of the tongues between the adults and the child – (The language of tenderness and of passion). *International Journal of Psycho-Analysis*, 30(4), 225–230. doi:10.1080/00107530.1988.10746234.

Freud, S. (1955). Fragments of an analysis of a case of hysteria. In J. Strachey (Ed. & Trans.), *The standard edition of the complete psychological works of Sigmund Freud* (Vol. 7, pp. 1–122). Hogarth Press. (Original work published 1905).

Freud, S. (1957). The future prospects of psycho-analytic therapy. In J. Strachey (Ed. & Trans.), *The standard edition of the complete psychological works of Sigmund Freud* (Vol. 14, pp. 139–152). Hogarth Press. (Original work published 1910).

Freud, S. (1958). Recommendation to physicians practicing psychoanalysis. In J. Strachey (Ed. & Trans.), *The standard edition of the complete psychological works of Sigmund Freud* (Vol. 12, pp. 109–120). Hogarth Press. (Original work published 1912).

Greenberg, J. R. (1986). Theoretical models and the analyst's neutrality. *Contemporary Psychoanalysis*, 22(1), 87–106. doi:10.1080/00107530.1986.10746117.

Greenberg, J. R., & Mitchell, S. A. (1983). *Object relations in psychoanalytic theory*. Harvard University Press.

Greenson, R. R. (1967). *The techniques and practice of psychoanalysis*. International Universities Press.

Hazell, J. (Ed.). (1994). *Personal relations therapy: The collected papers of H. J. S. Guntrip*. Jason Aronson.

Heimann, P. (1950). On counter-transference. *International Journal of Psychoanalysis*, 31, 81–84.

Kernberg, O. F. (1976). *Object relations theory and clinical psychoanalysis*. Jason Aronson.

Kohut, H. (1971). *The analysis of the self: A systematic approach to the psychoanalytic treatment of narcissistic personality disorder*. International Universities Press.

Lewin, K. (1935). *A dynamic theory of personality*. McGraw-Hill.

Poland, W. (1984). On the analyst's neutrality. *Journal of the American Psychoanalytic Association*, 32(2), 283–299. doi:10.1177/000306518403200203.

Racker, H. (1957). The meanings and uses of countertransference. *Psychoanalytic Quarterly*, 76(3), 725–777. doi:10.1002/j.2167-4086.2007.tb00277.x.

Schneider, K. J. (1998). Existential processes. In L. S. Greenberg, J. C. Watson, & G. Lietaer (Eds.), *Handbook of experiential psychotherapy* (pp. 103–120). Guilford.

Stewart, L. (2010). Relational needs of the therapist: Countertransference, clinical work and supervision. Benefits and disruptions in psychotherapy. *International Journal of Integrative Psychotherapy*, 1(1), 41–50.

Stolorow, R., Brandschaft, B., & Atwood, G. (1987). *Psychoanalytic treatment: An intersubjective approach*. Analytic Press.

Winnicott, D. W. (1959). Hate in the counter-transference. *International Journal of Psychoanalysis*, 30, 69–74. https://pep-web.org/browse/document/ijp.

Chapter 8

Relational Withdrawal, Internal Criticism, Social Façade

Psychotherapy of the Schizoid Process

> Solitude is independence. It had been my wish
> and with the years I had attained it.
> It was cold. Oh, cold enough!
> But it was also still, wonderfully still
> and vast like the cold stillness of space
> in which the stars revolve.
>
> Hermann Hesse

In one of Maryann's early psychotherapy sessions she cried, "I'm so confused. Sometimes I am two people or even three. I'm split inside. I can be nice to people but then I get so scared that I can't talk. I just hide. Then I beat up on myself for being so stupid. I don't know which is really me. I'm so tired of it all". Maryann's anguish touched my heart as she struggled to speak about her "split inside". Her words were an apt portrayal of the internal struggle that we call the *schizoid process*.

Schizoid is the Greek word for scissors: it means "to split". When I use the terms "schizoid process" or "schizoid syndrome", I am describing a person's tendency to withdraw from relationship, to live with an internal sense of personal isolation and self-criticism in order to avoid the potential stress of interpersonal contact. People who rely on a schizoid process to stabilize and manage internal stress are often introverted and live primarily in an internal world without much emotional contact with others, even family. They may have a well-rehearsed social presence, but the essence of who they are, their vulnerability, is hidden.

Many people who seek psychotherapy may exist somewhere on the schizoid spectrum – from *Schizoid Style*, to *Schizoid Pattern*, to *Schizoid Disorder*. Yet for many of these people their schizoid process may go unnoticed, even in their psychotherapy. The schizoid syndrome is prevalent in the lives of many psychotherapy clients but it is often not attended to because both a schizoid style and pattern are subtle; the clues are not obvious as they are with a schizoid disorder. After we had established a consistent working relationship, my client Maryann revealed, "I was an expert at hiding in plain sight. I simply told my former therapist what she wanted to hear".

DOI: 10.4324/9781003626718-8

With clients who have a clear diagnosis of *schizoid disorder*, their relational difficulties are often evident in the first session because they are unable to engage in interpersonal contact. Their tendency to withdraw emotionally is pervasive throughout all their relationships as well as in their relationship with the psychotherapist. They may have a number of acquaintances but they are usually without any meaningful relationships. People with a diagnosable schizoid disorder are more likely to avoid psychotherapy because it is too personal and intersubjective. If they do come for psychotherapy, they are reluctant to talk about their internal process and prefer to talk instead about their day-to-day activities. They often want specific solutions to a problem. Novels that portray a protagonist with a schizoid disorder provide us with insight about both their relational discombobulation and internal turmoil.

Hermann Hesse's novel *Steppenwolf* (1927/1963) tells the story of Harry Haller, a man with a schizoid disorder who wanders through his encounters with people like a bewildered alien, always a stranger in his community. He is prone to intellectualization but cannot tolerate interpersonal contact. As a result, his relational isolation and despair plague him with thoughts of suicide.

In Damon Galgut's (2010) autobiographical novel, *The Protagonist*, Damon reveals his personal anguish in his mix of first and third person voices as he wanders from country to country, split between his longing to be in relationship with the various people he encounters and his desperate efforts to withdraw into his internal sanctuary. In Conrad Aiken's 1934 short story "Silent Snow, Secret Snow" (1960), Paul, a sensitive adolescent boy, finds solace in daydreaming. He distances himself from the demands of school and family by withdrawing into a fantasy world of pure white snow – a world of silent snow that he must keep a secret. The first-person story of Paul, as well as each of the other two protagonists, provides us with a glimpse into their emotional and relational struggles. Unfortunately, none of these three stories address the qualities of relationship that the principal characters needed to heal from their internal distress.

Most psychotherapists are likely to have some clients who we can identify as having either a schizoid style or a schizoid pattern. The distinction between a style, a pattern, and a disorder is in the *frequency, duration*, and *intensity* of their tendency to engage in relational withdrawal, to suffer with internal criticism, and to maintain superficial relationships. The intrapsychic and behavioral manifestations are the same. The term *schizoid process* refers to an entire continuum of internal and social dynamics. It is used to describe the psychological process of anyone struggling within the schizoid syndrome.

Evidence that a client has a *schizoid pattern* is often apparent early in their psychotherapy as the client talks about current events while avoiding displaying any of their affect. They may talk about the people in their lives, but it is often without any emotional connection. For the first year of her therapy, Maryann used most of our therapy hours recounting – in great detail – the many novels she had read. She disregarded any inquiry that I made about her feelings or personal experiences while continuing to tell me about the stories in her books. It took me many months to decipher a pattern in the themes of her stories – authority, betrayal, and loneliness – that were metaphors about her life.

Clients with a schizoid pattern may not show evidence of it in the first few sessions, but the pattern will gradually become more evident as the therapeutic dialogue explores the quality of interpersonal contact in the client's life. A schizoid pattern will certainly become evident if the contact with the psychotherapist becomes emotionally intimate. Clients with a schizoid pattern will usually struggle to escape being emotionally involved in any intersubjective relationship.

I have found that a client's schizoid pattern is often first apparent through examining my own countertransference. Such clients often leave me with a sense that something important is missing. With such clients, my counter-transference reaction is to drift toward more cognitive and behavioral inter-ventions. I may lose my relational perspective, or I start watching the clock to see how soon the session will be over. My loss of interpersonal contact is engendered both by their superficial conversation and their fear (often unconscious and unexpressed) of a meaningful interpersonal relationship. Colleagues working with similar clients report that they feel inadequate, bored, or sleepy, and that they work harder and harder to make something happen.

It may be difficult to identify clients with a *schizoid style* early on in the psychotherapy. At first, they may have a compatible social presentation with a tendency to be shy, quiet, or introverted. However, when the client is stressed, or after they have been in psychotherapy for a while, the client with a schizoid style will display a tendency to withdraw from relationships, to be plagued by internal criticism, or to put on a social facade. They will talk about preferring to be alone, rather than being with people. They may find solace in reading, video games, or some solitary activity; alternatively, they may be busy with many energy-consuming activities.

Clients with a schizoid style often come to psychotherapy saying that they are depressed. As the psychotherapy unfolds with these clients, I have found that it is necessary to attend to the intense shame that they experience – a shame that is intrinsic to their depression. They are often afraid of being criticized and rejected for what they think, or how they behave; therefore, they report constraining themselves in social situations. They may be sad about past rejections, but compensate by anticipating further denigrating comments; hence, they do not reveal any vulnerabilities. Clients with a schizoid style struggle to comply with what others expect of them. They make efforts at fitting into what other people, including the psychotherapist, require. They disavow any possible anger at how they have been treated, because any protest may produce further criticism and rejection. The result of disavowing their anger and complying with others' expectations is their conviction that "there is something wrong with me".

In my practice of psychotherapy, I have found that it is necessary to provide sufficient attention (often repeated over many sessions) to five focal points that I consider essential in the therapeutic resolution of shame (Erskine, 1994, 1995). I will briefly spotlight them here. Shame is usually composed of:

- Hurt in not being accepted for **who I am**: i.e., "My worth as a human being is of less value"
- Fear of rejection for **how I am**: i.e., "My behavior means I'm not acceptable as I am"
- Disavowal of anger at not being accepted **as I am**: i.e., "I'll criticize myself so that you can never criticize me"
- Compliance with how **others define me**: i.e., – "I will be what you say I am"
- A belief that **"something is wrong with me"**

The term *schizoid process* depicts a "splitting" of the Self into various entities. The concept of "splitting" is borrowed from the early psychoanalytic literature and is used as a metaphor to explain our client's experience that their sense of Self is internally divided into diverse parts. Ronald Fairbairn (1954) used the term "splitting" to portray an archaic, self-protective polarization of a sense of self that is the result of overwhelming and conflicting affects (Rubens, 1996). R.D. Laing (1960) also used this concept in his book title, *The Divided Self*. Although the concept of splitting is not theoretically consistent with a physiological and relational perspective of psychotherapy, it serves as a useful metaphor in describing the client's internal sense of being segmented into various selves.

Therefore, I use the concept of splitting as a metaphor to describe how a child will struggle in their attempt to preserve their vitality and protect their vulnerability by dissecting their natural, whole Self into manageable parts. My clients seldom use terms like "splitting" or "schizoid"; they simply say, "I have different parts", or "I'm split inside". It is my conviction that each "part" requires its unique form of psychotherapy.

When we use the term splitting, we are describing a different dynamic than dissociation. As clients describe it, dissociation is a sense of "me" and "not-me", whereas splitting has a sense of "me" and "me" and "also me". Dissociation is often the result of physical and/or sexual trauma, persistent abuse, and a disorganized family environment. The splitting of a sense of Self usually occurs when children have parents who are consistently experienced as simultaneously *neglectful* and *controlling*. The result may be an *implicit fear of invasion*. Maryann described her mother as a "bee hovering around a flower, helping to pollinate, but always buzzing, pestering… and with a potential stinger. So, I learned to shut her out. I told her nothing. I wouldn't accept her pestering me and I didn't accept her helping me. I learned to live on my own".

Clients who rely on a schizoid process to manage their affect report that – in their childhood – significant caretakers were constantly misinterpreting their emotional expressions while controlling the child's sense of identity. In general, they report that their parents:

- Constantly misattuned to their affect and rhythm
- Were overprotective and authoritative
- Were critical of their behavior and their sense of "who I am"
- Failed to provide the tenderness and security necessary to heal from these traumatic relational ruptures

As a result, they are left with an implicit and intense fear of invasion. In response, they learned to "split off" any affective connection with their caretakers; they distanced themselves, as a way to manage their relationship; and they removed themselves from the intensity of this fear by splitting off their own vulnerability.

After a few years of psychotherapy, Maryann was able to summarize her schizoid process in her own words, "Even before I went to school my natural need to depend on my mother was continually met with a lot of fussing and smothering. She continually misinterpreted any emotions that I had. She was always controlling and invasive". Maryann went on to describe how, as a very young child, she sensed that "to be vulnerable was risky". She told several stories about how she developed patterns of relationship marked by a social facade and the absence of emotional expression.

When "splitting" is used as an attempt to self-stabilize, the vital core of the personality is withdrawn from the self that lives in the external word. The driving force is fear (Guntrip, 1961). Harry Guntrip, in a significant article about the schizoid process, says that a child "is capable of **fear** so intense that it can amount to fear of death in the absolute sense of annihilation" (Guntrip, as cited in Hazell, 1994, p. 161). Because of repeated criticism, control, and relational conflicts, a child under such stress may deny their need for security-in-relationship. Security may then be pseudo-accomplished through fantasies of being in a safe hiding place: a cave, wardrobe, closet, or womb.

People with a schizoid process may engage in *relational withdrawal*, a blankness or fantasy that does not involve real people. These clients described how they created a sense of security for themselves – a pseudo-security that requires no interpersonal relationship. They talk about their preoccupation in a world of constant work projects, excessive reading, video games, or TV. Some clients have described how they imagine being alone in their safe hiding place where their affect is diminished, "all is quiet", "there are no conflicts", "the rhythm of life is slowed down", and "the conflicts with my mother are forgotten". Marye O'Reilly-Knapp writes about her client's relational withdrawal, "In the withdrawn and hidden places there is only existence, with no true sense of self, and no sense of self with another. The person remains uninvolved, unintegrated, and lives in quiet desperation" (2001, p. 48).

It seems to me that many clients struggling with their schizoid process bring into their relationships with the psychotherapist a twin desperation: the desperate fear that they will be invaded once again, and the desperation of profound loneliness. Donald Winnicott (1988) summarized his patient's schizoid process as an attempt to regain psychological stability by creating "isolation in quiet". Guntrip summarizes the schizoid dilemma with, "They are caught in a conflict between equally strong needs for and fears of close good personal contacts, and in practice often find themselves alternatively driven into a relationship by their needs and then driven out again by their fears" (Hazell, 1994, p. 164, italics in the original).

Our clients' relational withdrawal may be stimulated by several factors:

- When there is external criticism and/or aggression. For example, one of my clients hides in her bed after her husband criticizes or shouts at her. She stabilizes herself by imagining that she is in her baby crib with padded sides all around her.
- When the pressure of internal criticism becomes oppressive. Another client struggling with his schizoid process suffered from constantly saying to himself, "I'm worthless" and "I don't deserve anything". In response, he felt a constant urge to hide from people.
- When the psychotherapy relationship is perceived as consistently providing protection; when there is sufficient security to reveal their secret place. *This withdrawal is for the purpose of physiological repair.* The client's therapeutic withdrawal is motivated by hope for healing contact but at the same time this relational withdrawal is laden with fear. There is a flickering sense of hope that the psychotherapist will understand their desperation, provide safety, and be attuned to their rhythm and affect. Simultaneously, they are afraid of possible criticism and invasion, a speed of interpersonal interaction that they cannot manage, and a demand that they be in a close relationship. Hidden beneath all of this is a fear of abandonment, so they are often the first to disrupt the therapeutic relationship.

Whenever I made inquiries about Maryann's feelings, I noticed that she would look toward the window. At first, I asked about what had occurred just before she averted her eyes but she was unable to answer. My attempts to get any answer were followed by her looking at the floor. She shrugged her shoulders and offered what seemed to be a superficial answer. Sometimes, she would tell me the details about a book she had read. I was left not knowing what was happening in her internal world.

Many clients who engage in a schizoid process will not reveal their relational withdrawal or talk about their secret hiding place, if the psychotherapist lacks attunement to their rhythm and affect, or if the psychotherapist is focused on interpretations, behavior change, or uses confrontation. With such therapeutic interventions the client will just turn away and will subtly withdraw. The child psychoanalyst Selma Fraiberg (1982/1983) identified how infants will "turn away" from interpersonal contact after they have experienced relational disruptions with their significant caretakers. The "turning away" from a parent who is invasive or controlling, when used repeatedly in early life, may become a pattern used in other significant relationships. Clients who rely on a schizoid process will internally "turn away" if there is a hint of control or invasion.

I eventually realized that Maryann's "turning away" was a clear indication that she experienced some uncomfortable disruption between us whenever I made a phenomenological inquiry. Over time she was able to tell me that my inquiries, such as, "What are you feeling now?" or, "What do you remember about...?" were understood by her to mean, "You are wrong for feeling what you are feeling" or, "You always exaggerate". She could not hear the caring and interest in my inquiry; she only imagined ridicule. Hence, she turned away or talked about one of the books she read.

Clients who use a schizoid process to self-stabilize often come to their psychotherapy because they feel depressed. They may appear to be adaptive with socially appropriate behavior but internally they have a vulnerable, frightened Self that is deeply hidden from interpersonal contact.

They are secretly lonely. Their relational needs force them to come out of hiding to make some superficial contact with people. Maryann's description of herself provides a good example. She was active in two charities. She organized fundraising social events for hundreds of people, she was an active board member in her professional association, and she attended many dinner parties, but she was often "secretly depressed". She said, "I prefer to just be left alone to read, but then I make all these social obligations that must get done".

Some clients who use a schizoid process have a social facade where their vulnerability is secret. Their *Vital & Vulnerable Self* is withdrawn and in hiding. They have a *Social Self* that is well rehearsed. Some clients may be able to engage in business and social activities effortlessly because they present themselves with a "social mask". This social facade helps them navigate a variety of interpersonal situations on only a superficial level. Harry Guntrip (1968) referred to this duality as the "schizoid compromise" where the person lives half in the external world and half in a secret hidden world.

Clients who have a schizoid process are perplexing to many therapists because they may:

- Have difficulty talking about needs, physiological sensation, and affect
- Forget what was discussed in previous sessions
- Be self-critical of any vulnerability, emotions, or the idea that they may have relational needs
- Be overwhelmed by shame
- Be frightened by phenomenological inquiry

- Fear dependence on the psychotherapist
- Have no memory of the interpersonal contact between self and the psychotherapist

This list of symptoms may apply to many clients, who would not be diagnosed with either a schizoid pattern or disorder, but who may rely periodically on a schizoid style when they are under stress.

Ronald Fairbairn (1954) described how children who have their affect and relational needs responded to with attunement and vitality will develop a "Whole Self". He used the term "libidinal ego" to describe the child's liveliness. This is what John Bowlby (1988) called a "Secure Self". This "Whole Self" is "Vital" and "Vulnerable", sensitive to both over- and understimulation, with a desire to explore, learn, and grow.

As I mentioned above, Fairbairn used the metaphor of "splitting" to describe his clients' internal struggles. "Splitting" is not real. People don't actually split their Self, but they may suffer with internal criticism and shame; they may actively keep significant feelings, needs, and internal dynamics a secret. The concept of "splitting" is a metaphor and, as a metaphor, it is a useful way for us to think about our clients and what is therapeutically needed in their relationship with us. In the section that follows, I will illustrate four types of "splitting" and share with you some of what I know about working with each aspect of the Self.

Figure 8.1 The Vital and Vulnerable Self

"Splitting": A Useful Metaphor

First Split

With repeated physical, rhythmic, and affect misattunements, developmentally unreasonable demands, and/or unrelenting criticism, a split may occur in the child's sense of Self. In response, a "Social Self" may be formed that hides the "Vital and Vulnerable Self". This first split is an attempt to be accepted, validated, and attached to caregivers. The child learns to adapt to what is expected because any form of self-expression or protest could be dangerous. Without the intellectual development to comprehend the ramifications, the child may conclude, "I will be what you want me to be".

Donald Winnicott refers to this split as "organization towards invulnerability" (Winnicott et al., 1992, p. 198), the creation of a "Social Self". It is as though the child is deciding, "If I am compliant, I am less likely to get hurt". Selma Fraiberg (1982/1983) described how very young children, even prior to the acquisition of language, learn to transform affect and behavior in order to be accepted, validated, and loved. Anger, fear, or unacceptable behavior may be split-off and replaced with a social mask of cooperation. This newly created "Social Self" maintains superficial relationships with people while the "Vital & Vulnerable Self" is hidden behind a social mask.

Figure 8.2 The 1st Split: The Social Self

Donald Winnicott called this "Social Self" a "false self" (1960), while Eric Berne called it an "adapted child" (1961).

While some pseudo-security is achieved by displaying a Social Self, the child remains anxiously attached because their emotional stability is always threatened. Sometimes, the "Vital & Vulnerable Self's" natural feelings, desires, and needs leak through the split and are expressed. The child then runs the risk of disapproval, rejection, and punishment. The fear of punishment leads to a second split. Maryann described herself articulately with, "I know I am segmented into parts because I'm not authentic with people. I am always acting smart and helpful, even when I don't know what is happening. I am always feeling pressured when I am with people. I work hard to please them but, at the same time, I long to be alone. But when I am alone, I'm either nervous or I just want to sleep. I don't know what I really want".

Second Split

As a way to maintain some attachment to their primary caretakers, the child will introject the thoughts, feelings, and behaviors of their significant others. Introjection is a self-stabilizing, unconscious identification with a significant caretaker that occurs in the absence of need-fulfilling contact (Erskine, 2003). Introjection functions to provide a false sense of attachment when the secure attachment is threatened.

Figure 8.3 The 2nd Split: Introjected Others Figure

With introjection vital aspects of the Self are replaced with characteristics of the significant other person. The introjected thoughts, feelings, and behaviors dominate the child's sense of self. Vitality is lost and the vulnerable child refrains from full self-expression. Unfortunately, since the parents have become internalized, these introjected others follow the child wherever they go. Instead of vitality the child feels shame and disappointment. Maryann said, "I cannot remember my mother's actual words but I just know that she wanted me to be perfect. She was always correcting the way I talked or looked so that her family and friends would think that she was a good mother. Right now, I can feel a pressure in my head to be social and happy looking the way mother always wanted me to appear".

Third Split

As children mature they become increasingly aware of the introjected attitudes of their parents. In order to stay attached to the parents a child will deny the effects of the parents' criticisms and controls. As a self-protective strategy they learn to criticize themselves. This self-criticism may be more demanding, intense, and continuous than the original criticism. With some clients we refer to this self-critical part as an "Internal Strategist". With other clients we call this the "Saboteur" because its purpose is to be more powerful than the introjected voices in order to maintain an illusion of attachment.

Maryann had volunteered a third time to organize a large function to raise money for a charity. For the next several weeks she was plagued by a loud internal voice that repeatedly said, "I won't do it right"; "I'll look foolish"; "I can't produce what they need"; "Stop being so tired and just push through it". She described the harsh bitter tone of her own internal voice.

As we examined what she felt and remembered, she realized that these were the same admonishments that she "lived with all the time in high school and at university. They are what made me get good grades, to be perfect".

This self-created "Saboteur" is clever in that it takes control by criticizing the "Vital & Vulnerable Self". The person becomes their own oppressor because the "Vital & Vulnerable Self" is frightened and goes into hiding; self-expression is perceived to be dangerous. Self-created criticism functions as both a deflection from awareness of the introjections and also as a way to have some control over difficult interpersonal situations. One client described their self-criticism as a "ghost that follows me everywhere", while another called it a "monster that hangs over me all the time".

The internal criticizer is controlling and despising of one's own relational needs, desires, and feelings. The constant self-criticism ensures that the person does not receive, seek, or even become aware of needs and feelings, except for the shame of having needs and feelings. It protects the "Vital & Vulnerable Self" from the criticisms of others but it destroys the very vitality it is trying to protect. Both the "Saboteur" and the "Social Self" function to anticipate and avoid real dangers of interpersonal conflict by inflicting an even more severe criticism on themselves.

During the second year of her psychotherapy, Maryann revealed some of her internal criticisms: "I'm not worth anything"; "I don't dare make mistakes"; "No one likes a depressive like me". Maryann often concluded her social activity stories with, "I'm just not good enough". These self-criticisms preceded and superseded any possible criticism from other people because Maryann strategically neutralizes any potential disapproval before it is ever made. However, rather than protecting her, each of these self-inflected criticisms increased her sense of "feeling pressured when I am with people".

Fourth Split

Under the intense pressures of either external criticism, introjected criticism, or the oppression of the "Internal Saboteur", there may be a fourth split in the person's sense of self. They may withdraw to a "Sequestered Self", where their vitality and vulnerability is completely disconnected from human contact in a search for quiet and peace. Marye O'Reilly-Knapp (2001) calls this fourth split the "encapsulated self", where the person withdraws into their internal world because they are convinced that there is no security-in-

Figure 8.4 The 3rd Split: Internal Saboteur

Figure 8.5 The 4th Split: The Sequestered Self

relationship. This withdrawal is like living in a secret and protective closet, cave, or castle where the client can hide from demanding relationships.

As our therapy relationship progressed, Maryann put into words her strong urge to withdraw from any human contact. "I hate the pressures I have always lived with. I don't want to be social. I just want to find a quiet place. Often I go to a toilet and sit there for 10 or 15 minutes just to escape people". On another day, she added, "Even though I am lonely I never want to be in relationship with a partner. I don't want them messing with my life. I just want to be left alone to read my books. Books never invade me".

Considerations for Psychotherapy

A unique form of psychotherapy is needed for the Self that emerges from each split. Some clients will require that we attend to the "Social Self" first. Other clients will require relief from introjected messages, attitudes, or criticisms of significant others before we can proceed. Usually later in the psychotherapy it will be necessary to address the functions of the self-created criticisms, and most will require careful attention to the "Sequestered Self". The various methods are not sequential. The focus of the psychotherapy may flow from one aspect to another and then back again. Some clients may be burdened by internal criticism and a compulsion to maintain a social facade while others will be secretly hiding from interpersonal involvements.

Adjusting the psychotherapy for each individual and their unique split of the Self requires that we think and work multidimensionally.

Each part of the Self has its unique pattern of relational attachment. In creating an effective in-depth psychotherapy, it is essential that the psychotherapist respond to the style of relational attachment unique to each part. The "Vital & Vulnerable Self" reflects securely attached relationships where parents were predictably responsive to the child's various needs. As a result, the person is interpersonally contactful and excited about exploring and learning. Even secure individuals need acknowledgement, validation, and ongoing responsiveness to their emerging relational needs.

Working with the first split: The Social Self is relationally attached by *hope* and *anxiety* because significant caretakers were *unpredictably responsive.* Out of hope and anxiety, they cling to dysfunctional relationships; they will adapt to the other at any cost. When our therapeutic work is focused on the "Social Self", I want to help the client acknowledge the various ways they have adapted. I validate the significance of compliance. I help the client explore the advantages of a "Social Self", such as: maintaining attachment; less possibility for humiliation; less punishment; or achieving some comforting attention. I also help the client recognize the various disadvantages of a "Social Self", such as: loss of joy; loss of vitality; emotional numbness; or loss of physical sensations.

I strive to help the client discover the vital aspects of the self that have been lost such as joy, anger, excitement, exploration, and their uniqueness. Much of our therapy time may be devoted to helping the client become aware of their body sensations, becoming sensitive to their various affects, and validating the importance of vulnerability. This includes helping the client discover their relational needs – both the needs of childhood as well as today's relational needs.

When working with the split between the "Vital & Vulnerable Self" and the Social Self, I often use the "empty chair" method to enable the "Vital & Vulnerable Self" to express body sensations, affects, and the homeostatic functions of splitting. I want to support the client's natural protests and to facilitate the client in identifying and expressing their physical and relational needs.

I might also use the "two-chair" method to externalize and resolve the intrapsychic conflict between the Social Self and the Vital & Vulnerable Self. It may be necessary for the client to physically express retroflected feeling and to actively protest to the introjected other(s) by defining one's self. Any of the methods that invite clients into interpersonal contact are effective in working with this first split. The Gestalt therapy methods of the "empty chair" and "two-chair" techniques are designed to clarify and resolve the intrapsychic conflict between a person's natural desires and the introjected attitudes of significant others (Perls, 1969, 1973; Perls & Baumgardner, 1975).

The "Vital & Vulnerable Self" is often confused, like a frightened child. Many of my clients learned to be compliant at several developmental stages. I find it necessary to talk to the child in my client about what they needed from an attuned parent. I want them to become aware of how they managed the criticisms and demands placed upon them. I aim to provide the quality or relationship that is protective of the client's exploration of change. I provide permission to be authentic, self-expressive, and intimate. However, I always want to assess the level of internal punishment before giving encouragement to change.

When working with the split between the "Vital & Vulnerable Self" and the Social Self, I encourage the client to express their relational need for self-definition and their need to make an impact. The expression of these vital needs can occur relationally between the client and a receptive psychotherapist, or to an imagined other, by using the "empty chair" method.

After several sessions in which I talked with Maryann about the absence of any joy in her life, her physical and emotional numbness, and her constant urge to either read or sleep, we contracted to do some two-chair work. I asked her to imagine her "Social Self" in one chair and her "Vital & Vulnerable Self" in the other. My role was to function like a cinema director, to suggest when she might change positions. We began with the "Social Self" boasting about having many friends and activities, how she received lots of attention and praise from acquaintances, and admonishing the other part of her for "hiding from people". Then I suggested that she change chairs so as to give her "Vital & Vulnerable Self" a chance to express what she was holding inside.

The Vulnerable Self talked about how burdened she felt with all the social activity, with "putting on a good face". As I encouraged her to put her inner sensations into words, she detailed her loss of hope and desire and then added, "I have no pleasure in life because you are always playing a role". At this point, I asked her to change chairs. We continued the dialogue, back and forth from one chair to another, for another 15 minutes, until the "Vital & Vulnerable Self" became a strong voice and proclaimed that "I have the right to be me. If I want to be social I will do it and if I want to be alone I will be alone... And, I appreciate how you can adapt to any situation; you are successful with people. I don't want to lose that skill but I also need to be alone, the freedom to be me". With this two-chair dialogue, we were facilitating an integration of these two divergent parts of her self.

Working with the second split: In the second split, the child has unconsciously identified with some significant others in order to disavow their needs and feelings and to, importantly, maintain a semblance of a relationship. Although they struggle to maintain attachment, their pattern is *avoidant* because significant caretakers were *predictably unresponsive*. They are attached via *neglect* and *aggression* – neglect and aggression that is often turned against the "Vital & Vulnerable Self".

When the internal conflict is between the "Introjected Other" and the "Social Self", I use phenomenological inquiry to identify how the client complied with messages and demands. I use historical inquiry to identify any criticism and control that may have been a part of their life. And I encourage them to talk about their fears, the lost opportunities, or punishments that they may have received for being authentic.

Sometimes, I might use a two-chair dialogue to externalize the introjected criticism and to facilitate the person becoming aware of the importance of a Social Self, or I may use myself as an *interposition* between the introjected other and my client's "Social Self" or "Vital & Vulnerable Self". I may engage my client in actual psychotherapy with the introjected other (see Erskine, 2015, Chapters 16 and 17, for a detailed description of these methods).

In the second year of Maryann's psychotherapy, once she seemed secure with me, I asked Maryann to imagine her mother sitting in a chair across from the two of us. I talked with Maryann about how I would support her, both as a child and as an adult. I encouraged her to tell her mother what she had never said aloud. At first Maryann was hesitant in talking to the image of her mother. After a few fearful interruptions she was able to say aloud, "You have always controlled me. I was never allowed to be me". I coaxed her to say it with the full intensity that she felt inside and she exploded with, "I want to be me. I want to make my own mistakes. I want to be me. But being me was not good enough for you". She stood up and shook her finger at the mother she imagined in the chair, "You are the one that's imperfect. I'm never good enough for you... but it is you who has a problem. You could never appreciate me".

Working with the third split: The self-created criticism of the "Saboteur" begins as a three-part strategy:

- To deny the emotional impact of the actual criticism from others
- To remain unaware of the internal influence of the introjected criticism
- To ensure that the "Vital & Vulnerable Self" remains protected, out of sight, and unexpressed

The relational attachment pattern of the "Saboteur" is disdainful. They undervalue relationships and inhibit sadness, fear, and intimacy while being full of rage. They have an implicit fear of vulnerability.

With several clients I have discovered that their internal criticism is a secret, as though they are ashamed of it. The constant internal criticism may be traumatic because there has been no reparative relationship that served to neutralize the toxicity of the criticism. I invite the client to say the criticism out loud so that I can hear and feel the impact of it.

I encourage them to amplify the volume and intensity of the internal criticism, to externalize what has been internal. I want the client to distinguish the difference between the self-created "Saboteur" and the "Introjected Voice". I may engage the "Saboteur" in a dialogue about the origin and purpose of the criticism. The tendency for self-created criticism often begins in early adolescence as a strategy to protect one's self from others' criticism, control, and rejection. I focus our therapeutic dialogue on the original purpose of the criticism and how that purpose no longer applies in the client's life today.

In the first year and a half of her psychotherapy, Maryann would allude to "an inner voice that controls all that I do". She was reluctant to give me any details about what the voice said. One day she uttered, "The voice always pressures me. I just want to escape into a good book". She then realized that she had two different sensations: the first was that she was ashamed of having the voice, and second, that she felt overwhelming shame with the criticisms the voice was saying. She was confused. "Sometimes I think the voice is my own and sometimes it's similar to my mother's harangues".

Over the next several weeks, I devoted some time in each session to give Maryann an opportunity to express internal criticisms out loud so that both she and I could hear them in their full intensity. Eventually she was able to voice several of her internal condemnations: "I'm a fake"; "I didn't do it good enough"; "I'll never make it"; "I look so awful that everyone will laugh at me".

As we explored the function of each of these self-created criticisms, Maryann became aware that she had created the voice "to beat my mother at her own game! If I criticize myself, I don't have to remember her criticisms". This led to her having a series of memories – memories that she had not previously had. "My mother was constantly invasive. I had to find a way to drown out her controlling voice". In a later session, she discovered that a second function of her self-created criticism was to "make me do what I didn't want to do. All through my life these internal criticisms pushed me to stay awake and study, to work hard, to put on a good face for people. The criticisms have helped me to be successful at work and in all my social activities because I am always working hard to adapt to the critics. I hate my self-criticisms yet I am afraid that if I give them up, I'll never be good enough. This is a shitty situation. I want to be free to be me".

Working with the fourth split: The "Sequestered Self" is hiding, longing for security, quiet, and escape from painful interpersonal relationships. The attachment pattern of the "Sequestered Self" is *isolated*. Relational withdrawal is used to manage their intense affect and to escape from either internal criticism or possible external criticisms. Psychotherapeutic methods that are effective for other parts of the Self may not be effective for the "Sequestered Self". The client withdrawing from interpersonal contact requires a unique form of psychotherapy to heal from the hidden wounds of cumulative relational failures. For a detailed case presentation on working sensitively with a client's "Sequestered Self" see the article entitled "Relational withdrawal, attunement to silence: Psychotherapy of the schizoid process" (Erskine, 2020).

When working with the "Sequestered Self", I focus on providing security within our therapeutic relationship. Once the client has some sense of security in our relationship, I proceed with helping the client to feel their physical sensations, affects, and memories. This is much deeper awareness work, often quiet and less conversational than when working with the loss of sensations in the first split. Although they do not trust, they need a psychotherapist who is reliable, consistent, and dependable. I invite them to withdraw while they are in our therapy sessions, to go to their "quiet place".

I recommend that they close their eyes and take a few minutes to feel the safety of being in their private place. I speak to them slowly and reassuringly with, "I'm staying right here" and "I'm listening to you, even when you are silent". I don't expect a response. I'm patient and provide time for the client to make internal contact with their body sensations, feelings, and memories without talking. While they are in their quiet, private place, I may speak to them in short validating sentences:

- "It is important to have a quiet place".
- "It is necessary to feel safe inside".
- "There is no need to hurry". "I am right here watching over you".

I have learned that when a client is in their sequestered place the best thing I can do is relax and not try to make something happen. I often do some deep, calming breathing while staying focused on the client's non-verbal experience. I create the time and place for them to feel both the security of their "quiet place" and my quiet, non-demanding presence.

When the client has a tendency to withdraw from interpersonal contact, phenomenological inquiry – effective with many other types of clients – may not be appropriate. They may become silent or provide only superficial responses because they experience inquiry as an invasion or a demand for the "correct answer". Instead of using phenomenological and historical inquiry, *therapeutic description* may be more effective.

Therapeutic description provides the client with validation of their often unspoken emotional and physical experiences. Therapeutic description is based on attunement to the client's rhythm, affect, archaic and current relational needs, and an understanding of their cognitive process. Therapeutic description provides a vocabulary for previously unspoken experiences to be acknowledged and eventually talked about.

Therapeutic description facilitates an interpersonal connectedness between client and psychotherapist by providing the client with a sense that "my therapist knows my internal experience, my fear of relationship, the safety in silence, the importance of hiding, and the depth of my loneliness".

Therapeutic description is not the same as explanations or interpretations that may be given to other clients to enhance their cognitive understanding of their psychological dynamics. It is about attuning our self to our client's non-verbalized sensations and experiences and helping the person form a language to talk about their physical and emotional sensations.

The effective use of therapeutic description requires that we use a tentative voice, not a voice of certainty, and watch for the client's physiological reactions of acknowledgement, disagreement, or nothing. Let's look at a few examples of translating phenomenological inquiry into therapeutic description. Rather than asking:

- "Why are you quiet?", a therapeutic description such as, "It must be important to be quiet", may be much easier for the client to accept.
- "What are you feeling?", it may be more effective to simply state a description, "It must be difficult to find words to describe what you are feeling".
- "What is happening in your body?", it may be more contactful with clients who tend to use relational withdrawal to say something like, "Your body must be tense holding all those feeling inside all the time" or "Being in a safe hiding place seems so necessary".

Throughout Maryann's time in psychotherapy there were many times when I witnessed her momentary withdrawal. I would inquire, "Where did you go?". In response she would immediately answer, "I was just thinking". If I inquired further, she would give me a deflective answer about something happening in her social life or what she had just read. I sensed that she was not "thinking" but that she was retreating to some internal place.

If I inquired with, "What just happened? You seemed to go away", her face would form a scowl and she would turn away in silence. I surmised that she heard each inquiry as an accusation that she was doing something wrong. I began making comments instead of an inquiry. For example, "My questions must seem invasive"; she responded by giving a "Yes" nod of her head. Whenever I would notice a brief retreat to her internal place, I stopped inquiring. Instead, I described what I imagined her experience to be, "It must seem necessary to have a private, quiet place". She again nodded a "Yes".

When I would see her withdrawing, I began making therapeutic descriptions such as, "It is important to have a safe place to rest", "It must be overwhelming listening to people", or, "I'm right here, even when you are quiet". My comments described her internal process and what she might need; they were not as invasive as my questions, and she remained free to stay in her safe internal place.

Maryann began withdrawing more frequently in our sessions. I think that her willingness to withdraw to her place of safety while being in my presence was now possible because of the non-judgmental, non-criticizing perspective that I brought to our psychotherapy relationship during the previous years. She now felt safe enough in our therapeutic relationship to allow me to witness her retreat to her "hiding place". People struggling with a schizoid process will withdraw when there is a threat of invasion, but they try to keep their withdrawal a secret. Yet, when they feel secure in a therapeutic relationship they will withdraw in search of healing – a healing that occurs through the psychotherapist's sustained attunement to the client's affect and rhythm.

I increasingly sat in silence and relaxed with my yoga breathing. I watched her intensely for any clues as to what she was experiencing and I periodically made comments like: "There is no rush. Take your time to be quiet"; "Having a safe place is so important"; or, "In a private place, no one can criticize or control". I watched her head and shoulders for the little nods of agreement; these were my guide to continue with my therapeutic descriptions. Sometimes there would be no nod. Then I would patiently wait in silence and, some minutes later, I could make a similar therapeutic description that I hoped would reflect her inner experience.

In each session, I would reserve time long before the end of the session for us to discuss what was occurring in the psychotherapy. She repeatedly informed me that my quiet, patient way of being with her was "a salve, a soothing ointment". Following another session, she said, "I had to invent a quiet place. Growing up I had no safe place in which to go. My mother was always hovering over me. But you are just there. You are not demanding anything of me. You are not actually with me but you are out there, safe. Like you are watching over my welfare".

With this kind of therapeutically supported withdrawal, Maryann began having vivid memories; she would withdraw into her quiet place for about ten minutes and then she would suddenly have a memory. As we continued the supported withdrawal her internal images were of an increasingly younger age. Her memories were not explicit, rather they were composed of impressions, body sensations, and procedural reactions. Through therapeutic implications, we were able to compose a story about her deep sense of loneliness.

In my experience as a psychotherapist there are many errors that I have made while working with several clients who use a schizoid process to stabilize their affect. I have been fortunate to have clients who have served as my teachers, who have helped me understand and appreciate the schizoid process and what they need in a healing relationship. Their honesty and ways of being in our sessions have periodically exposed dimensions of my countertransference that were not obvious with other types of clients, such as my desire to achieve a specific outcome and my urge to do the psychotherapy quickly. With such an internal urge it is impossible to attune to the clients' sequestered rhythms and affects.

I have learned that it takes patience and long moments of silence to reach the client's "Sequestered Self", and much longer to provide a consistently dependable healing relationship (Erskine, 2021). It is essential that we psychotherapists foster a sensitivity to the client's never-spoken, emotion-filled story; adjust our psychotherapeutic involvement to the rhythms of a frightened child; and attune to the clients' deep sense of fear and loneliness.

References

Aiken, C. (1960). Silent snow, secrete snow. In: *The collected short stories of Conrad Aiken*. World Publishing. (Original work published 1934). This story may be retrieved from https://fullreads.com/horror/silent-snow-secret-snow/.

Berne, E. (1961). *Transactional analysis in psychotherapy: A systematic individual and social psychiatry*. Grove Press.

Bowlby, J. (1988). *A secure base*. Basic Books.

Erskine, R. G. (1994). Shame and self-righteousness: Transactional Analysis perspectives and clinical interventions. *Transactional Analysis Journal*, 24(2), 86–102.

Erskine, R. G. (1995). A Gestalt therapy approach to shame and self-righteousness: Theory and methods. *British Gestalt Journal*, 4(2), 107–117.

Erskine, R. G. (2003). Introjection, psychic presence and Parent ego states: Considerations for psychotherapy. In C. Sills & H. Hargaden (Eds.), *Ego states: Key concepts in Transactional Analysis, contemporary views* (pp. 83–108). Worth Publishing.

Erskine, R. G. (2015). *Relational patterns, therapeutic presence: Concepts and practice of Integrative Psychotherapy*. Karnac Books.

Erskine, R. G. (2020). Relational withdrawal, attunement to silence: Psychotherapy of the schizoid process. *International Journal of Integrative Psychotherapy*, 11, 14–28.

Erskine, R. G. (2021). *A healing relationship: Commentary of therapeutic dialogues*. Phoenix Publishing.

Fairbairn, W. R. D. (1954). *Psychoanalytic studies of the personality*. Basic Books.

Fraiberg, S. (1982/1983). Pathological defences in infancy. *Psychoanalytic Quarterly*, 51, 612–635. Also published in 1983 (Fall) in *Dialogue: A Journal of Psychoanalytic Perspectives* (pp. 65–75).

Galgut, D. (2010). *In a strange room*. McClelland & Stewart.

Guntrip, H. (1961). *Personality structure and human interaction*. Hogarth.

Guntrip, H. (1968). *Schizoid phenomena, object-relations and the self*. International Universities Press.

Hazell, J. (Ed.). (1994). *Personal relations therapy: The collected papers of H. J. S. Guntrip*. Jason Aronson.

Hesse, H. (1963). *Steppenwolf*. Modern Library. (Original work published 1927).

Laing, R. D. (1960). *The divided self*. Tavistock.

O'Reilly-Knapp, M. (2001). Between two worlds: The encapsulated self. *Transactional Analysis Journal*, 31, 44–54.

Perls, F. S. (1969). *Gestalt therapy verbatim*. Real People Press.

Perls, F. S. (1973). *The Gestalt approach and eyewitness to therapy*. Science & Behavior Books.

Perls, F. S., & Baumgardner, P. (1975). *Legacy from Fritz: Gifts from Lake Cowichan*. Science & Behavior Books.

Rubens, R. L. (1996). The unique origins of Fairbairn's theories. *Psychoanalytic Dialogues: The International Journal of Relational Perspectives*, 6(3), 413–435.

Winnicott, D. W. (1960). *Ego distortion in terms of true and false self. The maturational process and the facilitating environment: Studies in the theory of emotional development*. International Universities Press.

Winnicott, D. W. (1988). *Human nature*. Routledge.

Winnicott, D. W., Shepherd, R., & Davis, M. (Eds.) (1992). *Psychoanalytic explorations*. Harvard University Press.

Chapter 9

Psychotherapy of Relational Withdrawal

Perspectives from a Client and Therapist

Christine's Preface

I am writing this chapter to share my therapeutic experience so that we, as professional psychotherapists, can refine our methods for clients who are silent about their internal process; I am referring to people who engage in a schizoid process by withdrawing from interpersonal contact, who are sequestered in an inner world of loneliness.

I have always felt a sense of aloneness deep inside. Even though I was surrounded by people, I felt empty, lost, and alone. From the outside, no one ever suspected that I always felt a vast distance between me and other people. My efforts to form some semblance of a social life focused on doing what I thought was expected of me. I masked the intensity of my emotions, a process that was exhausting me. So, I regularly felt like withdrawing, isolating myself, just to rest. But in those moments, I missed interpersonal contact; I lived a real paradox. For me, relating to others was either too intense and invasive, or not enough and boring. This inner conflict caused me to suffer. I was frequently overcome with shame and struggled with harsh criticism of myself, as if I was the one who didn't know how to relate to others. And that was true! I didn't know how to communicate my internal turmoil. But what I hadn't realized was that my internal struggle was an attempt to restore my integrity, damaged by the failure of the significant people in my early environment to respond to my needs.

I often tried to gain some relief from this emotional paradox during my psychotherapy. But talking didn't help. I masked my vulnerability with words. Thinking about myself was easy, much easier than truly feeling my internal sensations. Therefore, I talked about myself, often in a socially appropriate first-person voice, but inside it was as if I were talking about someone else. I was internally split off from my own liveliness.

In my previous psychotherapy sessions with Richard during a series of five-day professional workshops, I tried to accept his invitations to create real interpersonal contact. Sometimes I was able to have an authentic connection with him. But most of the time my internal sense of fear was stronger; I held

DOI: 10.4324/9781003626718-9

back from being fully present. Moreover, my ongoing therapist "fell into the trap" of accepting my false social-self because what I showed them was just a façade, far from who I really am.

When I started this particular workshop, I had no idea that I would work on my tendency to withdraw from intimate interpersonal contact. I'd been stimulated when reading Richard's book *Withdrawal, Silence, Loneliness* (2023) and I was excited by the opportunity to work with him. However, I was unaware that I was about to uncover a wounded, silent, lonely, curled-up part of myself.

The following verbatim transcript is interspersed with several descriptions of my internal experience and Richard's comments on the therapeutic process. In providing this unique form of research, we hope to provide our colleagues with a greater understanding of the importance of therapeutically focusing on the client's withdrawal into silence and their struggle with loneliness.

The psychotherapy with the sequestered self does not involve talking, thought or explanations, or any focus on behaviors. Rather the psychotherapy is focused on the client's internal body experience and dormant affect; a quality of interpersonal contact that heals early traumas. In the psychotherapy of the schizoid process words are of little importance, the quality of the relationship is central. It is the rhythm and the texture of the voice that guide the patient to discover his hidden place, to once again feel their dormant affects, and to "bring my vital self into the world". The vulnerable, ashamed, and lonely part of the patient experiences the harmonious respect of their boundaries through affect and rhythmic attunement, validation, and the unconditional acceptance. The following describes my personal journey into the psychotherapy of the schizoid process.

Richard's Preface

This article presents a unique form of psychotherapy research. Rather than using a parametric research design involving several participants, the single-person research format presented here makes use of three significant components: a verbatim transcript of a recorded psychotherapy session; a detailed description of the client's internal experience during and after the psychotherapy session; and the psychotherapist's reflections on what he was feeling and thinking. When we assemble a significant number of single-person research reports we will have further information to distinguish what constitutes an effective or ineffective psychotherapy for psychotherapy clients who are lonely, silent about their internal experience, and who self-stabilize by relying on relational withdrawal.[1]

This article also provides an example of psychotherapy with a client who engages in relational withdrawal. The one-hour psychotherapy session occurred in a five-day psychotherapy workshop for professional psychotherapists. The workshop includes teaching about psychotherapy theory and methods, demonstration of the methods with participants, and an exploration of what is effective and what is ineffective in the psychotherapy. Christine, the client in this verbatim transcript, has attended several previous workshops.

Session Transcript

The setting for this series of five-day residential professional training workshops is in a rural retreat center in France. The room is spacious, with 24 participants sitting in a circle. Christine chooses to sit on a large mattress in the center of the room, just in front of Richard's chair.

R: *[with a soft voice]* So what did you have in mind when you sat down here?
C: *[with a cheerful voice]* What came to my mind was my very first marathon with you, and the first words I said when we were doing the round were: "I don't have the words". *[laughing]* And... I have your book in mind that I am reading now, and I was wondering whether this time I would sort of be taking refuge in silence or whether I would be in another place.

[6 seconds silence]

R: *During this pause I am wondering if Christine is describing age regression to a preverbal level or if she is indicating that she withdraws to an inner place without words. Or both. I want her to feel secure in our relationship so that she can explore her inner world. I realize that she has attended other workshops in which she has alluded to using withdrawal to manage interpersonal relationships. Perhaps our relationship is sufficiently secure that this may be a good time for her to fully experience her private place with someone who is protectively present.*
R: *[with a softer voice]* What if we made it OK to take refuge in silence? And that I just accompany you... without... interfering? *[9 seconds silence]* You just close your eyes. And let's see if you can go... to that private place. And I am going to stay right here. I am not... doing anything fast or move toward you, but I am going to keep my eye on you and listen. Even if you are silent, I'll listen.

[12 seconds silence]

R: *I know from past experience with clients who engage in relational withdrawal that patience and tenderness are essential in providing the security that is necessary to appreciate and explore their inner world. Many clients who rely on relational withdrawal have lost touch with their own emotional rhythm. I want to provide a secure relationship that allows them to process their internal affect at their natural pace. This often requires "pregnant pauses" so that the client's affect-laden experiences can be expressed and integrated.*

C: *[with sadness in her voice]* I am hearing you from far away.

C: *My sensations change. My metabolism slows down: I breathe more slowly; my chest seems lighter. The silence in the room seems very present. I go inside of myself. Richard's voice now seems like it's far away. I barely hear him. I am withdrawing, but I don't know why.*

R: Yes, I am breathing, and move, and scratch a little bit, but I am listening to you, so there is no rush. *[6 seconds silence]* You can take all the time you need.

R: *I alert Christine that I might be rustling about. I don't want to startle her or distract her from her private place, so I give her a warning that I may make some sounds. It seems essential that I adjust myself to her natural rhythm.*

[5 seconds silence]

C: *The urge I feel in my body vanishes when I get permission to slow down. I no longer need to adapt or to submit myself to the rhythm of the world. Softness in Richard's voice pushes me to relax. As my defenses dissolve, I feel vulnerable, but I don't want to. A part of me tries to resist, but I need so much calm.*

C: *[with more energy in her voice]* I feel as if I'm in space, but there is no planet. And the space is thick.

C: *This silence becomes a friend, an envelope, a protection. I feel contained, safe, far from the outside world. Nothing seems important anymore. There is only me and Richard's distant voice. I sense my skin and my breathing. It is a relief to be only with myself without worrying about anything else.*

[2 seconds silence]

R: Just go ahead! Go into your space.

C: I am moving my arms. I am playing with that thick texture. I am playing all alone.

C: *Because nothing else but me exists at this point, I distract myself with my own body. It's funny. I feel free. This is an unusual feeling.*

[2 seconds silence]

R: *[with a sad voice]* All... alone...

R: *I repeat her words "all alone" and emphasize the sadness that I think her words convey. I do not want to make any explanation or ask any question that may distract her from her internal experience.*

[19 seconds silence]

C: *[with sadness]* There are no living beings around me. I don't even know they exist.

C: *Now, it gets uncomfortable. The loneliness that used to be pleasant is becoming unpleasant. I'm missing something, but I don't know what it is yet, so I prefer to stay alone. It is safer.*

R: *It seems important that Christine stay in her private place long enough to appreciate the functions of being sequestered. The relational withdrawal often provides a comfortable hiding place away from other peoples' potential invasion; it provides a pseudo sense of security. Relational withdrawal also provides a familiar lonely place –a place of desire for the other person's sensitive connection, yet simultaneously there is a fearful predictability that something will go wrong in the interpersonal contact, just as it has occurred in the past.*

R: *[in a higher tone]* Perhaps it is important... to have no one around.

[11 seconds silence]

C: Yes and no.

C: *The uncomfortable part of me grows. I feel split in two parts: one is seeking contact with others, and the other is frightened by them.*

R: *I am remembering Harry Guntrip's descriptive comment about how some clients are driven into hiding out of fear, and driven into personal contact out of loneliness (Hazell, 1994 , p. 164). This is the schizoid compromise: seeking contact with others and at the same time being frightened by them.*

[15 seconds silence]

R: *[with a low voice]* But it is so important to have a safe place.

R: *With this comment, I am validating the importance of her safe place.*

[4 seconds silence]

C: Calm.

[8 seconds silence]

R: Safe... calm.

[6 seconds silence]

C: *[with a softer voice]* You say "safe" but I can't even feel the fear or the danger even though I know they are there.

C: *Richard's words help me to clarify that it is fear that I am feeling. Emotions are stuck in my head, and I can't feel them in my body. I'm cut off. I have the impression that there's something wrong with me, that I should experience things differently. My situation now seems weird to me.*

R: *[in a low, barely audible voice]* How wonderful to have a place where you don't have to feel the fear, the danger. Just to float in thick space. Must be wonderful to have such a place.

R: *I am describing what I imagine a function of the withdrawal to be: a place without fear of danger.*

[6 seconds silence]

C: *[with a tremulous voice]* I feel touched that you said this, that you are joining me in there. I always had the impression that I had to choose to be there or on Earth with others... pretending. *[14 seconds silence]* I did not know that I had the right.

C: *I am close to crying. At this moment I start feeling ashamed, Richard makes it OK to feel that way. I feel like I am allowed to be who I really am. I start thinking that maybe I don't need to hide away from the world, that someone, at least Richard, wants to contact my genuine self, but I am still scared.*

R: I will accompany you. *[6 seconds silence]* But I don't want to invade your place.

C: I would like to invite you and to show you the somersaults I am doing in space. But I have the impression that if you are there, I won't be able to do it anymore.

C: *The presence of another freezes me. I can't be myself in the presence of someone else. I'm again cut into two parts, and it is painful.*

R: *[with a gentle and cheerful voice]* Yeah, so I want to sit right here, and listen to your description, and I will imagine it all with you.

R: *It seems essential that I not invade her private place, but that I am a witness to her sensations, affect, and images.*

[6 seconds silence]

C: *[with a more energetic voice]* So I am doing the starfish turning on itself... I am stretching... *[voice gets sad]* But it ends up being boring. I feel something is missing.

R: But it is so important in the beginning to amuse yourself... By stretching. *[14 seconds silence]*

R: *My words are meant to be validating of her experience because I am concerned that she may define her sensations as "something is wrong with me".*

C: Boring.

[20 seconds silence]

C: *[her shoulders retract, with a sad voice]* It is pulling in my belly… *[voice gets lower, almost whispering]* I have the impression that I am struggling with sadness.

C: *The top of my body stiffens. I stop moving. My breathing gets shorter. I can't think anymore. Sensations get more present, but I don't want them to.*

[12 seconds silence]

R: *[with a deeper and steady voice]* But the sadness is there. The loneliness. That you called boredom.

R: *I emphasize the sadness and loneliness that she previously said. I want her to feel the full sense of her sadness and loneliness and not transpose it to boredom. I reflect on Salma Fraiberg's (1983) description of how children will transpose their affect when a particular feeling does not elicit a contactful response from a significant other, such as transposing anger to fear or loneliness to boredom.*

[22 seconds silence]

C: *[starts crying]* Now I don't find it so entertaining. I have the impression that I have no choice.

R: *[with a low and soft voice]* No choice… *[11 seconds silence]* No choice… *[9 seconds silence]* But so important to have your private place.

R: *Again I am validating her phenomenological experience to lessen the likelihood that she will criticize herself.*

C: *[with a higher voice]* And the more you are saying this, the more I have the impression that I have no choice.

C: *I feel like a prisoner to myself. I feel a constraint, an impediment that I generate within myself, an impossibility of living. I feel in contact with Richard, but it's dangerous. Now it is more a conflict than a split. By now, both needs are available: withdrawal and contact.*

R: *[a little more animation in the voice]* Perhaps no choice. Just the need to escape to a private place… A quiet place.

R: *With my comment I want to validate the significance of her private, quiet place.*

[14 seconds silence]

C: *[with a relaxed voice]* The more you say this, the more I have the impression that the Earth is coming closer.

C: *By accepting my withdrawal, Richard shows me that I have the right to feel what I feel. He's not intruding. I have the right to refuse contact, and this is what allows me to consider it. He respects me, my needs and my rhythm. Now I feel in contact with him, but this time I feel safe. It's not what I expected; I expected to be forced. He's waiting for me. He's right there, available to me.*

[7 seconds silence]

R: It is so important to have a place to withdraw.
C: *[my upper body relaxes a little]* Yes.
R: Maybe nobody knows how important it is.
C: *[answers quickly]* You know... You know: I've read about it. And I can feel it now. And it is strange for me to feel normal in this.
R: *[speaks more softly barely audible]* Maybe there is a deeper hiding place... [8 seconds silence] When the external world gets too bad... [19 seconds silence]*
R: *My comment is based on my wondering if there is a deeper more sequestered place that she might retreat to, if her private place is threatened. Previous clients have talked about various levels of withdrawal depending on how critical or invasive they experienced the other person.*
C: *[crying]*
R: A place to escape criticism.
R: *I am again validating the significance of hiding to escape criticism. I made this comment about escaping criticism because I had the thought that she may be struggling with internal criticism – criticism that is either self-generated or criticism from significant others (Erskine, 2020).*

[26 seconds silence]

C: *[whispering, as if it were difficult to speak]* Yes, it is inside of me, in a tiny place, *[even softer whisper]* tiny as a bean.
C: *Inside me, I can see a hiding place. An authentic, secret, and precious place. I feel vulnerable, dependent, like a bean in Richard's hand: at his mercy. But this time, it doesn't scare me: it feels good to depend. I like feeling carried, but the more I feel dependent on Richard, the more I feel sad. Experiencing Richard's presence leads me to a place of abandonment inside myself. While feeling in contact with him, I sense more the relational emptiness and the absence within me.*
R: Well, I will stay right here with you. Right here, if you go to this little, tiny place.
C: *I have always believed that by being myself, I would lose others' presence. That's why I am pretending to be someone I am not with people. Richard accepts that I'm scared. He stands here, and I don't feel alone in my cave because he's there waiting for me outside. I feel I can be me without threat. I have the feeling that his presence is unconditional, and I feel accepted.*

Silence and slowness have something to do with this. By slowing down, Richard points out that I need to calm down my rhythm. I realize that my everyday rhythm is not my biological rhythm. To live in a hurry helps me from feeling this loneliness inside.

R: *My words "I will stay right here with you" are intended to affirm to her the security in our relationship.*

[15 seconds silence]

C: *[her back bends over] [whispering]* Are you sure?

C: *It's new and strange for me to feel unconditionally accepted. I want to believe that I can trust that presence. That nothing bad will happen to my feelings. But this is not what I am used to. I expect to be injured while making contact. Is it safer to believe it is dangerous?*

R: Yeah but take your time. I am in no rush.

[29 seconds silence]

C: *[seems to lose her balance]* I need to lay down.

R: Of course...

C: *[lies down in fetal position]*

R: *[with a lot of air in his voice]* I am going to move to get a pillow. *[puts a pillow under Christine's head]* I am going to watch over you to make sure that nobody interferes with your private place... *[37 seconds silence]*

R: I am still here...

C: *I feel like I'm fainting. My head spins a little. My body feels as heavy as a stone. I need to lie down, rest, and make it stop. I want to forget everything. I want to disappear from myself.*

   While I am vanishing, I can feel Richard standing here. He is the light of a lighthouse that I see through the fog. He seems far away, but this is the closest I can stand. He doesn't go beyond the distance I need, staying in the distance, but the more he respects that, the more I feel an emptiness. That is the lack of an attuned presence within me. I start feeling loneliness and isolation thanks to him, who makes me experience his listening, respect, and attuned presence.

R: *I am calm and patient, with no plan or desire for her to be different; I just want to meet her in her experience.*

C: *[continues to arch, begins to tremble, crying]* I would like to go inside of myself until it hurts.

C: *I feel rejection toward myself. I am willing to destroy not who I am, but the feeling of existing. I feel lonely. I feel stunted, pulled inside myself. My body is hard as a stone. My shoulders are tense.*

R: *[with a reassuring, higher-pitched voice, as if calming a child]* OK... I listen to that... *[16 seconds silence]* That must seem much better than all the conflicts outside. All those conflicts outside that hurt. So, it must seem so wonderful to go inside. *[with a soft voice]* I can sense you crying. *[1 minute silence]*

R: *I am sitting quietly and watching over her, much like I did when my children were sick with a fever. I can wait and respond to her when she is ready.*

C: *[starts shaking]*

C: *This shaking is the only clue of any life inside of me. My muscles tell me I am living because I don't feel it.*

R: I am right here with you, listening to you. Even if you are silent, I am listening because there is a big story in there. A story that may not have words. *[46 seconds silence]*

R: *In the last couple of minutes, I am using therapeutic description, statements that I hope describe her non-verbalized experience. I am not inquiring about her inner process because clients who are sequestered in their private place may experience inquiry as an invasion. I make non-definitive statements, in a tentative voice, and I watch her bodily reaction. When I said "all those conflicts outside that hurt... it must seem so wonderful to go inside" and "there is a big story", I am watching for muscle tension and small movements in her body. With each of these therapeutic descriptions she nodded her head. That head nod signaled to me that I was attuned to her experience.*

C: *[back, legs, and arms seem to relax gradually]*

R: *[with a very low and soft voice]* I am wondering if it gets lonely in there... *[higher-pitched voice]* Protective, maybe lonely!

[8 seconds silence]

C: But it is calm.

C: *The fear is gone. It leaves behind a sense of calm, as if I was awaking.*

R: Oh, it is so important, calm... *[18 seconds silence]* so important to have a private place that is calm.

R: *My intention is to acknowledge and validate the importance of her calm, private place. My commitment is to remain calm and attuned to her, to observe the subtle movements in her body, and to sense the various changes in her affect.*

[24 seconds silence]

C: It's different now. I am feeling wrapped up, and it is pleasant.

C: *I realize that Richard's words are the same as earlier, but it doesn't sound the same. Calm is no longer only inside my hiding place. It's in my whole body. I can feel my whole body now.*

R: *[very slowly]* Should I?

R: *At this moment I considered reaching out and gently touching Christine with my hand. I wanted to pair her "pleasant" feeling with comforting physical contact. I made a gesture toward her with my hand as I said "Should I?" It seemed to me that she did not recognize my gesture, therefore I assumed I had no invitation to approach her private space.*

C: As if your arms were around me. As if I were in your hand, tiny as a bean.

C: *I picture myself as a little bean, on Richard's palm, laying down here, vulnerable. I feel his temperature, his mellowness.*

R: *[with a very low and soft voice]* Safe from any hurts, safe from any criticisms...

C: *I finally feel secure. I can be held with no threat. I feel relaxed.*

[2 minutes and 20 seconds silence]

R: *My calm presence seems so important during these couple of minutes. I want to create an atmosphere in which she feels secure and completely accepted. I have no goal except to be fully present with her. I watch for the little movements that may tell a non-verbal story.*

C: *[left pinky finger starts moving]*

R: *[whispering]* Those fingers of your left hand tell us a story. *[13 seconds silence]* Pinky finger is telling us a story.

C: I think he is seeking something.

C: *My pinky finger is moving by itself. It's fun to move it even though I have no control over this.*

R: *[approving voice]* Mmm.

C: *Richard moves to sit next to me on the floor. Richard gently touches my pinky finger with his forefinger, moves his finger away, and touches my finger again. I grab Richard's finger. I then cry much harder, and finally I just sob with my whole body. Richard again touches my finger with his finger. He touches me gently, and then moves his finger away.*

   It is important that he doesn't push. I get an invitation; therefore, I feel allowed to refuse, but I don't. Then he touches me again, with his fingertip, leaving it to me to answer, which I do. Suddenly, I realize how much I need this contact and how much I miss it. I've been avoiding this until now. Feeling his skin and warmth on my skin makes me feel whole, as if I have the right to be in this world. It's as if the pieces of me were sticking back together.

[1 minute 18 seconds silence]

R: *[almost inaudible]* I hear you crying.

[15 seconds silence]

C: *[sobbing]*
R: Crying all alone.
C: *[cries harder, starts shaking]*
C: *This is more than I can stand. My muscles are shaking.*

[1 minute 13 seconds silence]

R: *I attentively and patiently watch over her. I am cautious about prematurely comforting her. I do not want to distract her from her intense emotional experience. I stay present with her as she shakes and sobs because I know that this therapeutically supported, cathartic experience will be healing.*
C: *[catches her breath]*
C: *I just climbed something, I came across, down to the other side. Something inside of me gave out: like an ending journey within my dark inside. My body has experienced those turbulences in order to integrate them. I just went through a painful memory and now I realize that it is over, that it is not occurring anymore. It is more than a relief: it is a digestion. It doesn't go out, it stays in but with a different shape.*
R: Mmm *[approval]*. *[slowly]* Yeah, your body wants to cry.

[2 minutes 35 seconds silence]

C: *[Christine pulls her hand grasped to Richard's finger to make it touch her forehead.]*
C: *I need to feel more of this contact, and I need it on my face. It calms the loneliness inside. My muscles relax, my breathing gets calm. My internal sensation begins to feel pleasant again.*
R: *[with an airy and soft voice]* A lot of emotions inside.

[2 minutes 51 seconds silence]

R: *[gets a chair and sits down without letting go of my hand]*
C: *I cling to his finger. It's as if I'm breathing through my hand, which is in contact with Richard's hand. My whole world is in this contact. I don't think about anything. I don't feel anything. Only this skin-to-skin contact exists for me.*
R: *[barely audible]* It's safe. You can come back in the world now. In the world of you and me.
C: *Richard brings me back to the present. I'd forgotten that I was here, in this workshop, surrounded by these people, and that it should end. But it doesn't scare me. His presence has infused into me. I can come back into contact with others now that I feel safe. It's as if a new envelope protects me without preventing me from opening up to others.*

[41 seconds silence]

C: *[speaking as a child]* I know that I have to let you go but I don't want to!
C: *I realize what's happening, and that the session has to end. It's not painful to contemplate separation, but I feel so good that I don't want it to end. I feel a deep attachment to Richard. As I go back to the surface, I realize how good it feels to be in this body and to be me. Now I have value, I feel worthy. I feel like laughing and having fun. I feel energy flowing through me. My body is still slow, but I feel full of life.*
R: *[with a soft voice, almost inaudible but higher pitched].* It's ok! No rush! *[11 seconds silence]* I am still listening to you, I am still there.

[10 seconds silence]

C: *[starts stretching]*
R: Yeah have a stretch... Stretch your back. Stretch your back; it got tense a little while. Stretch your other arm.
C: *My body isn't awake enough for the amount of energy flowing through it. I need to wake up every part of my body. I need to feel every muscle and to come out of the numbness.*

[Christine sighs with relief]
[1 minute 50 seconds silence]

R: *[whispers approvingly]* Mmm... Can you do it that loud?
C: *[blowing loudly]*
C: *Focusing on my sensations and on my body continues to bring me back inside myself.*

[22 seconds silence]

R: *[with a low voice, whispering]* To wiggle and stretch. Come back to this world.

[36 seconds silence]

C: *[blowing, breathing more slowly]*
C: *I feel much more air in my lungs. My chest seems bigger. I'm getting back the air I missed earlier.*
C: *[breathes loudly but speaks]* I can feel the mattress. *[7 seconds silence]* I am cold. *[6 seconds silence]* I can feel the light. *[6 seconds silence]* *[speaks louder]* I can hear my breathing. *[17 seconds silence]* I have the impression that I feel my heartbeat again. *[11 seconds silence]* I am not so sure that I feel like totally coming back. *[7 seconds silence]* There are beautiful things here, this makes me want to come back.

C: *I'm used to my hiding place. I know I'm safe in here. The outside world seems interesting but also new and worrying.*

R: *[barely audible]* This is so important to have a quiet place. A place to hide. A place to re-nourish.

[2 minutes silence]

C: *[breathing loudly and peacefully]*

C: *[opening her eyes]*

C: *The energy inside of me is too intense to keep my eyes closed. I need to see the light, and to move again. I need to interact with my surroundings. I feel joy.*

    Richard doesn't rush me. He follows my rhythm to come back. I feel an invitation, with no pressure.

R: *[looking at C with concern]*

C: *[with energy and sadness]* I feel like nobody has ever looked at me like you are doing now.

C: *I thought I was alone, but when I see Richard's concern, I realize that I'm not. I thought I was invisible in my hiding place, but I realize I'm not: he can see me. I feel important, worthy of interest. Richard's solicitude helps me to respect myself, to take care of myself, to stop adapting, and to be myself.*

R: Mmm *[approval]*... Perhaps... I am looking to really see you, to see your experience.

C: *[louder and quicker than before]* Without being intrusive.

R: I hope.

C: You are here, and I am there.

C: *At no time did I feel forced, obliged, or adapted. I was able to let myself listen to my body's needs, and I felt accepted in doing so. Paradoxically, being accepted at a distance makes me want to get closer. I feel like a scared animal, but Richard now seems totally harmless. I accept being approached. I now feel uniquely me, and therefore in existence.*

[18 seconds silence]

R: *[with a very soft voice]* And even when I touched you, I wanted it to be an invitation.

C: It was perfect.

Richard's Postscript

Throughout my years in practice, I have worked with several clients who use relational withdrawal as a way to self-stabilize (Erskine, 2021a, 2021b, 2021c, 2021d, 2021e). These clients have a particular need for a sensitive responsiveness to their fear-laden affect state – a state that is so dominant in the schizoid process and often related to non-verbal experiences. They also need a psychotherapist who is exquisitely attuned to their developmental level of functioning, especially to what Daniel Stern (1985) described in his writings as the emerging self, the core self, and the intersubjective self – those levels of developmental functioning that are pre-language. In fact, many clients who use relational withdrawal as an attempt to self-stabilize, in the presence of intense relationships, regress to pre-linguistic developmental functioning as a safety zone (Guntrip, 1968). Such clients require the psychotherapist's consistent attunement to their affective state, a sense of meeting their sadness with compassion, their fear with security, and their anger with a sense of being taken seriously in the expression of that anger.

Several clients have taught me about the importance of attuning to the client's affect and validating their subjective experience. When our psychotherapy focuses on the client's internal process, we are able to acknowledge and validate the psychological void that the withdrawn client experiences internally. What becomes evident in a phenomenologically focused psychotherapy is the sequestered, hidden, encapsulated affects of the client's self. With relationally withdrawn individuals, the affects of terror and rage have often never found their way into verbal dialogue with another person. We know from treating trauma victims that trauma remains traumatic in the person's life because of the failure of a healing relationship. Many people have traumatic experiences but do not remain traumatized because someone was there in a healing, supportive, and clarifying way that allowed the trauma to be integrated within the individual's experience (Erskine, 1993). So too for clients who rely on relational withdrawal; they need a supportive and validating other who is present and patient, without any plan that they change their behavior.

For clients who engage in relational withdrawal, the early relational failures are often the result of cumulative neglect – the repeated misattunements, disparaging comments, capricious punishments, and rejections of the child's relational needs – like grains of sand that pile up until they form a dune. The accumulation of missed attunements and missed connections creates the conditions wherein the child hides more and more in his own sequestered world while adjusting his behavior to provide what the other demands.

Interpersonal connections are a threat to the sense of self for clients engaging in relational withdrawal. They experience a great fear of contact; for such individuals, a genuine relationship seems dangerous. Metaphorically there is a "split" in a person's sense of self that occurs when the child's natural organismic functioning is repressed and denied – split off – and they adapt the social façade required by the grown-ups around them. The adaptive, social façade becomes "me", and the natural, fundamentally human part becomes "not me". What is natural is lost and disregarded so intensely that the person experiences no other way of being in the world. My psychotherapeutic experience has led me to believe that a patient, consistent, respectful, and attuned therapeutic relationship allows those hidden aspects that were made "not me" to become "me". Such a relationship allows the person to find out for themselves what is natural for them.

Christine's Postscript

I have always felt like I had a broken radar; I was unable to find a sense of direction to my true self. My internal experience was to secure safety in distancing myself from others because of the fear of invasion. I tried to make my own subjectivity disappear. I became passively willing to adapt my behavior to give others the illusion that I was connected with them. My capacity for self-definition surrendered to compliance and fawning in order to have some semblance of contact with people. The result was that I lost a sense of who I was in relationships with others. It was as though my center of gravity shifted away from me; it left me feeling an emotional numbness, almost depersonalization.

In the psychotherapy described above, Richard's absolute attunement to my unexpressed affect, moments of patient silence, and the absence of his making any demands was instrumental in removing any threat of invasion of my privacy. Along this process, my internal experience was that I could be myself, feel my mix of feelings, have my own rhythm, and establish my own balance between distance and interpersonal contact. I sensed that he provided exactly what I needed in order to feel secure. I became acutely aware of the pain I felt when I held myself in isolation. I experienced an unaware longing for interpersonal contact and explored what I could feel if I was safe with another person.

In choosing to engage in a developmentally based, relationally focused psychotherapy, the goal I set was to allow myself to be fully in the presence of an intimate other. My description of this psychotherapy process may not seem significant to some readers, but the hour of therapy that I have just described has fundamentally changed my life. Richard understood and accepted my predisposition to withdraw from interpersonal contact. He was aware that somewhere within me there was a dormant desire for intimate connection. He resonated with both my urge to withdraw into a safe hiding place as well as my need for person-to-person relating.

Interestingly, this piece of therapy has left me with a sense of calmness in my body, while it has also significantly diminished my sense of shame. It is a privilege to share my therapeutic journey with you.

Note

1 For two other client reports, see chapters 14 and 15 in *Withdrawal, Silence, Loneliness: Psychotherapy of the Schizoid Process* (Erskine, 2023).

References

Erskine, R. G. (1993). Inquiry, attunement, and involvement in the psychotherapy of dissociation. *Transactional Analysis Journal*, 23(4), 184–190. doi:10.1177/036215379302300402.

Erskine, R. G. (2020). Relational withdrawal, attunement to silence: Psychotherapy of the schizoid process. *International Journal of Integrative Psychotherapy*, 11, 14–28.

Erskine, R. G. (2021a). Depression or isolated attachment? Part 1 of a 5-part case study of the psychotherapy of the schizoid process. *International Journal of Integrative Psychotherapy*, 11, 28–40.

Erskine, R. G. (2021b). Internal criticism and shame, physical sensations, and affect: Part 2 of a 5-part case study of the psychotherapy of the schizoid process. *International Journal of Integrative Psychotherapy*, 11, 41–55.

Erskine, R. G. (2021c). Isolation, loneliness, and a need to be loved: Part 3 of a 5-part case study of the psychotherapy of the schizoid process. *International Journal of Integrative Psychotherapy*, 11, 56–65.

Erskine, R. G. (2021d). Therapeutic withdrawal and painful memories: Part 4 of a 5-part case study of the psychotherapy of the schizoid process. *International Journal of Integrative Psychotherapy*, 11, 66–74.

Erskine, R. G. (2021e). My mother's voice: Psychotherapy of introjection: Part 5 of a 5-part case study of the psychotherapy of the schizoid process. *International Journal of Integrative Psychotherapy*, 11, 75–88.

Erskine, R. G. (2023). *Withdrawal, silence, loneliness: Psychotherapy of the schizoid process*. Phoenix Publishing.

Fraiberg, S. (1983). Pathological defenses in infancy. *Psychoanalytic Quarterly*, 51, 612–635. doi:10.1080/21674086.1982.11927012.

Guntrip, H. (1968). *Schizoid phenomena, object-relations and the self*. International Universities Press.

Hazell, J. (Ed.). (1994). *Personal relations therapy: The collected papers of H. J. S. Guntrip*. Jason Aronson.

Stern, D. N. (1985). *The interpersonal world of the infant: A view from psychoanalysis and developmental psychology*. Basic Books.

Chapter 10

The Truth Shall Set You Free

Saying an Honest "Goodbye" Before a Loved-One's Death

Before the death of a loved-one, some clients suffer from a variety of symptoms related to grief. These grief-related symptoms may include denial, bouts of intense sadness, often alternating with periods of emotional numbness, confusion, avoidance of, or anger at, the dying person, repetitive arguments, a general sense of helplessness, or feeling overwhelmed and stressed. Many people experience intense anticipatory grief before a loved-one dies.

John Bowlby (1961, 1980) was one of the early psychologists to study the process of mourning and described grief as resulting from the loss of attachment. Parkes (1972), and later Parkes and Weiss (1983), made use of Bowlby's ideas about attachment and loss and proposed a theory of grief that included four stages: shock-numbness, yearning-searching, disorganization-despair, and reorganization. Kubler-Ross (1969) popularized the idea that grief occurs in distinct stages and outlined five stages: denial, anger, bargaining, depression, and acceptance. Axelrod (2006) makes the point that not everyone will experience all five stages of grief, and that it is not necessary (or expected) that one will go through the stages in any particular order. The Yale Bereavement Study (Maciejewski et al., 2007) examined the concept of stages of grief and found that many people seemed to progress through various stages and that "yearning was the dominant negative grief indicator" (p. 716). Friedman (2009) challenged the notion of stages of grief as a simplistic taxonomy that does not allow for individual variances in the process of grieving. He suggested that each person grieves in his or her own unique way.

When clients experience anticipatory grief, they may exhibit some of the same psychological dynamics described by "stage" theorists, but their emotional reactions do not seem to pass through distinct stages. In my clinical experience, clients experiencing anticipatory grief often display a mix of emotional reactions. With some clients, there is an orderly progression from one emotion to another. With other clients, their reactions seem to oscillate from one extreme to another in a matter of minutes. They may be resentful, appreciative, despairing, openly angry, nostalgic, compliant with family traditions, and/or also yearning for some words of acknowledgement

DOI: 10.4324/9781003626718-10

or love. Frequently, grieving clients will focus on one specific emotion and disavow other thoughts and feelings. Whether we organize our psychotherapy to attend to each "stage" of grief, or instead focus primarily on our clients' emerging experiences of emotions, our clients often need us to attend to their "unfinished business" with the dying person.

Other authors, writing on the therapeutic treatment of grief, have focused on various treatment models (Clark, 2004; Hensley, 2006). These models emphasize: accepting the loss; the treatment of anger and despair; understanding the necessity for supportive and caring relationships; providing a suitable amount of time for healing from the loss; and developing new interests and activities (Greenwald, 2013; Wetherell, 2012); the use of expressive methods in the resolution of grief (Goulding & Goulding, 1979; Perls, 1969, 1975); attention to the need for supportive relationships in the family, in therapy, and in the community (Olders, 1989); and how grieving may potentiate other mental health issues (Greenwald, 2013). However, the psychotherapy literature does not seem to address the treatment of grief that may occur in anticipation of the death of a loved-one.

Sigmund Freud (1917/1957) addressed the topic of grief by clarifying the difference between mourning and melancholia. He describes melancholia as being "marked by an ambivalent relationship where there is a love and hate reaction to the other person that is often accompanied by anguish and a diminished sense of self-esteem; it is pervasive, unconscious, and continuous. He describes mourning as a common and regular "reaction to the loss of a loved person" (1917/1957, p. 243). Freud goes on to describe mourning as a conscious response to a specific death. Unlike melancholia, he considers mourning non-pathological because it is a normal reaction to events and is generally overcome given enough time. During the mourning period, the person realizes that the loved person is truly gone, an acceptance of the loss eventually occurs, and slowly the person returns to their customary way of living.

Fritz Perls (1975), in teaching about the psychotherapy of grief, defined grief as "unfinished business" and used his "empty chair" method to help the client gain "closure" on his or her grief. He made a distinction between pseudo-grief and genuine grief. He defined "pseudo-grief" as "feeling sorry for one's self" and "holding on to unexpressed resentments". He challenged clients to develop "self-support" and take responsibility for living in the "now". When clients expressed genuine grief, he considered it a natural process of mourning the loss of someone and responded with genuine concern.

I learned about the psychotherapy of grief while watching Fritz Perls use his "empty chair" method to help people complete what he called the "unfinished business" of grieving (Perls, personal communication, September 28, 1967). Perls would ask the grieving person to use the "empty chair" and fantasize that the significant "Other" was sitting in front of him or her. He would then encourage the client to speak to the image of the other, just as though they were actually sitting in the chair, and to be fully vocal, and to use body gestures that conveyed the fullness of their emotions.

When teaching about the psychotherapy of grief, Perls accentuated how grief was maintained by "holding on" (a physical retroflection) to old resentments and anger. He also highlighted the importance of unexpressed appreciations. He taught that the resolution of grief is in the expression of both resentments and appreciations. However, in practice, Perls often gave greater consideration to the grieving client's expression of anger and resentments, than he did to the expression of appreciations. In both *Gestalt Therapy Verbatim* (1969) and *The Gestalt Approach and Eye Witness to Therapy* (1973), Fritz Perls provides numerous examples where he also used the "empty chair" method to resolve clients' psychological conflicts.

In the early 1970s, a few transactional analysts who had trained in Gestalt therapy with Fritz and/or Laura Perls began to use the "empty chair" technique to facilitate a client's resolution of "unfinished business" – the psychological issues related to either archaic or current interpersonal conflicts. Erskine and Moursund in *Integrative Psychotherapy in Action* (1988/2011) provide several clinical examples that illustrate both the use of the "empty chair" method and the integration of a variety of Gestalt therapy interventions with Transactional Analysis and contemporary psychoanalytic theory. Bob and Mary Goulding, following Perls' examples, included a section in their book *Changing Lives Through Redecision Therapy* (1979) that illustrates the use of the "empty chair" method to resolve what they also call the "unfinished business" of grief (pp. 174–184). Their brief therapy vignettes show that they also emphasize resentments and anger and give only cursory attention to appreciations.

Although Fritz Perls gave most attention to the expression of anger and resentments, I have personally found it necessary to create a therapeutic balance between emotional polarities such as unacknowledged anger, resentment, and bitterness on one side of the scale; and unrealized dreams, precious experiences, unexpressed affection, and loving memories on the other side in order to make it easier for the client to balance things out. I organize my therapeutic interventions to interweave each of these many emotions into the relational discourse. Sometimes, we focus on one emotion until it is well expressed, then I may draw the client's attention to another end of the emotional spectrum, and then back again, always searching for and interweaving the unexpressed emotions, striving for a healing balance.

The Premise of "Unfinished Business"

Intimate and meaningful conversations are essential in the resolution of grief; ideally such intimate conversation would occur before the actual death of a loved-one. After the death of a loved-one, the grief is often potentiated by "unfinished business" – the emotional pain of what had happened and/or the regret of what never happened – and thoughts of "I wish I had said more", "If only we had had a real conversation", "I never told him (or her) how much he (or she) meant to me", or "I never really told them the truth about myself". When intimate and honest conversations happen before the death of a loved-one, the grief, after the death, is much easier for the remaining individual to assimilate and resolve. When such meaningful conversations do not happen before the death of the loved-one, the after-death experience of grief is often intensified and prolonged.

The psychotherapy technique described in this article is about creating an appropriate opportunity for the expression of feelings, making interpersonal contact, and "truth telling" – ideally before the other person dies. It is based on the Gestalt therapy premise that it is necessary to make "full contact", to have a real "hello", before we can say "goodbye" (Perls et al., 1951). Ideally, I prefer that the psychotherapy pave the way for sincere face-to-face conversations between my client and the dying person, while he or she is still lucid.

Many clients need a significant degree of encouragement and therapeutic support in order to engage in a meaningful dialogue with the "Other" person. For some clients, our psychotherapy provides an emotionally filled rehearsal (or practice session) that makes intimate and honest communication more possible before the loved-one dies. In some situations, the actual expression of true emotions, full interpersonal contact, and expressing one's own "truth" to the other person is not a viable option. The other person may be in a coma, suffering from dementia, or be emotionally unable to have a meaningful conversation. Because of archaic intrapersonal patterns and long-held beliefs such as, "I have no right to say what I feel" or "Others are more important than me", many clients are extremely reluctant to initiate such intimate and meaningful conversations (O'Reilly-Knapp & Erskine, 2010). However, there is often a hope that intimacy might happen, or an existing grief that intimate, truthful interactions have never happened – yet.

Clients may be inhibited in communicating meaningful experience because they believe that being honest with the other person will upset, hurt, or even possibly kill them. Many families have forged a system that does not allow for such intimate conversations. At the time of the impending death, the loyalty to such a family system may even be intensified. In each of these situations, it may be therapeutically possible for the psychotherapist to facilitate a meaningful conversation – in fantasy – by using the "empty chair" method. In working with the client's fantasy, through the client imagining the other person sitting directly in front of them, we can create the possibility for a plausible interpersonal contact – contact that may not be possible in reality – thus an imaginative contact, but one that can conceivably heal deep relational wounds.

The resolution of grief involves restoring the individual's capacity for full internal and interpersonal contact – the capacity to say an authentic "hello" before a genuine "goodbye". When working with unexpressed experiences, it is important that the person fully gives voice to their many different internal feelings, needs, thoughts, and assumptions that have never been properly expressed. This is what my clients call "truth telling" – it is the verbal (and sometimes physical) expression of the unsaid and often unacknowledged feelings, thoughts, attitudes, associations, and reactions that the person has kept locked-up internally.

Telling one's own "truth" – one's personal narrative – is an essential factor in making sense of a complex relationship, completing significant unfinished experiences, and providing an end to (or reduction in) grieving (Nelmeyer & Wogrin, 2008). "Truth telling" is not about the citation of facts or verifiable information that can be confirmed by others. It is a "narrative truth", the expression of one's own internal experiences and his or her personal endeavors in order to make emotional "meaning" (or sense) out of those experiences (Allen, 2009; Burgess & Burgess, 2011).

"Truth telling" involves translating affect, physiological reactions, and relational experiences into language and expression and honestly stating or sharing what may have never been expressed in a significant relationship. Many clients are not accustomed to sharing their private thoughts. I encourage clients to speak with candor and physical expression. Such "truth telling" is the opposite of the inconsequential conversations (platitudes, business, gossip, "safe" topics, etc.) that many people have throughout their lives. Inconsequential conversations begin as self-protective measures to maintain an emotional relationship but, over time, they can erode intimacy and inter-personal contact; they might even inhibit the expression of Self in the relationship. When we psychotherapists emphasize "truth telling", we are inviting the client to attend to, and express, the interrupted expression of feelings, attitudes, and physical gestures. It is these interrupted or withheld gestures, words, and affects that interfere with the capacity to say "hello" and "goodbye".

A Case Example

Jason's brother, Andrew, had a brain tumor. He had been in a slow process of mental and physical deterioration for over two years. As his only living relative, Jason had, for the past two years, assumed the responsibility for his older brother's living arrangements, medical care, and financial needs. A year before, the doctors predicted that Andrew would die within a month or two. Instead of dying, Andrew continued to live but his physical capacities had worsened.

Jason is a member of a psychotherapy group that meets for one six-hour day each month. He has attended the past 13 such monthly sessions. In the sixth and seventh sessions, he talked to the group members about his brother's illness and about his frustration and exhaustion in continually having to care for his brother. Jason reported to the group that, through the relational group process, he had felt understood, supported, and encouraged and thus more able to continue his responsibilities for his brother. I had also encouraged him to have several "truthful conversations" with Andrew. In the eleventh session, Jason reported that he found it "impossible" to say anything meaningful to his brother. He again expressed to the group his despair and his annoyance at Andrew and he told the group that he wished his brother would "get it over with and die". He then wept, and said that he yearned for his brother to say "some kind words to me" or to "just show that he loved me".

In this, the thirteenth session, Jason began by saying that his brother could no longer speak or even feed himself. Jason had now lost all hope that Andrew would acknowledge him in some loving way. Jason was despondent; his body was rigid. I asked Jason if he was willing to use the "empty chair" technique to have a "heart-to-heart" talk with Andrew. At first, he was reluctant to imagine his brother sitting in front of him, or to express what he was feeling. I assured him that I and the other group members were there to support him and help him express any or all of the feelings toward Andrew and about himself that he had rigidly held inside. His tight fists revealed some of his unexpressed emotions. I pointed out that, in previous sessions, he had made some angry and caustic comments about his brother that I thought might have represented some degree of unresolved resentment. After some group discussion about his body tension, he agreed to experiment with visualizing his brother and to tell him honestly about their relationship.

We began with my using a quasi-hypnotic introduction: "Jason, close your eyes and imagine your brother is in his hospital bed, with perhaps only 30 minutes to live. He can hear you fully, but he cannot talk. This is your last opportunity to say all the important things that you have never said to him. The important point is that you be truthful and not leave anything out. I will be right here to back you up. Just look at his image (in your mind's eye) and tell him the truth about your relationship".

Jason hesitantly told his brother how much he had always admired and loved him. I encouraged him to keep talking to the image of Andrew and to tell him everything. He told Andrew how he had looked up to a brother who was five years older and very athletic. As he started to talk about Andrew in the third person I encouraged him to keep visualizing his brother and to "talk to him" directly. He went on to tell Andrew how he had longed for "good times" with him. I prompted him to talk about some of the "good times" and mention some of the important things that they had done together. Jason had great difficulty recalling any pleasant moments, though he described some of the games that they had played together and the one time when his brother had defended him from a bully on the playground.

Jason was struggling to recall shared experiences that were pleasurable or intimate. So, I suggested that he switch and tell Andrew what was missing in their relationship. Jason expressed his yearning for a "kind and loving" brother. He spoke about how he, as a boy, waited for Andrew to come home and play with him. He expressed how disheartened he was that Andrew had either ignored him, or even sometimes hit him. Jason described bitterly how, as a boy, he had longed to share a bedroom with Andrew, but how Andrew had actually "tortured" him. He went on to tell his brother how, as an adult, Andrew had misused him by borrowing money and not repaying it; how he expected Jason to take care of his "financial mess", but never said "thank you".

Jason's face had turned bright red; the veins in his neck were bulging; his fists were pushing against his chair. It was clear that he was physiologically still containing his anger. I put a large cushion on the chair and suggested that Jason begin each sentence with the words, "I don't like it that you...". Jason began to shout out several things that he detested. He hit the cushion and screamed at his brother, "I don't like the way you have always treated me", and reiterated several painful events in their relationship. He then added, "I have always loved you. I always wanted you to like me. I hate the way you used me and treated me. I have always kept quiet and waited for you to be good to me. Now I know that you will never change".

He continued to shout and pound the cushion for a few minutes and then he began to weep. He said many of the same things again, but this time he was full of sorrow. He lamented, "I longed for you to be my brother but most of my life you hated me. I have been so good to you, but you never acknowledged it. It is time for me to say goodbye now to all my hopes. I will never have the brother I wanted. You have been a real shit to me. Now I want you to die and to get all this torment over with. Go now! Find the peace you never had in life. It is my time to be free of you. I want to be with people who like me". Jason's body relaxed and his face returned to a normal color as he quietly cried for several minutes. Later in the day, he looked much livelier. The next day he telephoned to say that he had had the best night's sleep in two years.

Conclusion

The case of Jason illustrates the transformative power of "truth telling" and the importance of actively expressing emotions that have been, until now, inhibited and contained through emotional constraints and physical tensions. The therapeutic use of imagination, the "empty chair" method, and the psychotherapist's caring and supportive involvement, all provide the client with an opportunity to have a quality of interpersonal communication, at least in fantasy, that has not yet been possible in their reality.

Earlier in this chapter, I outlined several models for the treatment of grief that are described in the professional literature. The case example used in this chapter illustrates the integration of a number of these therapeutic approaches, most notably:

- The acknowledgement of disavowed feelings
- The use of expressive methods in the healing of emotional pain and anger
- Providing the time and space for the person to tell his or her story and to finish any "unfinished business"
- Providing a supportive relationship by way of the group members' and psychotherapist's involvement
- Assisting the client's movement through various emotional responses, such as denial, despair, yearning, anger, and the reorganization of a sense of self

In my years of treating clients suffering from anticipatory grief, I have found that it is often necessary for the client to establish a balance between the emotional polarities of anger, resentment, and bitterness, with memories of precious experiences, unexpressed affection, and love. As described in this chapter, "truth telling" to the imagined other in the "empty chair" is an effective method for the resolution of anticipated grief. It is essential that the psychotherapist encourage and support the client's "truth telling", whether it be only in fantasy to a mental image in an "empty chair", or whether eventually it is face-to-face with a real person. The purpose of this type of psychotherapy is to restore the individual's capacity to have an honest and meaningful "hello" before engaging in a genuine "goodbye".

References

Allen, J. (2009). Constructivist and neuroconstructivist Transactional Analysis. *Transactional Analysis Journal*, 39, 181–192.

Axelrod, J. (2006). *The five stages of loss and grief.* Psych Central. psychcentral.com/lib/the-5-stages-of-loss-and-grief/000617

Bowlby, J. (1961). Processes of mourning. *International Journal of Psychoanalysis*, 42, 317–339.

Bowlby, J. (1980). *Attachment and loss.* Basic Books.

Burgess, A. G., & Burgess, J. P. (Eds.) (2011). *Truth.* Princeton University Press.

Clark, A. (2004). Working with grieving adults. *Advances in Psychiatric Treatment*, 10, 164–170.

Erskine, R. G., & Moursund, J. P. (2011). *Integrative Psychotherapy in action.* Karnac Books. (Originally published by Sage Publications in 1988).

Freud, S. (1957). Mourning and melancholia. In J. Strachey (Ed. & Trans.), *The standard edition of the complete psychological works of Sigmund Freud* (Vol. 14, pp. 243–258). Hogarth Press. (Original work published 1917).

Friedman, R. (2009). Broken hearts: Exploring myths and truths about grief, loss and recovery. *Psychology Today.* psychologytoday.com/blog/broken-hearts/200909/no-stages-grief

Goulding, M. M., & Goulding, R. L. (1979). *Changing lives through redecision therapy.* Brunner/Mazel.

Greenwald, B. (2013). *Grief issues in the psychotherapeutic process.* www.uic.edu/orgs/ convening/grief.htm.

Hensley, P. L. (2006). Treatment of bereavement-related depression and traumatic grief. *Journal of Affect Disorders,* 92, 117–124.

Kubler-Ross, E. (1969). *On death and dying.* Macmillan.

Maciejewski, P. K., Zhang, B., Block, S. D., & Prigerson, H. G. (2007). An empirical study of the stage theory of grief. *Journal of the American Medical Association,* 297 (7), 716–723.

Nelmeyer, R. A., & Wogrin, C. (2008). Psychotherapy for complicated bereavement: A meaning-oriented approach. *Illness, Crisis, Loss,* 16, 1–20.

Olders, H. (1989). Mourning and grief as healing processes in psychotherapy. *Canadian Journal of Psychiatry,* 34, 271–278.

O'Reilly-Knapp, M., & Erskine, R. G. (2010). The script system: An unconscious organization of experience. In R. G. Erskine (Ed.), *Life scripts: A Transactional Analysis of unconscious relational patterns* (pp. 291–308). Karnac Books.

Parkes, C. (1972). *Bereavement: Studies in grief in adult life.* Tavistock.

Parkes, C. M., & Weiss, R. S. (1983). *Recovery from bereavement.* Basic Books.

Perls, F. S. (1969). *Gestalt therapy verbatim.* Real People Press.

Perls, F. S. (1973). *The gestalt approach and eyewitness to therapy.* Science & Behavior Books.

Perls, F. S. (1975). *Legacy from Fritz.* Science & Behavior Books.

Perls, F. S., Hefferline, R. F., & Goodman, P. (1951). *Gestalt therapy: Excitement and growth in the human personality.* Julian Press.

Wetherell, J. L. (2012). Complicated grief therapy as a new treatment approach. *Dialogues in Clinical Neuroscience,* 14, 159–166.

Chapter 11

Saying an Honest "Goodbye"

Three Case Examples

A sense of emptiness, interpersonal deprivation, and "unfinished business" persist with anticipatory grief because the opportunity for full expression of one's inner experience is often missing in the relationship. Telling one's own "truth" – one's personal narrative – is an essential factor in "making meaning", completing significant unfinished experiences, and providing an end to anticipated grieving (Erskine, 2014). The resolution of anticipatory grief involves restoring the individual's capacity for full internal and interpersonal contact – the capacity to say an authentic "hello" before a genuine "goodbye". This article presents three case examples that illustrate the use of the Gestalt therapy method of the "empty chair" (Perls, 1969, 1975), in conjunction with the relational perspectives central to Integrative Psychotherapy (Erskine et al., 1999; Moursund & Erskine, 2003).

Linda's Reparation

Linda was a client whom I had seen in individual therapy once a week for six years. When she began her therapy with me, she was 33 years old and had been a patient for a year and a half in a clinic that specialized in the treatment of borderline disorders. Linda had been referred to that clinic by her physician after Linda had told him about the discord and arguments she was repeatedly having with her husband and father. After a few months, Linda abruptly quit her therapy at the clinic because she "felt criticized and defined". She complained about the "cold" way that the two clinic therapists had treated her.

Early in our therapy together, Linda would often find something wrong with the way I had said something. She would complain and argue with me that I should "have said it in a better way". She would alternate between what she called her "sweet and nice self" and her "angry self". I paid careful attention to the potential unconscious communications in her expression of her two selves. During the first three years, much of our therapy focused on working within the transference and countertransference matrix. I often inquired about Linda's relationships with her family members and we

DOI: 10.4324/9781003626718-11

explored how she stabilized and regulated herself when relational disruptions occurred. Two significant developments emerged as a result of our therapeutic focus on her physical sensations and body tensions, relational needs, explicit and implicit memory, and our transference and counter-transference dynamics. Linda stopped arguing with both her husband and me, and the center of her attention shifted toward her anger at her father and the inappropriate sexual touches that she had received from him when she was 11 and 12 years old.

For the next year, our psychotherapy focused almost exclusively on Linda's troubled relationship with her father. Linda had never forgotten his sexual molestation of her. She said, "I always put it out of my mind" and "I wondered if I had exaggerated how bad it was". In the psychotherapy, she expressed her rage at her father for touching her vagina and rubbing her developing breasts. She was sure that they had never had sexual intercourse, but she was hurt and angry at his "violation of my love". She had never told her mother because her father had said that it was a "secret – just for the two of us". What had previously appeared to be behaviors typical of borderline personality disorder now seemed to be the reactions of a woman who had been sexually traumatized as a child.

As a result of our psychotherapy, she realized that many of the arguments that she had with her husband and her attempts to "push his affection away" were an enactment of her desire to push away her father's sexualized touch. She related being "acutely uncomfortable" with her husband's sexual touch, comparing it to her father's "violation" of her. Shortly after getting married, she had confronted her father about his sexual abuse when she was a pre-teenager. He told Linda that she was "crazy". He said: "You have always exaggerated. We were only affectionate with each other". Linda came away from this altercation feeling hurt, scared, angry, and with "an urge to argue with everyone".

In the fourth year of therapy, Linda's father was dying of cancer. She had expressed a great deal of anger in our therapy sessions; she had cried and longed for "a father who I could trust". She was – effectively – grieving in anticipation of his death. I now encouraged her to talk to him, to tell him what she had missed in their relationship, and to tell him her truth – even if he accused her of exaggerating. She was reluctant to do this and we debated about the importance of her again telling her "truth" to him before he died. We agreed that a strong confrontation, like she had had several years before, would not work. In compromise, she decided to talk to him about many of her fond memories. She had three private conversations with him where they talked about their wonderful memories of the things they had done together over many years. As a result, she was feeling much closer to him and, at the same time, knew that she was holding in a lot of resentment. In between these meetings with her father, I talked to Linda about the importance of "truth telling" and eventually bringing her whole story into the relationship.

In the fourth conversation with her father, she obliquely referred to his seductive touching of her. He blurted out, "I have been waiting for you to bring that up. I am so sorry I fondled your body. I was wrong in doing that". He continued to apologize to her, both for his inappropriate sexual touching of her when she was a child, and for how he had denied her accusations several years before. Later, in therapy, Linda said that she was greatly relieved because the only reparation she needed was for him "to admit the truth of our relationship. That I loved him and that he exploited me because of it". She said, "I needed him to admit that I had not exaggerated anything – that I am not crazy".

Linda spent many nights holding her semi-conscious father's hand before he died. She seemed to be at peace with him and, shortly afterwards, I encouraged her to tell the full story to her mother. Again she was reluctant, but eventually agreed because, "the secret has created a distance between us". Her mother was shocked, hurt, angry, and dismayed. The two women wept together over the unnecessary distance that the "secret" had created between them. Linda continued in therapy for another year. We often talked about the new sense of affection that she and her mother had for each other. We periodically reviewed how important it was for her to have had the "truth telling" with both her father and mother.

Martha's Lament

Martha was a conservatively dressed, 53-year-old woman, with strong religious convictions. She has previously attended six intensive group therapy sessions, but seldom contributed her perspective to the group's discussions. Martha said that her silence was because she feared criticism. In the fifth session, she expressed anger at the therapist for a comment he had made. The therapist attended to her anger, took her perspective seriously, and invited her to tell him more about her anger. Within a short time, she was shouting vehemently to an image of her mother in an empty chair. During the sixth session, she reported a sense of internal relief after she had expressed her previously contained anger.

In this current group session, she is sitting with slouched shoulders, looking sad. As she begins to speak, her voice is slow-paced and mournful. The following is an edited transcript of a 46-minute individual therapy session that occurred during an intensive therapy group. Martha begins her session by describing her mother's failing health. She tells the group how she is responsible for making her mother feel good and that "my inner state is terrible, unbalanced when I can't make her feel good". Martha continues to describe her inner demands to preserve her mother's "well-being no matter what".

THERAPIST: So what would you say to her if the doctor called you today and said, "Come to the hospital, she's had another heart attack and she's got only 30 minutes to live?". {*The therapist's question is designed to stimulate a "creative emergency", an opportunity for the expression of that which has been inhibited.*}

MARTHA: Well, maybe... I would just say what I say to her all the time.

THERAPIST: Now you have the opportunity to say something different... to be fully honest with her. So just close your eyes and imagine that you are sitting next to her hospital bed... and this is the moment to say the truth. Tell her everything, particularly the things that have never been said, including all the way back to your childhood. Just go ahead and talk honestly to her – because she's going to die in half an hour. So you don't have to worry about hurting her. The most important thing is the truth telling. {*Here the therapist is using "therapeutic direction" to encourage Martha to engage her mother in a uniquely different and contactful way. He emphasizes that truth telling is important. The experience of talking to the image of the person in an empty chair allows the individual to express, in the safety of fantasy, what they did not do in reality.*}

MARTHA: Mama... throughout my whole life I've dedicated my time to you, all my efforts. I've given you all the affection, all the care, I was able to give – but I never dared to tell you *[her voice drops]* that you didn't parent me well. Not long ago, you told me that you didn't know if you had done a good job in raising me. So, instead of answering you, I told you how much I loved you... but I didn't tell you that you hadn't cared for me or raised me well. *[Martha is tense, she squeezes her interlaced fingers; her shoulders are hunched].*

THERAPIST: Tell her what you did not say that day. Just close your eyes and tell her your experience. {*The therapist is encouraging Martha to go beyond her usual mundane conversation, to express herself fully.*}

MARTHA: I didn't want to hurt you Mom, the same way that I've never wanted to hurt you, so I shut up. But...

THERAPIST: But, the truth is... {*Here the therapist is "priming the pump"; he is encouraging Martha to say what has never been said. He does not provide the content; he provides only the impetus to move her to tell her full story.*}

MARTHA: The truth is... that I carry on my shoulders the responsibility for your well-being. Your whole life has been very hard, so I tried to take care of you. In taking care of you, I haven't allowed myself to live my own life. *[Martha's voice becomes more forceful]* I've missed... too many things. Mostly, I miss having a real mother... a loving mother.

THERAPIST: Keep going. There's so much more to say. Right from your heart. {*The therapist is again encouraging her to speak honestly. He does not define what she might say; he only encourages her to continue.*}

MARTHA: Mother, you've been a child. You've been a childish mother all my years. You relied upon me since I was born. You used me to feel good about yourself. {*For the next several minutes Martha goes on to tell the image of her mother about her emotional pain and a sense of being "unprotected" and "unimportant" to her mother.*} *[She whimpers]* The only way I could be anything was to comfort you. *[The therapist continues to keep Martha focused on her own experience with "tell her what you feel".]*

MARTHA: Your family, Mama... I know they were more important than me. *[Martha weeps.]* I've asked you many times to pay attention to some of my needs. You tell me my needs are nonsense, that I am very silly, that I was a very strange girl when I asked for your attention and caring. *[Martha continues to cry for several minutes]*.

THERAPIST: And tell her what happened when she labeled you like that... when she defined you that way. {*Here the therapist is helping Martha to define and articulate her own experience.*}

MARTHA: Mother, when you define me in that way, I always have hurt and anger inside. And when I try to tell you about my hurt or anger, you criticized me. Many times, instead of listening to my needs, you scoffed at me or said, "You're just like your father".[Martha's voice is much stronger]THERAPIST: And tell her what happens deep inside you when she scoffs or defines you like that. {*The therapist senses that encouraging Martha to be angry again at her mother will be less healing than helping her become aware of and express her sadness and loss.*}

MARTHA: When you defined me that way... and you say it with such a scornful tone... I hurt... I wonder, "Am I a very bad person?"

THERAPIST: Tell her about that hurt and internal doubt. {*The therapist encourages her to elaborate on two focal points: hurt and internal doubt. Whichever Martha follows, she is likely to express what she has previously inhibited in conversations with her actual mother.*}

MARTHA: For a long time, Mama, I've had a very big inner conflict, always questioning myself. When I would receive a compliment from someone I found it hard to accept because I always hear your words and scornful sound.

THERAPIST: Tell her about the inside, what happens inside when you believed Mama's definition of you.

MARTHA: When you define me in that scornful tone or say that my anger is just like my father, I have a terrible pain... and a terrible fear of losing you... that you wouldn't love me... of not deserving you. I hurt.

The therapist has been observing Martha's tense shoulders and encourages her to describe her physical experience. As Martha becomes aware of the "weight" on her shoulders she begins to weep. Although Martha is conscious of sadness, the therapist wonders if they have skipped over the anger, and so he suggests that she tell mother "about all that sadness and anger that you've keep a secret". Martha continues to express both her pain and anger at her mother's superficial behaviors. She blurts out, "I always thought that I was a big mistake: the Bad One". The therapist encourages her to articulate how these beliefs form a life script: "I feel worthless". "I am no good". "I am not loved, Momma".

The therapist then prompts her to tell her mother the whole story, the story that Martha has kept a secret. With a mix of tears and anger, Martha then tells her mother about the cruel treatment that she received from an aunt, and how her mother defended the aunt, instead of protecting Martha. The therapist suggests that Martha tell her mother what she needed from her.

MARTHA: As a child, Mama, I needed your protection. I would have liked you to play with me, to take me to the park, to take care of me... but you left me in her care. She was a bitter woman, who scolded and hit me. She used to criticize me and humiliate me... and her humiliations have been a huge burden in my life.

THERAPIST: And what I needed from you, Mama... {*The therapist is steering the therapy in a natural progression from anger, to sadness, to an expression of needs.*}

MARTHA: What I needed from you, Mama... was for you to protect me from her. But you only lived to please her. Nobody else existed for you but her. I was insignificant... unless I catered to you.

THERAPIST: Tell her how you experience that inside... when she was busy pleasing your aunt and did not attend to you. Tell her what happened to that little girl. {*The therapist now focuses on how Martha coped as a child, what meaning she ascribed to mother's behavior.*}

MARTHA: I felt worthless, Mama: I was no good... I cannot forgive you for the way you treated me.

THERAPIST: "Worthless..." {*Here the therapist underscores what Martha has just said: "worthless". Such underscoring will help Martha continue with her narrative truth.*}

MARTHA: Yes, that robbed my spontaneity.

THERAPIST: "Robbed my spontaneity". {*The therapist again repeats what Martha has just said and thereby acknowledges that her words are significant. Such acknowledgement provides an encouragement to the client to continue telling her personal story.*} And I remember once... {*Martha opens her eyes and looks at the therapist. The therapist senses that it is not yet time to stop the conversation with mother. Martha may have more to say to the image of her mother. When she is finished expressing her feelings and narrative to mother, there will be time for real interpersonal contact between client and therapist.*}

THERAPIST: Close your eyes again and tell it to Mama. Tell Mama about that memory. {*Martha continues to tell the internal image of her mother more about her pain with the aunt's cruelty, her anger at mother's defense of the aunt, instead of protecting Martha, and the pain of the "scorn and humiliation" she received from both her mother and aunt.*}

THERAPIST: Tell her your truth. Keep going. It's so important, before you say goodbye to Mama, to have this opportunity for truth telling... Even if it's telling Mama about your anger and pain... Even if it's telling Mama about what you dislike. {*Martha continues to talk to the image of her mother in the empty chair. She expresses anger that her mother "would not let me be me". She describes her mother's lack of affection and how her mother continually defined Martha, not only when she was a child but even today.*}

THERAPIST: And what I want to tell you now, before you die is...

MARTHA: What I want to tell you, before you die, Mama... is that I also have the right to live, that I love life. I love people and that I would like to be able to experience all that in peace, without questioning myself whether I've done enough, whether I've done it well or not, whether I should have done this or that, without being in a constant doubt. You demanded that of me and now I do it to myself. I am just like you... I demand things from myself... even if I don't want to do them.

THERAPIST: Tell her what that sentence means, "Now I do it to myself"... explain to her what that sentence means. {*The therapist is highlighting Martha's awareness "I do it to myself". Martha's awareness may be the first step in resolving her constant internal criticism and resulting shame. Martha's internal criticism will certainly be an important issue to return to in future therapy but now it seems important to attend to her awareness, "I do it to myself".*}

MARTHA: Now I'm the one demanding of myself. It's an internal demand, Mama... A constant internal criticism. *[Her voice becomes sorrowful].* And that internal demand never satisfies you... *[a pause of 6 seconds]* ... It's a repeat of all your criticism... criticism and a lack of acknowledgement from you. You have never valued me for who I am... not even what I do for you... I have the feeling that all my effort was useless. Now there is no need for my internal demands.

THERAPIST: Tell her what you're aware of now that she's about to die.

MARTHA: *[after 8 seconds, she speaks with a sad quivering voice]* ... I've asked you so many times to understand me and what I get instead is criticism. You told me many times, "You're so exaggerated". "Here you go again, always with the same things, you're so silly..." I've received so little love from you... and I needed it so much. *[She weeps].*

THERAPIST: *[after 10 seconds]* ... So, tell her what you're going to do with that internal criticism.

MARTHA: *[after another 10 seconds]* *[her voice is now firm]* ... Mama... When I criticize myself, when I'm self-demanding... I will STOP... because I am being LIKE YOU... and... each time, I'll put more strength into a tolerant, more human part of myself. Each time, I'll love myself more. Each time, I'll value myself more. *[Her voice is stronger]*.

THERAPIST: As I put you in a grave, Mama...

MARTHA: *[after 5 seconds]* ... *So, as I put you in the grave, I wish that you have eternal peace [5 second pause]* ... I intend to live my life in peace, without demands. You are about to die and I will live.

THERAPIST: Just imagine... you could put all that criticism in the grave with her... all her critical words, all her scornfulness, and all your self-criticism, and all your self-doubt. You could bury all of that negativity with her.

MARTHA: It's a good idea. I can put it all in your grave Mama... and I won't have to live with any of it.

THERAPIST: One important thing before she goes... tell her what you appreciated about her. Tell her what you love about her.

MARTHA: What I like most about you, Mama is your sense of humor... how funny you are, your ability to relate to others... that playful part of you... even if you didn't use it with me.

THERAPIST: Tell her what else you love about her. *[Martha is shaking her head, at a loss to find something more she loves or appreciates about her mother. Two minutes go by without her saying anything.]* ... She's going to go in a minute.

MARTHA: Nothing else comes to mind. I'm cleaned out. I only want to speak the truth.

THERAPIST: Then, continue to tell her your truth... You have just a moment before you say goodbye.

MARTHA: *[after 11 seconds]* Everything I'm saying is true, Mama... *[Her voice is strong]*. It's what I've experienced and what I've felt... *[pause of 10 seconds]* ... Mama, I just need the right words from you...words like a message from the Bible. I need a biblical message, like: "Only say the word and I shall be healed" *[pause of 10 seconds]* ... Mama, please tell me that I am loved... then I will be free.

THERAPIST: *[after 35 seconds]* ... She will be gone in a minute.

MARTHA: *[after 9 seconds, in a very soft and plaintive voice]* ... She will never tell me that I am loved.

THERAPIST: Then all you can do is say your truth... and then say goodbye.

MARTHA: *[after 11 seconds]* Everything I'm saying is true... *[Her voice is strong and clear]*. It's what I've experienced and what I've felt.

THERAPIST: You may open your eyes, when you're ready. *[after a pause of 11 seconds, Martha opens her eyes and looks directly at the therapist]* ... Since you've asked for something from the Bible, may I give you a quotation? *[Martha nods her head in agreement]* "You shall experience the truth and the truth shall set you free". I think the quote is from the Gospel of John *[for 30 seconds Martha and the therapist gaze into each other's eyes]* ... Martha, it is the truth that will set you free. *[Martha nods her head]* ... Now would you like to begin the important part of the therapy?

MARTHA: I don't understand you.

THERAPIST: I think the important part is yet to come. It may be important to have a truthful conversation with the real woman before she dies.

MARTHA: I've tried many times but she doesn't want to. She tells me I'm silly. She tells me not to say things that will upset her. She says that my emotions have always hurt her.

[Martha is shaking her head in a gesture of "no"]

THERAPIST: Are you saying that she doesn't want to know the truth? *[Martha nods]* ... Well, I believe you! ... There are some people who have built such a wall against intimate contact... that they won't hear the truth. Other people need the truth; most people need the truth so that they can live, and even die, in peace.

MARTHA: I would like to be really truthful with both of my parents but they didn't want to hear my truth. They only want to tell their own story. *{Since Martha has continued to shake her head in a gesture of "no", the therapist changes directions. If it is impossible for Martha to have an honest conversation with her mother, then it is essential that she express her "truth" to the members of her group and experiences full interpersonal contact with those who want to know her.}*

THERAPIST: Then it is important that you share your story with us... that we become the witnesses to your story... Just take a moment and look around at your witnesses in this group. Can you do that? Just look around at all these witnesses.[Martha blows her nose as she looks at some of the people in the room]MARTHA: It really touches me to look at them. *[Martha moves to see them better]*. It touches me and at the same time it's hard. It's hard for me to look at their faces.

THERAPIST: I think the difference between the people in this group and the mother you were talking to is in their eyes... what I see in their eyes is compassion and interest in your story. That's why I wanted you to look in their eyes. *[after 30 seconds Martha makes eye contact with a few people in the group]* Does anybody want to say anything to Martha?

Several group members begin to speak at once about their feeling and reactions. A lively group process continues wherein some people express their sympathy and others identify with her plight.

Tessa's Clarification

Tessa was physically abused by her mother: she had a vivid memory of many severe beatings; of her mother burning her with cigarettes (she had scars to show); and of being tied to a bed while the mother was out for the night with various men. We spent three years deciphering the implicit and explicit memories embodied in her many physical sensations and gestures. Tessa would often write "horror stories" for me to read. Each of these stories contained an encoded account of her experience of physical abuse, emotional cruelty, and degradation. Our coconstructive decoding of her horror stories was the way she was finally able to construct a somewhat consistent narrative of her life. Tessa had not seen her mother all the while she was in therapy. In the fourth year of therapy, Tessa's mother was dying of liver disease. She discovered that her mother did not have much time to live. Tessa had expressed a great deal of anger throughout the ongoing therapy and she had also grieved for "the love of a mother that I had never had".

I thought that she might benefit from a possible reconciliation with her mother and I encouraged her to have an honest conversation, while her mother was still lucid. When Tessa entered the hospital room, her mother criticized the way she was dressed, insulted her, and asked for money. Tessa spent several hours with her mother wherein she attempted to talk about her childhood. She told her mother about being tied to the bed. The mother answered, "You had fits. Something was wrong with your brain. There was nothing else anyone could do for you – you were such a bad child". Tessa described the beatings she had received. Her mother justified the beatings and had no empathy or remorse. When Tessa showed her the scars from the cigarette burns, the mother accused Tessa of having done it to herself.

Tessa returned to therapy heartbroken and angry. She was angry at her mother's callous and humiliating comments, and she had hoped that her mother would express regret and ask for forgiveness. She wept with the painful realization, "We will never have a relationship". She was also angry at me and screamed, "Truth telling doesn't work".

Later, in therapy, she said that – no matter what she had said to her mother that day, even if she had been very complimentary and kind – she knew that her mother would insult and blame her. She concluded that her mother was now, and had always been, "self-centered and cruel". She did not speak to her mother again before her mother died. We continued the therapy for another two years and, during this time, she periodically said that the hospital conversation with her mother was very clarifying. She was now certain that none of the physical abuse was her fault. She no longer criticized or blamed herself.

Conclusion

In Tessa's situation the idea of "truth telling" did not have the desired effect of repairing a ruptured relationship, as it had for Linda. Truth telling and open-hearted conversations are possible only when the other party is receptive to a meaningful dialogue. If the other person is closed to interpersonal contact, such truth telling may still have some benefits, as it eventually did for Tessa. Over time, Tessa experienced a sense of clarification and an end to self-ridicule.

For many clients having an honest, face-to-face, and intimate conversation with the significant other before he or she dies is the most effective way of resolving anticipatory grief and decreasing the intensity of grieving after the person dies. Martha was unwilling to have a direct conversation with her mother. She was certain that her mother would be unreceptive to any truthful or intimate dialogue. Instead, we used the "empty chair" and Martha's imagination to create the quality of interpersonal contact in fantasy that was not possible in reality. In all three of these examples, the "truth telling", in its various forms, either resolved resentment, repaired a ruptured relationship, or provided a sense of clarification. To quote the Gospel of John (8:32), "The truth shall set you free".

References

Erskine, R. G. (2014). What do you say before you say goodbye? Psychotherapy of grief. *Transactional Analysis Journal*, 44(4), 279–290.

Erskine, R. G., Moursund, J. P., & Trautmann, R. L. (1999). *Beyond empathy: A therapy of contact-in-relationship.* Brunner/Mazel.

Moursund, J. P., & Erskine, R. G. (2003). *Integrative Psychotherapy: The art and science of relationship.* Brooks/Cole-Thomson Learning.

Perls, F. S. (1969). *Gestalt therapy verbatim.* Real People Press.

Perls, F. S. (1975). *Legacy from Fritz.* Science and Behavior Books.

Chapter 12

Relational Group Process
Developments in Group Psychotherapy

In *Transactional Analysis in Psychotherapy: A Systematic Individual and Social Psychiatry*, Eric Berne (1961) began his chapter on "Group Therapy" (p. 165) by stating, "Transactional Analysis is offered as a method of group therapy because it is a rational, indigenous approach derived from the group situation itself". He wrote that a Transactional Analysis group is different from other groups that are based specifically on theoretical concepts of a group as a "metaphysical entity" (such as psychodynamic group analysis), those designed to force growth (such as encounter groups), or those that use "opportunistic" techniques (such as Gestalt therapy groups).

Berne went on to describe what he meant by a rational approach: "The objective of Transactional Analysis in group therapy is to carry each patient through the progressive stages of structural analysis, Transactional Analysis proper, game analysis, and script analysis, until he attains social control" (1961, p. 165). Berne's rational perspective and structured approach make sense when we consider that his examples in Chapters 9 and 10 (see Berne, 1961) came from his experience with his borderline women's group or from the hospitalized patients described in Chapter 15 of his work (D. Kupfer, personal communication, September 16, 1969). Rational understanding and social control are essential early therapy goals with such patient populations.

Berne (1961) provided a conceptual foundation for a transaction-by-transaction approach to group psychotherapy. He described how he made use of therapy by interpretation to analyze each group member's actual transactions, to identify life-script patterns, and to provide alternatives to psychological games. Berne's writings about group psychotherapy also illustrated a specific and useful model of therapy through the group members' interactions with each other. The central methods in his group therapy were his explanations of complementary, crossed, and ulterior transactions and his theoretical interpretations about the ego states involved in games, transference, and scripts. Berne's therapeutic effectiveness as a group psychotherapist seemed to lie in his integration of two models of group psychotherapy: therapy through the group and therapy by interpretation.

DOI: 10.4324/9781003626718-12

What I find significant in Berne's (1961) opening statement is the phrase "indigenous approach derived from the group situation itself" (p. 165). This intriguing phrase has led me to experiment with a number of ways to make use of the healing and growth-enhancing power that is indigenous in a secure and effective group situation. I have searched for models of group psychotherapy that are effective for clients suffering from prolonged stress, cumulative neglect, acute trauma, and/or repetitive humiliation. This chapter is written to describe various influences, experiments, and discoveries in searching for that indigenous, growth-enhancing group therapy experience and in developing a Transactional Analysis model of therapy through a relational group process.

Developments in Group Psychotherapy

The history of the development of group psychotherapy is a long and fascinating story comprising many contributions, concepts, and models (Bion, 1989; Ormont, 2003; Rutan & Stone, 1993; Yalom, 1995). The annals of both the American Group Psychotherapy Association and the International Group Psychotherapy Association are replete with rich examples of the effective use of various models. Rather than recounting this history in detail, I will describe just a few models that have influenced my professional practice as a transactional analyst. These models may be described as therapy by the group, therapy by interpretation, therapy in the group, and therapy through the group. My experimentation with and application of these models in psychotherapy, education, and organizational consulting have influenced the development of an integrated model that I refer to as relational group process.

Therapy by the Group

In the 1930s, Alcoholics Anonymous (AA) began as a leaderless group. AA is based on the theory that alcoholism is a disease and individuals need group support to stop drinking. A 12-step program shapes the methods of the group; every aspect of the group is determined by one of the 12 steps. Members are encouraged to practice one of the steps daily and to tell their story in meetings, often repeatedly, while others listen respectfully. AA is a prime example of therapy by the group.

In the early 1970s, O. Hobart Mowrer (1972) increased the scope of the AA model to include the group treatment of depression and anxiety. Along with a focus on honesty and responsibility, he placed equal emphasis on integrity and the personal involvement of each group member in helping other group members live up to the 12-step program. Although Mowrer's integrity groups were originally designed for the treatment of acute depression and anxiety, his ideas and methods were also used in group therapy with a general adult population.

For two academic terms, Dr. Mowrer and I co-led a group of university graduate students in which we experimented with using a combination of integrity group concepts and Transactional Analysis theory. Each week the two-hour group would begin with a 20-minute introduction to a transactional analysis concept such as ego states, crossed and ulterior transactions, strokes, the OK Corral, time structure, games, or script. Although I taught a substantial amount of Transactional Analysis theory to the groups, we did not make use of interpretation in the way Berne had. Instead, we used a therapy-by-the-group model to explore how the Transactional Analysis and AA concepts could be used in the group members' lives to enhance each person's sense of honesty, responsibility, and integrity.

At the University of Chicago in 1945, Carl Rogers and Robert Neville developed non-directive group therapy to treat war neurosis. This form of therapy by the group was influenced by the work of Harry Stack Sullivan and emphasized a democratic process of equality and encouraging group members to share their traumatic stories and feelings with each other. By telling these stories over and over again while receiving empathic responses, the traumas of war were healed (Neville, personal communication, September 20, 1967).

In non-directive group therapy, the leader's role is to model empathy, congruence, and unconditional positive regard for group members. He or she does not offer interpretations. The therapy is not determined by a theory of motivation, personality, or psychopathology but by the idea that people need to be authentic with each other about their emotional experiences (Rogers, 1951, 1961). In my first two years as a group psychotherapist, I used this model exclusively. Over the years, I have often returned to this model when shame is a central issue, when the power of group members' empathy and identity are essential for the healing of trauma and neglect, or when other models seem too deterministic.

Therapy by Interpretation

The types of groups just described are different in principles, methods, and therapists' tasks from psychoanalytic group therapies that emphasize the importance of the therapist's interpretations. Several types of psychoanalytic groups began in the 1950s under the initial influence of Wilfred Bion at the Tavistock Clinic in England. The analyst's task was to interpret group members' behavior according to the ideas of certain psychoanalytic theorists (particularly Sigmund Freud, Anna Freud, and Melanie Klein) and the basic assumptions proposed by Bion (1970). Group members were encouraged to talk to each other, and it was assumed that, in the course of the group's discussion, each member's childhood transferences and psychopathology would be disclosed through his or her interactions within the group.

In such groups, the leader spoke only to make theoretically based, authoritative interpretations of group members' pathological motivations for their behavior (often in the last few minutes of each session). For example, interpretations of an individual's behavior might be attributed to unresolved aggression, envy, Oedipal sexual attraction, or infantile transference that was revealed behaviorally through dependency, fight or flight, pairing, and/or oneness (Banet & Hayden, 1997). In psychoanalytic groups, the authority of theory may, at times, appear to take precedence over group members' phenomenological experience.

In my experimentation with the therapy-by-interpretation model, I found that the use of authoritative interpretation may have the positive effect of arousing group members to think about their motivations, behaviors, and transference. It may even produce some adaptive changes in behavior. However, such theory-determined interpretations may also have a negative effect in that they may be quite distant from the client's subjective experience (hence not so useful), are often shaming to an individual group member, and may also provoke other group members to either withdraw or conform to some theoretical expectation or norm. It has thus been my practice to abstain from using a therapy-by-interpretation model and instead focus on an intersubjective understanding of each client's motivations, affects, and behaviors as well as a coconstructive understanding among group members about their interpersonal relationships.

The 1960s were a rich time of development in group therapy. Three trends emerged, often overlapped, and influenced each other: therapy by interpretation, therapy in the group, and therapy through the group. During this time Berne made use of a modified psychoanalytic model to analyze group members' transactions to determine which were transferential and which were not. He primarily focused on the transferences between group members that resulted in psychological games and reinforced life scripts. An example of his use of Transactional Analysis theory in group therapy can be found in his description of his weekly group of mothers of disturbed children at Atascadero State Hospital (Berne, 1961, p. 176).

In contrast to the psychoanalytically based group therapists of his time, Berne was active in the group's discussions, making theoretically based explanations, confrontations, and interpretations (Berne, 1966) during the process rather than waiting until the end as was done in most psychoanalytic groups. Even though he was active in the group's process and fostered a sense of equality by engaging group members in making contracts for behavioral change and in talking directly to each other, "his primary methods were explanation, confrontation, and interpretation" (Rosenfeld, personal communication, November 18, 1976). Although Berne did not make psychoanalytically based interpretations about an individual's pathological motivations, focusing instead on group members' transactions with each other, both his Transactional Analysis groups and psychoanalytic groups can be seen as following the model of therapy by interpretation.

Therapy in the Group

Also during the 1960s and early 1970s, Fritz Perls (1967, 1973) developed a model of therapy in the group in which the psychotherapist did individual psychotherapy with one person in the group while other group members observed. Group members participated both vicariously and through their supportive statements at the end of the work, but there was little in the way of group interaction. The psychotherapist was highly directive of psychotherapy by encouraging the client to do psychological experiments, to be expressive, and to explore unfinished emotional experiences.

Perls's Gestalt therapy groups pioneered the idea of therapy in the group and had a large influence on how Transactional Analysis and other forms of group therapy were conducted during the 1970s. The use of a Transactional Analysis model of therapy in the group is illustrated in Changing Lives Through Redecision Therapy (Goulding & Goulding, 1979) and Integrative Psychotherapy in Action (Erskine & Moursund, 1988/2011). I have often used such individualized in-the-group therapy methods, particularly in therapy marathons, to stimulate profound change in a client's life script. Group members benefit by identification and through group discussion at the end of the work. However, in such groups there is a dearth of interpersonal contact unless the psychotherapist encourages whole-group interaction following the individual therapy.

Therapy Through the Group

Another trend in the 1960s was influenced by the emergence of encounter groups, which emphasized interpersonal growth and the development of human potential (Egan, 1970). Encounter groups began as a form of human relations training and were not originally proposed as a form of psychotherapy. Over time, however, the model of interpersonal growth was used in various clinical settings as a form of therapy through the group.

Encounter group theory was based on a cybernetic model that suggested that we all affect each other in a myriad of ways. This is articulated in the notion that one person's behavior in the group directly influences the behavior of the others. We are all constantly influencing each other both consciously and unconsciously. Encounter groups focused on various group members describing the behavior of each of the other group members and how that behavior affected them. Each member in the group was encouraged to give feedback to other group members and to be highly vocal, confrontive, or even aggressive in describing others' behavior. Direct confrontation was seen as a form of authenticity. Both individuals' behavior and their possible lack of emotional expression were seen as their problem, which was to be fixed through group interaction. This theory is based on the idea that people are often out of touch with themselves and need an intense encounter with others to become authentic (Egan, 1971). Unfortunately, the lack of respect that often characterized feedback among group members and a heavy focus on behavior change made these groups shaming and traumatizing to some participants. They were not appropriate for clients with developmental neglect or acute trauma.

I have often experimented with the use of dyadic, small-group, and whole-group encounter exercises (as well as physical movement, dance, and psychodramatic enactments) to facilitate clients' discovery of their own potential and to heighten their awareness of how they have an impact on others. I found it essential when using this model of therapy through the group for the psychotherapist to maintain a protective environment that clearly communicates respect for each person's uniqueness.

The Feedback and Person-Centered Dialectic

By the 1980s, many group psychotherapists were influenced in some way by the various models I have just described as they experimented with different trends in interpersonal relations and group psychotherapy. I was influenced too and searched to find a form of group psychotherapy that was effective in changing the relational patterns of my clients' life scripts. I looked for a model that was relational and coconstructive and that made full use of the therapeutic potential indigenous in group members' interactive processes. I experimented with Transactional Analysis in the styles of a feedback and a person-centered approach to group psychotherapy. These two trends reflect important developments in group psychotherapy and represent opposing poles on a continuum of therapy through the group.

In a similar vein, Kapur and Miller (1987) presented a research study comparing the therapeutic factors central in Transactional Analysis and psychodynamic therapy. They described how "TA clinicians place strong emphasis on encouraging patients to achieve greater insight into their behavior" but place little emphasis on group interaction (p. 298). In contrast, psychodynamic group therapists emphasize a group process that facilitates universality, altruism, and cohesiveness. According to Kapur and Miller, the aim of psychodynamic group therapists is "to knit the group together and provide this as the therapeutic basis for personal change" (p. 299). They surmised that the high value placed on interpersonal feedback in Transactional Analysis groups might account for the low level of altruism in them when compared to psychodynamic groups. They suggested that Transactional Analysis group therapists should integrate procedures that "foster group cohesiveness and universality by varying therapeutic techniques, decentralizing leadership, and promoting free interaction among group members" (p. 299).

Many current Transactional Analysis and other theoretically oriented psychotherapy groups make use of a feedback approach to facilitate group interaction. Although such an approach is interactive, it often either reflects the leader's theoretical perspective or the opinion of a particular person or collection of people. Candor and bluntness are encouraged. The emphasis is on the speaker's perspective, which is considered bona fide and more significant than listening to and learning from others in the group. The therapeutic intent of the feedback is to influence and modify group members' script-determined behaviors and relational patterns. The social message is, "This is how you affect me", and the emphasis is on change.

Confrontation from the group leader or from one group member to another is considered essential to the therapy process. Such bluntness is often regarded as an expression of the speaker's genuineness and the "reality of how I see you". In a feedback-oriented group, the focus is on each member's perception and interpretation of other group members' behaviors. The feedback may not accurately describe an individual's subjective and internal experience, but it reflects how another group member perceives him or her. Candor is often encouraged and is defined as speaking congruently of one's own feelings, interpretations, and opinions about another group member's behavior. For example, one person might describe or interpret another with a statement such as, "You are angry and withdrawn. You always feel superior".

Theoretically, the advantage of the feedback model is that it provides the perspective and opinion of the group leader or of one group member to another. When someone makes a pronouncement, the recipient is expected to respond as though the original speaker is describing reality or the only truth (Banet & Hayden, 1997). Self-reflection in accordance with the confrontation is encouraged, whereas explaining one's subjective experience may be defined as being defensive (Bion, 1989).

One of the disadvantages of a feedback-oriented group is that little attention is given to an individual's inner processes (such as fear, shame, uncertainty, etc.) that may be manifested in the expression of what may appear to be, for example, anger, withdrawal, or superior behavior. Groups that rely on frequent use of a feedback model may change members' script-determined behavior but may also increase members' sense of shame and being misunderstood within the group. Rather than inviting intersubjective connection and real interpersonal growth, the feedback approach may trigger compliance and/or withdrawal.

In contrast, a person-centered psychotherapy group attends to how each member's subjective experiences are manifested in the group (Rogers, 1961). It places the therapeutic focus on each individual's phenomenological process and the importance of sharing one's subjective experience with an interested and involved listener (Snygg & Combs, 1949). In a person-centered group, one's personal perspective, opinion, or interpretation is seen as inadequate for understanding other group members. There is, therefore, an emphasis on inquiry, understanding, and attunement with others' inner experience, a resonance with their affect, self-perspective, and how they make meaning. It is based on the leader and each group member assuming, "I know nothing about the other person's inner process; my observation and interpretation are not enough to understand the experience of the other person".

One of the principles of a person-centered group is to learn to see and experience the other as he or she experiences himself or herself, to enter vicariously into the other's subjective experience. Careful listening and respectful inquiry are viewed as essential for knowing the other (Rogers, 1970). Empathy with other group members' stories and attunement to others' affect, rhythm, and mode of cognition is given central importance. Confrontation is generally not part of person-centered groups. The assumption is that when people experience being truly known, without interpretation or ridicule, their levels of stress and shame decrease, and they can more freely express themselves and resolve psychological issues (Bozarth, 1986).

One disadvantage of the person-centered model is that it may over-emphasize subjective experience and the importance of empathy. It may not sufficiently attend to the effects of a group member's behavior on others. By emphasizing each member's internal, subjective experience, such groups may miss giving adequate attention to the person's behaviors, including the effect of crossed transactions, projections, and misinterpretations; the impact one member may have on another; or the behavioral dimensions of life scripts. Another disadvantage is that group members may be nice to each other rather than authentically expressing what they perceive. When the group is nice, significant aspects of group members' script-determined behaviors may not receive therapeutic attention or the opportunity to be resolved.

My practice of group therapy has been influenced by a professional desire to resolve the dialectic between using a feedback and a person-centered approach, and I have experimented with bringing these perspectives into a therapeutically effective synthesis. In my view, clients need an approach that includes the central elements of both approaches. Such a synthesis provides the therapeutic environment in which clients can learn to relinquish their old life-script patterns; consistently engage in complementary transactions; live lives that are free from early survival reactions and parental introjections; avoid psychological games; be aware of themselves, others, and their environment; and have lives rich in intimacy. I think that the solution to the polemic between these approaches lies in the skillful integration of the two modes. The goal is to develop an effective therapy that is coconstructive and relational, that is truly indigenous to the group.

Relational Group Process

Relational group process emphasizes transaction-by-transaction inter-personal contact, the processes of intersubjective relating, and the reciprocal and mutual influence of each group member on the other members. The focus of both the group therapist and group members is on the interplay between the present moment and the emergence of unconscious relational patterns that may be an expression of archaic experiences. Group members learn to relate to each other through acknowledgment, phenomenological inquiry, validation, and normalization. The healing of anxiety, depression, cumulative neglect, and trauma becomes possible through group members' contactful, caring relationships that attend to each person's subjective experience and relational needs (Erskine et al., 1999). Relational group process is an implementation of Buber's (1923/1958) I and Thou philosophy.

The Therapist's Tasks

When using a relational group process model, my intention is to combine the best of both the feedback and the person-centered models. One of the leader's responsibilities is to encourage all group members to attend to each person's phenomenological experience and to participate actively by providing respectful responses. An important focal point of the therapy is the creation of an intersubjective experience wherein each member is fully involved with each other member.

I often begin a relational group process by teaching the importance of a coconstructive mission within the group. This is accomplished by encouraging group members to be empathic, to listen, to inquire, and to resonate with others. Group members learn, and hopefully appreciate, others' perspectives and feelings. They are encouraged to be responsive and to speak about their perceptions of, feelings about, and reactions to each other.

When group members are attuned to each other's affects and relational needs and are respectful in their transactions with each other, the quality of feedback they provide becomes a valuable asset in promoting growth. An effective relationally oriented group will include some feedback, but it will be given in a way that is respectful and attuned to the recipient's affect. This respect is based on the awareness that one's comments may not accurately describe the other's experience. It is in integrating the person-centered and feedback trends of working in groups that we create a viable "us", a shared experience rather than just a "you" or a "me" perspective.

This reciprocal process of respectful involvement with other group members' perspectives enables everyone in the group to elaborate on and enrich the expression of their own experiences. Relational group psychotherapy provides group members with the opportunity to express themselves, to be understood, to grow in emotional attachment, to develop their unique identity, and to express their own integrity.

In relational group process, the therapist has several tasks, including introducing principles and practices that validate the individuality and importance of each person and the multiple relationships in the group; providing a sense of cohesion, continuity, and stability; and encouraging group members to question and challenge their own and others' beliefs, fantasies, and behaviors. The therapeutic dialogue is built on honesty, responsibility, integrity, and courtesy. Truth telling, about one's self and how each person experiences the other group members (and the leader), is an important characteristic of such groups.

Effective relational group process often provides a contrast between an individual's current relational experiences and his or her internal psychological processes of implicit and procedural memories, script conclusions and beliefs, projections and expectations, and archaic forms of self-regulation. It emphasizes the importance of phenomenological inquiry, each group member's relational needs, and the reparative power of people's genuine interest and involvement.

Another task for the relational group process leader involves teaching and emphasizing the importance of active listening, acknowledgment, and normalization. In these groups, normalization does not refer to placating or minimizing the significance of a problem but to recognizing that the psychological function of the person's affects, fantasies, self-protective processes, script beliefs, and modes of coping are normal and a means of self-stabilization within a historically stressful, neglecting, or traumatizing family or school context.

Relational group process also takes the psychotherapist out of the role of interpreting and out of the position of working individually with each person. Instead, the leader focuses on facilitating relationships between group members, teaching about human needs and relationships, and guiding and facilitating involved relationships among group members. The image I use is that of an orchestra conductor who maintains the rhythm, adjusts the volume, gestures to various musicians when it is time for them to play their solos, and facilitates the orchestra members in playing in harmony with each other.

Healing relationships in groups are based on caring involvement while working together for the common benefit of all. An additional task of the group psychotherapist is to facilitate group members in inquiring about each other's phenomenological experience and to draw out those who are not actively participating or may be reluctant to talk about what they are feeling. For example, in a group session Charles spoke about how stressed he felt during the painfully protracted illness and eventual death of a dear friend. His grief was intense. He then thanked the group and the psychotherapists for encouraging and supporting him in talking about it, even though he had hesitated to do so. He described the relief he felt after talking and crying about his pain and how his feelings of grief had shifted to appreciating the way his life had been enriched by the friendship. With the group leader's encouragement, Charles then inquired about the experiences of two individuals who had not spoken in the group during this time and had recently experienced the death of loved-ones. They said that they found it difficult to speak about death and their lost relationships because of the fear of being overwhelmed with intense sadness. However, witnessing Charles's emotion-filled story helped them feel more able to express some of their own grief. This led to the whole group talking about the importance of interpersonal connections, loss, sadness, and how they each had a history of distracting themselves from the intensity of their feelings. This illustrates one of the important tasks of the group psychotherapist, which is to help group members become aware of their own relational needs while being respectful and responsive to the needs of others in the group.

In this situation it seemed wiser to encourage Charles to inquire about the experiences of the other two group members. As the group therapist, I was building on the empathy and identification that existed between these three people and wanted to strengthen the bonds between them. I was also focused on setting a model of involvement within the group. With other clients I may be the one who initiates an inquiry rather than coaxing a group member to do so. That depends on the quality of connection a person has with other group members and/or his or her need to rely on me to demonstrate my interest in his or her emotional experience. With someone else, I might inquire about his or her phenomenological experience of remaining silent, the importance of silence, and/or the quality of security that is needed.

In relational group process I want to establish a cultural framework in which each member will be actively involved with other group members without a loss of anyone's individuality. Each therapeutic intervention is based on a split-second evaluation of the relational needs of each person and of the group as a whole. In the situation just described, the two group members who had not spoken did not require a challenge in order to express their silent grief. They needed another person who was also acquainted with grief to reach out, ask about their feelings, and show an interest in their stories. It is through courteous and respectful transactions such as these that universality, cohesiveness, altruism, and intimacy are fostered.

Principles of the Model

A guiding principle of relational group psychotherapy is respect for each person's phenomenological experience. Through positive regard, understanding, kindness, and compassion, each group member establishes interpersonal relationships that provide affirmation of others' uniqueness and integrity. Integrity is perhaps best defined in Shakespeare's (1600/1982) words in *Hamlet*: "To thine own self be true, and it must follow, as the night the day, thou canst not then be false to any man" (Act 1, Scene 3).

Interpersonal contact between group members is the therapeutic context in which each person explores his or her feelings, needs, memories, and perceptions. This does not mean that relational group process is all about being nice and superficial with one another. On the contrary, when we use the best of a feedback model, the result may be uncomfortable discussions, challenges to the other person's perspective, or confrontation of behavior. In using a combination of the person-centered and feedback models, trust is built when the discussion, challenge, or confrontation is done with honesty and respect for the other's perspective – a respect that builds trust in the relationship and fosters each person's sense of integrity.

Confrontation, when used in relational group process, is done with sensitivity to the potential shame it may cause and an awareness of potential retraumatization. As a group psychotherapist, I encourage members to obtain the other person's consent before making a confrontation, for example, "I have something to say to you that may be uncomfortable. Do you want hear it and discuss your reactions?" I also lead group members to engage in phenomenological and relational inquiry following a confrontation with comments such as, "How did you experience what was said to you? What meaning do you make of the fact that I said it now and not before? Is it possible that I have misperceived you and do not understand your experience?" When confrontation is accompanied by respectful, courteous inquiry into the current quality of an interpersonal relationship, the possibility of shame diminishes, and integrity is strengthened for each person involved in the exchange.

Confrontation is only useful in group psychotherapy when the person receiving it experiences the confronter as being invested in the recipient's welfare. If that sense of interpersonal connection and collaboration is missing, then confrontation creates interpersonal conflict. The result may be resistance, resentment, and an interruption in the working alliance within the group. Therefore, it is essential that the group psychotherapist develop a relationally focused culture within the group, one that fosters attunement, understanding, acceptance, and interpersonal involvement among the members.

Developing a relationally focused culture occurs as the group therapist models and teaches about interpersonal contact and respect, focuses group members' attention on their own and other members' relational needs, explores possible breaches in relationships among members, and fosters group members' investment in resolving misunderstandings. Confrontations between group members are inevitable in therapy groups. The effective therapist uses the perceptions of the whole group to work with the individuals involved: to help the person doing the confronting to discover the motivations underlying it and to help the person receiving the confrontation to explore his or her feelings, associations, and self-protective reactions. As a group builds experience together, it forms cohesion and intimacy. As that happens, confrontations can occur with sensitivity, respect, and inquiry. It should be noted that the traditional feedback and person-centered models are incompatible if used interchangeably and prematurely. It is only when a group has established mutual trust and a shared purpose that confrontation may be integrated effectively into a relational group process.

In a relationally focused therapy group, the therapist is not the only one to support and encourage group members to express what they are feeling and thinking. Group members' inquiry of and empathy with each other, and their encouragement for everyone to be heard, may constitute important psychologically supportive transactions when they express a shared experience of similar loss, stress, neglect, or trauma. In an effectively conducted group, several elements occur synergistically:

- Group members talk authentically about their experiences, perceptions, and affect. Other group members fully listen and think about how the other's perceptions compare and contrast with their own.
- New experiences emerge in the form of communal experiences that are uniquely different from what each individual has previously known.
- New understandings come into view, script beliefs change, and new emotional experiences occur as old relational memories are contrasted with what is transpiring relationally in the group.

These new experiences are uniquely individual and simultaneously uniquely relational. In creating a shared experience, the group constructs a place that belongs to no one in particular and yet to each and all, a creative place of relationship.

The Therapeutic Process

Relational group psychotherapy often begins with recognizing each person's needs and feelings. The leader often encourages group members to focus on each person's need for security, that is, the freedom to be as he or she is, without criticism, ridicule, or put-downs. One of the first steps in healing stress, undoing cumulative neglect, and resolving trauma is for each person to be assured that he or she will not be shamed in the group. This is often accompanied by encouraging group members to talk about past humiliating experiences and how they were hurt, angry, or remain fearful in a group. Group members may be invited to remember emotionally laden experiences in which they did not feel secure with the goal of creating a safe space in which they can share their fantasies, attend to body sensations, and describe specific relational disruptions that occurred in their family, with friends, or at school. It is important to create the quality of relationships within the group that facilitates members talking about how they coped with fear, anger, relational disruptions, childhood neglect, a broken heart, or traumatic experiences.

The goal is to foster understanding of how implicit memories and archaic ways of relating may be reenacted within the group, in families, and in everyday life. The group provides a safe place in which to experiment with new behaviors, attitudes, and relationships. The emphasis often shifts between what the person needed from significant others in original script-forming situations and what he or she currently needs from other group members. Such conversation may move from one group member to another with a focus on the type of security and interpersonal relationship each needs from the other.

For example, in a group that had met for several sessions, discussion among the members seemed to be rather superficial. I was disheartened when several group members avoided any emotionally charged topic. Some members repeated old stories, a few appeared to be shy, while a couple of members only talked about current events. Everyone avoided talking about early childhood script-forming experiences. Following one such session, I was quite troubled by the absence of any emotional expression or interpersonal contact in the group. I felt ashamed of my impoverished therapeutic work in the group and sought consultation with a colleague. She reminded me of the research I had done on shame. I realized that no one in the group had ever spoken about shame, even though most of the members were displaying symptoms of debilitating shame. Each person, including me, was living his or her distress in silence (Erskine, 1994/1997).

I began the next session by saying that I had realized that no one had used the word shame in our previous sessions. I then described my sense of shame when I knew that I was not doing a competent job and expressed my fear of their potential ridicule. After my comments, there were several minutes of silence. Then the group members spoke of their own shame and how they often felt that there was something wrong with them. Over the next several sessions, each group member talked about how he or she had been blamed or humiliated in school, in previous groups, and in his or her family. These discussions led them to recognize how each person needed safety in the group and the opportunity to express who he or she was, without ridicule. Through my therapeutic inquiry the various group members also explored how their tone of voice or choice of words may stimulate shame reactions in other group members. As an outcome of these discussions some of the group members pledged to each other that there would be no shaming transactions and, if such transactions inadvertently occurred, the group would be committed to resolving the conflict. The group culture changed as they each talked about humiliating experiences, how they thought the others might reject them "if you knew" the painful childhood memories that had previously remained secret in the group. The group became lively and an interpersonally connecting, healing place.

Often discussions about security lead to someone's need for validation and affirmation by other group members. For many, behavior or ways of making meaning were discounted, ignored, or in some way not validated in previous relationships. The lack of validation is often shaming and adds to stress. Validation is provided when we find value in what the other is saying.

As mentioned earlier, an important mission of relational group psychotherapy is to provide each member with a sense of validation. A case in point: Frequently a group member will say something that is full of emotion and others will remain silent. Although group members may think that they are being respectful, silence in such instances is often experienced by the speaker as a lack of validation of his or her affect and/or sense of self. The person may begin to doubt himself or herself and what he or she is saying; internal stress, shame, and withdrawal may result. It is the leader's responsibility to identify such moments when there is a lack of validation and to encourage members to speak about what they are feeling in response to the person. Such feeling-based responsiveness provides indispensable validation.

Each of us needs to rely on others who are stable, dependable, and protective, who provide understanding, support, and guidance. An interpersonally contactful psychotherapy group can fulfill these needs when members consistently respect each person's affect, fantasies, and self-protective processes. The group provides a protective function when the setting is secure and offers the necessary attunement and involvement to understand the emotional expression or implicit memory that a member is experiencing. In some groups the significance of the larger unconscious story that a member is enacting in his or her behavior and the importance of group members' patience and acceptance is a way to provide stability and dependability.

All of us need to have our personal experiences confirmed, which occurs when we are in dialogue with someone who understands because he or she has had a similar experience. The group leader watches for and encourages members to talk about how they identify with what a person may be saying that is similar to their own experience. Frequently the conversation then flows between several group members, with each contributing the uniqueness of his or her own experience. It is in the shared experiences that people do not feel alone or worry that they are strange or crazy. Shared experiences are an important antidote to shame and an important way to reduce stress. The group's cohesiveness and the members' sense of belonging and universality are enhanced when members' personal experiences are confirmed.

Along with encouraging such confirmation, the group therapist supports each person in the group in expressing his or her uniqueness. People have the relational need to know and express their own self-definition, individuality, and distinctness while receiving acknowledgment and acceptance from others in the group. Self-definition is the communication of one's self-chosen identity through the expression of preferences, interests, and ideas without humiliation or rejection. The relational group psychotherapist encourages each person's expression of identity and integrity and the group's normalization of everyone's need for self-definition. In some family and school situations, children's attempts at self-definition are ridiculed or punished. When self-definition is thwarted, internal stress increases and a sense of one's self is lost. An effective group leader facilitates each individual in defining his or her self in relationship with others.

All people have the need to make an impact on others with whom they are involved. This need begins with an infant's first cry and continues throughout life. An individual's sense of competency in relationship emerges from attracting the other's attention and interest, influencing what may be talked about, and effecting a change of emotion or behavior in others. Attunement to a group member's need to make an impact occurs when other group members allow themselves to be emotionally impacted by the speaker and to respond with compassion when the speaker is sad, to provide an affect of security when the person is scared, to take the other seriously when he or she is angry, and to be excited when he or she is joyful.

Many people in group need others to initiate contact and reach out in a way that acknowledges their presence and demonstrates their importance in the relationship. The group psychotherapist models initiation, teaches about the importance of initiation, and encourages members to initiate with each other. So often people are hesitant to initiate because they think that they may be invasive or rescuing or they remember rules from school that prohibited children from talking to each other during class. Various initiations that group members make with each other often reduce group members' stress or sense of being alone. For example, a group member may say to another, "I noticed that you have been silent for a while. I would like to know what you are experiencing". This is an invitation to be fully involved together in the therapeutic process.

The need to express thankfulness, gratitude, and/or affection is also important in human relationships. When group members provide a sense of security, validation, stability, and dependability, when they have a shared experience, an opportunity for self-definition, a chance to make an impact, and show initiation with each other, individuals are often grateful and want to express their affection. The effective group leader facilitates expressions of thankfulness and gratitude as group members celebrate their accomplishments and successes together.

Conclusion

In my years of experimentation with group psychotherapy, I have found that a group based on the principles of relational group process is an effective venue in which to communicate Transactional Analysis concepts. It is through the development of trust, a shared relationship, validation, consistent reliability and security, and ongoing responses to each individual's relational needs that the indigenous healing and growth-enhancing power of the group is actualized in the lives of each member. Such respectful group involvement puts an end to group members' sense of shame and rectifies cumulative neglect, dissolves chronic stress, and heals trauma.

The development of this model of group therapy is not complete; it remains an active experiment. It must be continually refined according to the unique composition of each group, in response to the specific relational needs of its members and the cultural context of each group, and through the values and skills of the group leader.

I am intrigued by what other aspects of this model are yet to be developed: Are there more efficient and effective ways to resolve group therapy problems such as differentiation, inclusion, passivity, competition, envy, or confluence? What is the right balance between the therapist's attention to an individual member's script issues and the ongoing processes of the group? When is it appropriate to include experiential methods, supportive regression, body therapy, and/or redecision therapy within a relationally focused group? What are the short- and long-term effects of being a member of a relationally focused group? There is a plethora of research possibilities. I hope others will join me in experimenting with the various aspects of relational group process as a way to apply these concepts in group psychotherapy.

References

Banet, A. G., & Hayden, C. (1997). A Tavistock primer. In J. E. Jones & W. Pfeiffer (Eds), *The 1997 annual handbook for group facilitators*. University Associates.

Berne, E. (1961). *Transactional Analysis in psychotherapy: A systematic individual and social psychiatry*. Grove Press.

Berne, E. (1966). *Principles of group treatment*. Grove Press.

Bion, W. R. (1970). *Attention and interpretation: Scientific approach to insight in psychoanalysis and groups*. Basic Books.

Bion, W. R. (1989). *Experiences in groups*. Tavistock Routledge.

Bozarth, J. D. (1986). The basic encounter group: An alternative view. *The Journal for Specialists in Group Work*, 11(4), 228–232.

Buber, M. (1958). *I and thou*. (Trans. R. G. Smith). Scribner. (Original work published 1923).

Egan, G. (1970). *Encounter: Groups for interpersonal growth*. Brooks/Cole.

Egan, G. (1971). *Encounter groups: Basic readings*. Brooks/Cole.

Erskine, R. G. (1997). Shame and self-righteousness: Transactional Analysis perspectives and clinical interventions. In R. G. Erskine (Ed.), *Theories and methods of an integrative Transaction Analysis: A volume of selected articles* (pp. 46–67). TA Press. (Original work published 1994).

Erskine, R. G., & Moursund, J. P. (2011). *Integrative Psychotherapy in action*. Karnac Books. (Original work published in 1988).

Erskine, R. G., Moursund, J. P., & Trautmann, R. L. (1999). *Beyond empathy: A therapy of contact-in-relationship*. Burnner/Mazel.

Goulding, M. M., & Goulding, R. L. (1979). *Changing lives through redecision therapy*. Brunner/Mazel.

Kapur, R., & Miller, K. (1987). A comparison between therapeutic factors in TA and psychodynamic therapy groups. *Transactional Analysis Journal*, 17, 294–300.

Mowrer, O. H. (1972). Integrity groups: principles and procedures. *The Counseling Psychologist*, 3, 7–33.

Ormont, L. (2003). *Group psychotherapy*. Jason Aronson.

Perls, F. S. (1967). *Gestalt therapy verbatim*. Real People Press.

Perls, F. S. (1973). *The Gestalt approach and eyewitness to therapy*. Science and Behavior Books.

Rogers, C. R. (1951). *Client centered therapy*. Houghton Mifflin.

Rogers, C. R. (1961). *On becoming a person*. Houghton Mifflin.

Rogers, C. R. (1970). *On encounter groups*. Harrow Books.

Rutan, J. S., & Stone, W. N. (1993). *Psychodynamic group psychotherapy* (2nd ed.). Guilford.

Shakespeare, W. (1982). *Hamlet. The Arden Shakespeare*. (Ed. H. Jenkins). Methven. (Original work c. 1600).

Snygg, D., & Combs, A. W. (1949). *Individual behaviour: A new frame of reference for psychology*. Harper.

Yalom, I. D. (1995). *The theory and practice of group psychotherapy*. Basic Books.

Chapter 13

Contact and Relational Needs in Couple Therapy

An Integrative Psychotherapy Perspective

"Contact" is a core concept in Integrative Psychotherapy; we believe that establishing and maintaining full contact – full awareness of internal and external events – is a *sine qua non* of mental and emotional well-being (Erskine & Moursund, 2011; Erskine et al., 2023; Perls et al., 1951). For couple therapists, this notion of contact is centrally important for it determines the quality of the relationship, as well as the psychological health of the individual partners.

In a healthy couple relationship, the internal and the external facets of contact are interdependent, interrelated, and mutually causal. Contact with one's partner requires contact with one's internal processes, for only as one is aware of those processes can s/he share them with a partner. And, conversely, full internal contact is supported and expanded by contact with a partner who is interested in and sensitive to internal experiencing – of both self and partner.

Therapy with couples brings to the foreground specific experiences which we call *relational needs*: the needs of one person with regard to the behaviors of another. In this context, what is desired and needed includes both external behaviors and internal responses: we want those with whom we share our lives not only to behave in certain ways with us, but also to experience certain internal reactions to us (to care about us, to sympathize, to be interested). Internal and external contact are inextricably bound together, needed by each partner in him- or herself, and in/from their partner.

When external contact is distorted or broken – when relational needs are not responded to appropriately – the relationship is damaged. Damage occurs when one partner fails repeatedly to respond in the needed way; it also occurs when the partner does make an appropriate response, but the response is missed or mis-perceived by the other. The critical factor is not what "actually" happened, but rather the experience of need acknowledged or need missed. If I believe you to be unaware of or uncaring about what I need from you, I am not likely to experience our relationship in a positive way. I won't trust you, won't be willing to be vulnerable in your presence, and will be increasingly reluctant to respond to what you need from me. Conversely, if I do experience you as noticing, being interested in, and

DOI: 10.4324/9781003626718-13

responding to my relational needs, I am likely to feel safe with you and increase my attention to your needs.

Notice that nowhere in all of the preceding have we suggested that partners must or should always satisfy their partner's relational needs. To "respond" to a need may indeed mean acting so as to satisfy it, but it may also mean simply acknowledging it, recognizing it as a valid internal experience, while at the same time being unable or unwilling to fulfill it. Couples who recognize and respond to each other's relational needs, sometimes attempting to meet them and, at other times, simply acknowledging them, are likely to have a healthy relationship; couples who always feel compelled to meet those needs in each other are in danger of falling into confluence (Perls et al., 1951).

While it is neither realistic nor healthy to expect one's partner to meet all of one's relational needs all the time, it is equally unrealistic and unhealthy for the partnership when no relational needs are met by one's partner or when specific needs are chronically neglected. There are many things that I can't or won't always do for or with my partner, and there may be some things that I will seldom do (even though I may recognize and even sympathize with his or her desires for them). But, for the most part, it is essential that I gain satisfaction and pleasure from activities that are need-meeting for my partner, as well as for myself – or why should we bother to be in a relationship at all? A subtle challenge for any partnership, then, is to find a healthy and comfortable balance between those relational needs that are met within the partnership and those that are met elsewhere.

The Eight Relational Needs

At this point, it may be useful to get more specific about what we have thus far referred to generally as "relational needs" (Erskine, 1998; Erskine & Moursund, 2011; Erskine et al., 2023). There are probably as many different ways of describing relational needs as there are people in relationship. Humans are remarkably creative in how they relate to each other and describe their relationships (Stewart, 2010). The concept of relational needs has been applied in both individual and group psychotherapy (Erskine, 2015, 2019, 2021) and validated via empirical research (Pourová et al., 2020; Toksoy et al., 2020; Žvelc et al., 2020).

In our work with clients, both in private practice and in our workshops, we have noticed that eight particular relational needs keep coming up again and again. Let's take a look at what they are:

1 **Security:** In a relationship, one needs to feel secure in order to thrive. One needs to know that the relationship is a safe place to be who one really is, to show all of oneself without fear of losing the other person's respect and liking. Security requires more than verbal reassurances. It is

the visceral experience of having one's vulnerabilities respected and protected. It grows out of repeated experiences of sharing a new aspect of self and discovering that the relationship is still there, still solid, still OK.

2   **Valuing:** The need to be valued, cared about, thought worthy, is an obvious part of any relationship. Why would one want to be in relationship with someone who didn't value or care about or respect him or her? But "valuing" as a relational need goes even beyond this general sort of caring about. It has to do with one's psychological process being understood and that process being valued. Not just (or even necessarily) what one does, but why they do it, is the key to valuing. When I am valued in a relationship, I know that my partner expects and believes that whatever I do must have a reason that makes sense to me, and that s/he wants to understand the sense-making of my behavior.

3   **Acceptance:** Being cared for, respected, needed. And not by just anybody – by a reliable, stable, and protective partner, a partner from whom one can draw strength, and whom one can care for, respect, and need in return. This kind of acceptance allows each partner to support and to accept support from the other. It keeps in balance the kind of emotional "taking turns" that is essential if all of the other relational needs are to be dealt with in a fair and satisfying way.

4   **Mutuality:** The need for mutuality is the need to be with someone who has walked in one's shoes – who understands what one is experiencing because s/he has experienced something similar, in real life or imagination. Part of this need arises from the natural desire to not have to explain everything fully, to be understood without words. And part of it has to do with being able to believe that the other person really does understand and accept and value: if you have been there too, then of course you know what it's like for me – and I am not alone.

5   **Self-definition:** Self-definition in a relationship involves experiencing and expressing one's own uniqueness, and having the other person acknowledge and value that uniqueness. In some ways it's the mirror image of the need for mutuality: the need to be different, as contrasted with the need to be similar. We need our partners to acknowledge our differentness, our disagreements, and even our irritation or anger, when these emerge as a facet of our individuality. When this happens, each partner can grow and individuate with full support from the other.

6   **Making an impact:** An essential part of any meaningful relationship is the ability to have an impact on the other person: to be able to change their thinking, to make them act a different way, to create an emotional response in them. And not only to cause these effects in the other, but to be able to see the effects, to be shown that something has happened to the other person in response to one's input.

7   **Having the other initiate:** A relationship in which one partner must always make the initial approach, always initiate, always take first step,

will eventually become dissatisfying if not painful for that partner. We need our significant others to reach out to us in a way that acknowledges and validates our importance to them, to demonstrate their desire to be involved with us.

8   **To express love:** In any close, positive relationship the participants experience caring, affection, esteem, and appreciation for each other. Expressing these feelings is a relational need; not doing so requires that one push aside and deny the internal experience. When we deny the need to express love we also fail to express self-definition within the relationship. Part of who I am with you is how I feel about you, and – if I am to be fully contactful – I must be able to express those affectionate feelings.

And what about the need to be loved? The need to be loved is fulfilled within the relationship when all eight of the other needs are satisfied, at least some of the time.

Relational Needs Unmet

One of the things that interferes with appropriate, timely and satisfying responses to relational needs between partners is the fact that each partner is an individual, following his or her own experiences from his or her own point of view and with his or her unique history. Relational needs are not always complementary; what I need and want from you at any given moment may be quite out of sync with what you need and want from me. In a healthy relationship, such mismatches are temporary and time-limited. Partners learn to take turns, to put their own needs to one side for a while and attend to the other, with the certainty that the partner will soon do the same for them.

When relational needs are consistently not responded to in relationship one or both partners are likely to become irritable, indifferent, or depressed. The longer this situation exists, the more acute the discomfort. Over time, a relationship in which one or both partner's relational needs remain unmet will become toxic. Contact between the partners becomes a source of pain rather than of pleasure and satisfaction and the partners act so as to protect themselves from that pain. The ways in which the protection manifests itself form a familiar list of relational disruption: withdrawing, criticizing, accusing, arguing. Each disruption leads to a further reduction in contact with even less likelihood of meeting relational needs.

When couples seek therapy, it is almost certain that one or both partners are not getting their relational needs met within that relationship, and that one or both are creating some form of contact distortion as a consequence. Rudolph Dreikurs (Dreikurs & Soltz, 1964), in his studies of children's behavior, developed a hierarchy of behavior dysfunction which seems to apply to adult relationship ruptures as well. Initially, when a partner feels needy and that need is not met, s/he is likely to act so as to get the other partner's attention. "Notice me! Notice that I need something from you!" the behavior says. If the partner notices, and responds, the relationship has a good chance of getting back on course. Over time though, if the partner fails to notice and respond, the partner with needs-not-met moves into some sort of attempt to gain power. Either "I'll make you notice" or "I'll stop needing you at all (by getting my needs met elsewhere, or by being so powerful I don't need anybody)". Power-seeking behavior tends to be more aggressive, more attacking, than attention-seeking behavior in both children and adults.

If power-seeking fails too, the next step in the hierarchy is likely to be a quest for revenge. Revenge-seeking, however it is acted out, is of course likely to damage the relationship even further. Worse, it sets up a dynamic in which the revenge-seeking partner feels that s/he cannot accept what was once so badly needed because that would be tantamount to giving up the possibility of "getting even" with the partner who is now seen as the source of pain.

Revenge does not nourish; it may provide momentary distraction but it leaves the original need untouched. People who stay in a revenge-motivated relationship eventually reach the stage of despair, in which the only thing left is proving (to the other and even to self) that everything is truly hopeless, that they are without worth, and that nothing really matters.

So, what can be done to reverse this dismal progression? The thrust of the therapeutic intervention depends, logically enough, on where a couple is in the hierarchy. If one or both partners has reached the fourth stage, the stage of despair, the therapist's efforts will be designed to restore a sense of worth and a sense of hope; nothing else will make much difference until this is at least partly accomplished. The revenge-seeking partner must be persuaded that his or her self-interest is best served by finding a way to respond, and be responded to, in the relationship, rather than by lashing out and punishing. S/he must be encouraged to choose meeting current needs over being "right" or evening the score and to accept the fact that no amount of vengefulness now can change the partner's past behaviors. Power-seekers need to find alternative ways of interacting with and impacting their partners. The partners of power-seekers need to learn that it is possible to respond to their partner's needs while at the same time maintaining their own boundaries and integrity, that is, not to cave in and also not to withdraw. And attention-getting is usually the least difficult of all, for it simply involves teaching the partners how to ask for attention in ways that their partner can hear, can notice, and respond to their requests.

Origins of Couple Dysfunction

While all of above is very logical and useful in terms of setting an overall frame for therapeutic intervention, it is still not very specific. In order to choose a particular intervention, another facet of diagnosis is useful: let's consider how the rupture of relational need-meeting gets started in the first place.

1   The simplest situation is that of ignorance: one or both partners honestly don't know what is happening between them, or what to do about it. They know that they are unhappy but they don't know the source of the unhappiness. They know that they are often disappointed in or irritated with their partner but they don't know why. Or the "why" is always related to some specific incident, and they see no underlying pattern.

2   Sometimes this not-understanding is related to a more deeply rooted lack: one or both partners have no sense of what relational needs are all about. They have never learned to identify their own relational needs nor to attend to the relational needs of others. They may have grown up in families in which such needs were never recognized or in which people were criticized for needing anything from each other. Such people cannot ask for what they want because they don't know that they want it; and they are often similarly deaf to the requests of others. Talking to them about their relational needs is like discussing the difference between red and green with someone who is color-blind.

3   Both of these varieties of dysfunction are often learned and reinforced during the early history of a relationship. Couples tend to train each other during the early courting process; they learn what works with the other person, what to expect, what is expected of them, and how to make up for not getting what they really want. The map is drawn, the familiar routes become well-worn and invariant, and nearly impenetrable walls grow up around the unexplored areas. It is as though the map is a non-verbal contract, and when one partner fails to respond as the other expects, the contract is broken.

4   Another factor in the evolution of a relationship has to do with the kinds of self-protective patterns each partner has learned throughout his or her life. Both bring to the relationship unconscious expectations and core beliefs that may form their life scripts (Erskine, 2008, 2009, 2010). In a relationship, these individual life scripts become interlocked. One partner, for instance, may bring to the relationship a basic belief that he is stupid and unable to figure things out, that his relational need for valuing can never be satisfied. The other partner may have decided, and believed for years, that nobody can really understand her, and that her need for self-definition cannot be met in a relationship. What a splendid fit! The "stupid" partner cannot be expected to understand his partner, because after all he's incapable of understanding. Moreover, it's useless to even try to understand because nobody could possibly value his feeble and doomed-to-failure efforts at the impossible. The other partner will never challenge that belief, because she knows that nobody will ever understand her anyhow. She cannot ever feel supported for being herself in a relationship, because that self cannot possibly be understood. Each partner's belief supports and reinforces the other's in a kind of mutual

dance of dysfunction (see Chapter 7 in Erskine, 2025 entitled "The script system: An unconscious organization of experiences").

5   In addition to problematic patterns in the relationship itself, a partner may be trapped in their own history of dysfunctional relationships and be literally unable to attend to the needs and demands of the partnership. For such a person, the individual life script pattern may need to be addressed before couple work proper can begin: notice, though, that word "proper". Work on a partner's individual script pattern can be and often is done in the context of couple work, with the other partner there to observe and support the work (Kadis & McClendon, 1998). Also, since partners' scripts nearly always interlock, change in one will inevitably invite change in the other, as both partners begin to understand how their old script beliefs are reinforced by interactions in their current relationship.

Discussing the ways in which a therapist facilitates changes in an individual life script is beyond the scope of this paper; the reader is referred to our previous writings (Erskine, 1997; Erskine & Moursund, 2011) and most especially to both *Beyond Empathy: A Therapy of Contact-in-Relationship* (Erskine et al., 2023) and *The Art and Science of Relationship: The Practice of Integrative Psychotherapy* (Erskine & Moursund, 2023) for detailed discussion of our theory of individual therapy. Let's turn our attention back to the couple work, with partners who are able to invest energy in improving their relationship.

Intervention Strategies

Analysis. The first step in intervention is analysis: getting a clear sense of what unmet relational needs are in the foreground and what contact disruptions have developed as a result of these unmet needs. When the therapist has a sense of how these dynamics are working themselves out, s/he can help the couple to begin to understand what is happening. Teaching a concept is probably the easiest of interventions and may be sufficient to help the couple to initiate small changes which can take on their own momentum over time.
Using/creating examples. The effect of pointing out patterns, and how they are enacted in the relationship, is further strengthened by using both naturally occurring and therapist-prescribed interactions between the partners to enhance their awareness of relational needs in themselves and each other. They can share those awarenesses with each other and check on and correct their partner's perceptions. They can learn to inquire about their partner's inner experience and to value that experience even when it doesn't match their own perception of what is happening. Teaching and practicing the skill of inquiry is, in fact, a central focus of our work with couples.
Safety. It is necessary to provide a safe therapeutic environment when we invite the partners to explore new ways of listening and responding to each

other. We do not allow partners to take revenge or to punish each other (either accidentally or deliberately) as they experiment with new behaviors and new vulnerabilities. On these occasions we may intervene, attending to the relational needs of each partner, making sure that neither is neglected. Then we encourage each person to take turns being the focus of the other's inquiry. We model contactful self-disclosure and we consistently translate non-verbal into verbal communication, encouraging both partners to "talk straight" with each other.

Flow of the process. Couple work in which relational needs and their satisfaction are seen as the core of the relationship, and the key to both partners establishing and maintaining internal and external contact, is a constantly shifting kaleidoscope of patterns and interactions. The focus moves from the perceptions and needs of one partner, to those of the other, to those of both partners in relationship – and back again. Nothing is static; as one set of relational needs is dealt with, another can move into the foreground. Like a child walking upstairs with a yo-yo, the momentary ups and downs are parts of an upward progression. Even though the relationship may seem to worsen at times, the overall trend is positive, toward healthy growth and contact. As one partner learns that his or her current relational need can be met in the relationship, s/he is energized and encouraged (literally, infused with courage) to let go of some bit of protective armor, to allow himself or herself to be more aware of what s/he is experiencing and of what his or her partner is experiencing as well. In so doing, s/he is able to respond to that partner's relational needs in a more contactful way. Changes in each support positive change in the other and the downward spiral of dysfunction is reversed.

Conclusion

There is no panacea here, no "magic" that is guaranteed to mend broken relationships or to create positive change overnight. Some relationships are remarkably resistant to change; some partners are so damaged by their own pain, so stuck in power-seeking or revenge or despair, that they have little or no concern for the well-being of the partnership. Nevertheless, we believe that attention to the interaction between relational needs and contact can help the therapist to focus on those aspects of a relationship that are most malleable, most open to intervention. It allows us to encourage, even in difficult relationships, the kinds of small changes that allow the partners themselves to cultivate and build upon their success.

References

Dreikurs, R., & Soltz, V. (1964). *Children: The challenge.* Hawthorn Books.
Erskine, R. G. (1997). *Theories and methods of an integrative Transactional Analysis.* TA Press.

Erskine, R. G. (1998). Attunement and involvement: Therapeutic responses to relational needs. *International Journal of Psychotherapy*, 3(3), 235–244.

Erskine, R. G. (2008). Psychotherapy of unconscious experience. *Transactional Analysis Journal*, 38(2), 128–138.

Erskine, R. G. (2009). Life scripts and attachment patterns: Theoretical integration and therapeutic involvement. *Transactional Analysis Journal*, 39(3), 207–218.

Erskine, R. G. (2010). Life scripts: Unconscious relational patterns and psychotherapeutic involvement. In R. G. Erskine (Ed.), *Life scripts: A Transactional Analysis of unconscious relational patterns* (pp. 1–28). Karnac Books.

Erskine, R. G. (2015). *Relational patterns, therapeutic presence: Concepts and practice of integrative psychotherapy.* Karnac Books.

Erskine, R. G. (2019). Relational group process: Developments in a Transactional Analysis model of group psychotherapy. *International Journal of Psychotherapy*, 23 (3), 41–60.

Erskine, R. G. (2021). *A healing relationship: Commentary of therapeutic dialogues.* Phoenix Publishing.

Erskine, R. G. (2025). *Relational patterns, therapeutic presence: Concepts and practice of Integrative Psychotherapy.* Routledge Mental Health Classic.

Erskine, R. G., & Moursund, J. P. (2011). *Integrative Psychotherapy in action.* Karnac Books.

Erskine, R. G., & Moursund, J. P. (2023). *The art and science of relationship: The practice of Integrative Psychotherapy.* Phoenix Publishing.

Erskine, R. G., Moursund, J. P., & Trautmann, R. L. (2023). *Beyond empathy: A therapy of contact-in-relationship.* Routledge Mental Health Classic.

Kadis, L. B., & McClendon, R. (1998). *Concise guide to marital and family therapy.* American Psychiatric Press.

Perls, F. S., Hefferline, R. F., & Goodman, P. (1951). *Gestalt therapy: Excitement and growth in the human personality.* Julian Press.

Pourová, M., Řiháček, T., & Žvelc, G. (2020). Validation of the Czech version of the Relational Needs Satisfaction Scale. *Frontiers in Psychology.* doi:10.3389/fpsyg.2020.00359.

Stewart, L. (2010). Relational needs of the therapist: Countertransference, clinical work and supervision. Benefits and disruptions in psychotherapy. *International Journal of Integrative Psychotherapy*, 1(1), 41–50.

Toksoy, S. E., Cerit, C., Aker, A. T., & Žvelc, G. (2020). Relational Needs Satisfaction Scale: reliability and validity study in Turkish. *Anatolian Journal of Psychiatry*, 21 (Supplement 2), 37–44. doi:10.5455/apd.115143.

Žvelc, G., Jovanoska, K., & Žvelc, M. (2020). Development and validation of the Relational Needs Satisfaction Scale. *Frontiers in Psychology*, 11. doi:10.3389/fpsyg.2020.00901.

Chapter 14

Reflections on Supervision in Integrative Psychotherapy

In writing a chapter for a professional publication it is customary to include an appraisal of the relevant literature. However, in reviewing the articles on psychotherapy supervision published over the past four years in the *International Journal of Supervision in Psychotherapy* (Volumes 1–4, 2019–2022), it does not seem necessary to make evaluative comments about this series of articles. Each article clearly defines the professional perspectives of the authors and each has been a valuable contribution to the field of supervision.

Although the practice of supervision in psychotherapy and counseling has now become a professional discipline in and of itself, the need remains for psychotherapy supervisors to have a variety of approaches to assist psychotherapists and counselors in developing professional competence. In this chapter I will simply use the term "psychotherapy supervision" but the ideas are relevant to other professions such as counseling, coaching, and human resources consultation.

This chapter describes what I have learned in 50 years as a psychotherapy supervisor and how I currently practice supervision. I want to share with you a framework of supervision that I have found useful in organizing my approach to psychotherapy training, case consultation, and supervision according to supervisees' level of professional skill and acumen. Supervision can be highly effective in promoting competent, ethical psychotherapists when the supervisor varies the supervisory approach according to the individual's phase of professional development.

As I engage in any case consultation I am faced with a series of reflective questions:

- According to the professional development of this particular supervisee, is it beneficial to use the supervision session to teach various psychotherapy concepts and methods or is it more advantageous to enhance the supervisee's self-confidence as a psychotherapist?
- With this particular supervisee is it my task to challenge the supervisee to reach a new level of knowledge and competence? And do I do this through consistent inquiry, by sharing my knowledge and experience, or

DOI: 10.4324/9781003626718-14

by guiding them to readings or other training activities? Or a combination of all three?

- When is it best to facilitate the supervisee's appreciation and use of their responsive countertransference in order to enhance their capacity for empathy, involvement, and attunement to their client's developmental level?
- With this supervisee is the supervision session a suitable environment to enable the supervisee in identifying and resolving any possible reactive countertransference?
- Is it beneficial to engage the supervisee in their own psychotherapy to resolve any reactive countertransference that may interfere with their practice of psychotherapy or is it more advantageous to focus on the supervisee's acquisition of psychotherapy skills and knowledge?

Beginning Phase of Supervision

Skill Development

When I have a supervisee who is in their initial phase of training in psychotherapy the aim of supervision is on developing their therapeutic skills. The supervisee who requires skill development may be either a new psychotherapist or an already skilled therapist who has decided to enhance their effectiveness in utilizing a new approach, such as working within a relational perspective, using a child development framework, integrating body-oriented therapy, or resolving cumulative trauma. Therefore, the initial focus is on the trainee's acquiring of information, techniques, and the perspectives that can be gained from a supervisor's years of experience.

During this phase of the supervisee's professional development, I may do a lot of teaching as an integral part of the training and/or supervision session. The purpose of the teaching is to complement and enhance what the supervisee already knows and to stimulate the supervisee's thinking about ethics. Particularly during this phase I want to help the supervisee strengthen their skills in making interpersonal contact, develop their capacity for affect and rhythmic attunement, and consistently use phenomenological inquiry. Some of this is conveyed via my modeling with the trainee how to use both phenomenological and historical inquiry, when to acknowledge and normalize the client's experience, and how to sustain a sense of therapeutic involvement.

In this early phase and throughout the supervision, I use internal awareness exercises to facilitate the supervisee in focusing on their moment-by-moment physiological and affective experience when talking about their client (Perls et al., 1951). Periodically I ask the supervisee to assume the same body posture as their client, to center their attention on the body tensions and physiological sensations, to fully imagine themselves in their client's situation. If done well these awareness exercises result in the supervisee's increased capacity for physiological resonance, rhythmic attunement, and empathy with their client's affect.

I may also encourage the supervisee to take the time to observe what is occurring externally, without assigning any value or interpretation. I remember Fritz Perls instructing the Gestalt training group to begin our training sessions with "right now I am aware of" as we used our eyes, ears, and skin to receive impressions from the environment. Then Fritz had us focus on our physical sensations, then on our affect. Eventually we moved rapidly between internal and external awareness. Such shuttling between internal and external contact stimulates the capacity for therapeutic presence. Masa and Gregor Žvelc have elaborated on the use of various awareness exercises in their book on mindful and compassionate supervision (2023).

In this early phase of supervision, I often focus on refining the supervisee's observational skills about the client's body gestures, voice tone, cognitive style, and affect. And then correlating these observations with various theoretical frameworks that the supervisee may have learned in their training program, such as: attachment patterns; interruptions to contact; ego states; the script system; or other theoretical models wherein the psychotherapist can organize their observations to form treatment options. I periodically suggest specific readings and invite the supervisee to discuss the readings and how the ideas may apply to their client.

Skill development can be accomplished through a number of different formats. My preference is to encourage the supervisee to spontaneously talk about their relationship with their client and what may be perplexing to them. While they are doing this, I am attending to how they present their client, what they know and seem to not know, as well as what they are revealing about themselves. I engage the supervisee in a dialogue about their emotional reactions and understandings about their client; I use the opportunity to either teach a concept or support their growing self-confidence as a psychotherapist.

I ask some supervisees to write a formal case report that describes the client's presenting problem, family and school history, and a description of the psychotherapy methods the supervisee had been using. The time and thought that goes into a written report helps many supervisees to have a more thorough understanding of their client and what that client may need in their psychotherapy.

Other supervisees find that a written case report is not as effective as a spontaneous discussion or reviewing recordings of their therapeutic work. With such supervisees I have invited them to bring audio or video samples of their psychotherapy work. These recordings provide us an opportunity to hear not only what the therapist is saying but also the prosody of their communication, the subtle rhythm and sound of what they are saying. We can then stop the recordings and consider alternative ways of being in relationship with the client.

When engaging the supervisee in a spontaneous discussion or when listening to recordings of the supervisee's psychotherapy sessions I am also observing how the supervisee shapes their dialogues with their clients. I want to assess if they are engaging their clients in a confirmatory or exploratory conversation. I pay attention to the possibility that the supervisee may be making theory first and foremost by selecting evidence that confirms a particular theory. Such confirmatory interventions may occur with inexperienced psychotherapists who want to apply the theories that they are learning to every client. For example, when I was initially learning Transactional Analysis, I defined clients' behaviors in terms of ego states and therefore missed many of the subtleties of what they were unconsciously communicating. As I acquired phenomenological and relational perspectives my therapeutic dialogue became more exploratory – we talked more about the client's subjective experiences; theory was less important than the clients' awareness of their physiology and affect or what was happening within our therapeutic relationship.

In my practice of psychotherapy supervision, I want to foster the supervisee's capacity to invite their clients into an exploratory dialogue. I emphasize the importance of the supervisee's sustained inquiry into the uniqueness of each client's phenomenological and developmental experiences. Often, I model the skills of acknowledgement and validation and how they are central in an involved inquiry by giving hypothetical examples of how I might use phenomenological, historical, and relational inquiry with a client. In many situations I model an exploratory dialogue by inquiring with the supervisee about their own internal process.

Although using audio or visual recordings may be time consuming, they are a good way for the supervisee to enhance their capacity for both understanding and empathy. Another way to enhance the supervisee's capacity for empathy and to stimulate an understanding of their client's level of developmental functioning is to have them role play the client with the supervisor or another trainee and then talk about their experience of being "in the client's shoes". I periodically use a two-chair method to have the supervisee shuttle between being in the client's chair and the therapist's chair. When the supervisee is in the client's chair, speaking as though they were the client, I encourage them to talk about how they perceive their psychotherapist, what is missing in their psychotherapy, or what they don't like about what the therapist has done. The use of the two-chair methods often leads us to a new supervisory discussion and an increased sensitivity to the relational needs of their client.

Whether the supervision in done individually or in a group each of these supervisory formats are followed with a discussion of the interventions used, possible alternative interventions, the client's emotional and behavioral reactions to the methods used, and the theoretical concepts that apply. I may ask the supervisee a number of stimulating questions, such as:

- In your perception, what unconscious story is your client presenting?
- How do you understand your client in terms of the theory you are using?
- Where is the client open and where are they closed to contact: affectively, cognitively, behaviorally, physiologically, or relationally?
- If we use that specific theory, what type of intervention may be needed to help the client reach a resolution?
- When you imagine your client as a child what is happening to them and what does that child need in a reparative relationship?

These types of supervisory questions lead us to dialogue about various viewpoints for understanding the client's psychological functioning as well as providing opportunities for modeling, sharing experiences from the supervisor's professional past, or role playing the client to facilitate the supervisee in identifying with the client and the quality of interpersonal contact that the client may need.

In my supervisory practice I find that it is often necessary to reteach concepts and interventions which the supervisee has learned previously but with the focus on how the concept or method may be applied in this specific therapy situation. By applying theory-into-practice the supervisee gains a thorough understanding of how the theoretical concepts are useful with their particular client.

I may follow such a case consultation with reading assignments that may be helpful to understand the ideas discussed. And I ask them to return to supervision to discuss what they find meaningful in the readings. These collegial discussions are particularly growth-producing during the supervisee's early phase of professional development. With some supervisees I have requested that they listen to recorded samples of their therapy several times between our supervisory sessions, each time listening to their work from a different theoretical perspective.

An essential focus of my supervision in this early phase of professional development is on my facilitating the supervisee's capacity to make full interpersonal contact, to be fully present with and for their client. This is based on the assumption that presence and involvement are the essential factors in effective psychotherapy (Erskine, 2025). I give a lot of attention to the supervisee mastering the skills of phenomenological, historical, and relational inquiry. I emphasize the relational methods of acknowledgement, validation, and normalization (Erskine et al., 2023). Throughout this skill development phase of supervision my goal is to help the supervisee acquire the relational skills of attunement to the client's affect, rhythm, level of development, style of cognition, and relational needs (Erskine & Moursund, 2022). I want the supervisee to have awareness of both their client's relational needs as well as their own (Stewart, 2010).

The trainee can be guided to identify areas in which their client is open to contact and where a person is closed to contact, whether it be cognitive, affective, behavioral or physiological (Erskine & Moursund, 2022). For example, some clients may be resistant to behavioral changes until they first receive information that explains the problem or their psychodynamics. Others may need to express pent up emotions before they can process information about their dynamics and still others may need to change behavior first and then later cognitively process the meaning of that change.

Skill-development is important in the first phase of supervision; it provides the supervisee with a solid foundation for applying theory into clinical practice while also providing the supervisor with needed information regarding the professional strengths of the supervisee and those areas where further teaching is necessary. Over the years I have erred when I have prematurely focused on building the supervisee's confidence before the supervisee has formed a thorough foundation in understanding personality theory, therapy concepts, and various methods. I have found that my job as a supervisor is to determine whether inadequate therapy is the result of lack of skill that requires further teaching, simply the lack of confidence that comes through successful experiences, a personal therapy problem, or some combination of these.

Since the primary focus at this skill development phase is on increasing the trainee's level of information on how to do psychotherapy, I generally do not focus on any possible countertransference unless such countertransference is interfering with the supervisee's capacity to be fully present and therapeutic. At this phase of professional development, it is often best to encourage the supervisee to engage in their own psychotherapy.

Confidence Building

Once the supervisee has acquired an understanding of personality theory and has mastered the capacity to be fully in relationship with their clients, the aim of supervision is on facilitating the supervisee's sense of ease in using their various skills as well as a general sense of confidence and well-being as a psychotherapist. The supervisee may have acquired sufficient information and therapeutic acumen but may lack the confidence to use it, so the supervisor's task is to help the supervisee appreciate and use what they have already learned. In this phase the supervisor provides approval and support for that which the supervisee has done well.

The advantage of this confidence-building approach is that it minimizes the supervisee's possible inhibition of their own potential. Sometimes I have chosen to temporarily ignore what has not been done well with the purpose of diminishing any self-rebuke or sense of inadequacy that the supervisee may have. With some of these supervisees I have had to reteach skills or concepts that the supervisee has not assimilated.

As in the previous phase of supervision, I find it desirable at this phase to identify the supervisee's self-rebuke, inhibition, shame, or over-exuberance, and to then encourage them to address it in their own psychotherapy.

Usually, I do not attend to these types of personal issues in this confidence-building phase of the supervision. These two phases, skill-development and confidence-building, are not necessarily sequential; I tend to shuttle between these two phases in accordance with what the supervisee presents.

In this confidence-building phase I guide the supervisee to use the concept of an "inward eye" – to take whatever occurs in therapeutic situation and to look inward – to be in contact with their own affect, memories, beliefs, and fantasies. And simultaneously be able to observe the client's behavior, to inquire about the client's phenomenological experience, and to understand what is being communicated within a theoretical context. It is this ability to be in contact with one's own internal experience and the uniqueness of the client's experience that is the basis for empathy and the creation of a healing relationship.

Intermediate Phase

Thinking Theoretically and Skill Refinement

After the trainee is confidently using the psychotherapy skills learned previously, supervision is geared to building an identity as a therapist and refining the supervisee's approach to psychotherapy. Here the supervisor focuses on enhancing the knowledge that has been assimilated and stimulating thinking about therapy from new perspectives. One way is to ask the trainee for self-evaluation, either directly or through two-chair work where they become the supervisor and give their self-feedback about the quality of their involvement with their client. Some of the advantages of this approach are that it stimulates thinking; the supervisor gets further understanding of the supervisee's process of reasoning; it disarms seeing the supervisor's comments as criticism; and it avoids having the supervisor on a pedestal as the person who knows everything. The disadvantages include the trainee being too harsh in the evaluation or not thorough enough in self-confrontation – however, both provide the supervisor with significant information.

Another important approach at this level of training is to contract with the supervisee for what they want in the supervision. The advantage of this approach is that the supervisee feels in control of the supervisory process by defining their own professional goals; however, it may also carry the disadvantage of leading the supervisor away from other important areas. Contracts for supervision can be made either before or after the supervisor has watched or heard the recorded work or listened to an entire case presentation. The supervisor needs to avoid too tight of a contract so there is the flexibility to comment on other relevant observations for which the trainee may not have asked for feedback.

A question that helps to refine the therapist's approach is, "What would you do differently if you could do this therapy over?" Or alternatively, "What will you do next time you work with this client?" Here the aim is in planning treatment and exploring with the supervisee options for treatment interventions. This is a time when supervisors could insist that trainees bring recordings of their "worst" therapy sessions for supervision. The supervisor's task is to work with the supervisee to learn from their mistakes and to develop new options in the psychotherapy.

Often the problem at this skill-refinement phase is not in the actual interventions used but in the sequence of interventions. A concept borrowed from parametric statistics of "Type A – Type B errors" may be useful in setting priorities for what is said or done therapeutically. When the therapist makes interventions to correct Problem A, they may reinforce Problem B. For example, if someone's script beliefs are "I'm helpless" and "No one understands me", the therapist may temporarily not address the client's sense of helplessness while instead creating the quality of relationship that dissolves the client's belief that "no one understands me". The trainee thus learns how to evaluate which problem can be held in abeyance while another problem receives immediate focus.

The supervisee's psychotherapy approach can also be expanded by encouraging a discussion of the theoretical basis for interventions used. This can help solidify the frame of reference and develop facility in putting theory into practice. Once the supervisee can adequately explain what is being done from a specific theoretical position then it may be profitable to have them explain how they might work with the same client using a different theoretical concept, leading eventually to the ability to explain the work from multiple frames of reference. In this way the trainee can be stimulated to make use of what was learned in earlier training and supervision while providing the supervisor with information as to what areas of theory or practice need further concentration in teaching or reading assignments.

A way to consolidate and help the trainee retain what was learned from the supervisory process is to ask for a summary after a period of feedback and discussion. The advantage of the summary is that it provides immediate clarification of what the trainee has identified as important in the supervisory process and can alert the supervisor as to the feedback that might be avoided; it is an assessment of progress at different stages of professional development. The same approach of consolidating learning may be used at the beginning of a supervisory session with a question such as "What did you learn from the last supervision?" This question serves to provide continuity from one session to another and may be particularly effective in helping the trainee gain a perspective for ongoing treatment planning.

Written assignments may also be used to help maximize the gain in learning. Many trainees report that they have learned significantly from answering the specific questions following a supervision session:

- What was the problem presented?
- What did I learn from working with the client and from the supervision?

- What did I learn about myself?
- What will I do differently next time?

The advantage of writing a paragraph or two on each of these questions is that it can fix certain points as important in the mind of the supervisee and pro-vides an ongoing record of professional growth. As the trainee reads through the file, areas of growth can be identified, as well as areas of resistance to supervision and where there may be an issue requiring personal therapy. The supervision log increases self-reflection and self-awareness and fosters thinking about alternative perspectives. As a result, it is useful in establishing a sense of confidence and competence. When the supervisor periodically reads the supervisee's log, a written response of appreciative support of strengths or a challenge to take the next step in learning can be added.

Therapy for the Trainee

An integral part of supervision involves the resolution of a supervisee's own issues which may be an interference in working effectively with clients. The supervisor may find it necessary to focus on the difficulties in the supervisee which inhibit their optimum effectiveness as a psychotherapist and then, through contractual arrangement, may proceed therapeutically with the supervisee. These issues might be unresolved conflicts from the past or the lack of awareness of that which has been introjected and not thoughtfully rejected or assimilated as one's own. Often the supervisor sees the super-visee's internal dysregulation or the areas of relational conflict between the supervisee and their client that never emerge in the supervisee's individual psychotherapy. Therefore, the supervisor may be in the best position to therapeutically address these issues of countertransference.

I think of countertransference as either responsive to the client's therapeutic needs or as the reactions of the therapist to the client that are the result of the unresolved conflicts within the therapist and may include their beliefs and memories as well as their hopes and plans for the future (Erskine, 2024; Racker, 1968). The aim of providing some psychotherapy for the supervisee, that is contracted for within the supervisory relationship, is to develop the supervisee's integrated sense of Self so that the supervisee can use their whole vital Self as their most powerful tool in psychotherapy. This is accomplished through resolving whatever reactive countertransference issues interfere with full contact between the supervisee and their client.

While listening to the supervisee present a case I may ask myself the ques-tion, "In addition to telling us about the client, what is the supervisee revealing about their Self? For example, one trainee described her client as being "scared to death" to get angry. In our supervisory dialogue we discovered that she was hesitant to encourage any expression of anger. With further inquiry I discovered that the supervisee had been afraid, throughout her early adoles-cence and as a young adult, to be angry with her invalid mother for fear she would die. After identifying this as a personal therapy issue the supervisee agreed to work on it immediately in the supervision session. I facilitated the supervisee in dealing with her unexpressed anger with her mother and her childhood belief that "expressing anger is dangerous". I think that it is part of the supervisor's task to be sensitive to what is avoided or not talked about in supervision such as anger, money, health, or sex and how such avoidances might reflect unresolved therapy issues in the supervisee.

Supervisees will periodically present a client or select a recording of their psychotherapy sessions that describes an aspect of their own personal difficulties. This may be evident in the supervisee's not hearing incongruities in clients' statements, agreeing with script beliefs such as, "There's nothing I can do", or the failure to see the parallel process, or how the problem the client is describing is occurring in the relationship with the therapist. Personal problems may also be evident in how the therapist designs treatment plans. If, for example, a therapist continually uses one approach with all clients, such as behavioral change contracts or emotionally expressive work, the supervisor might question whether that approach is what the supervisee needs and is projecting onto the clients, or is a way of avoiding something that is needed personally.

Whether the supervision is in the form of formal cases presentations, spontaneous discussions, attending to audio or visual recordings, or observing the supervisee actually conducting psychotherapy with a client, I think of five areas in which the supervisee's personal issues may be revealed:

1   Contact – Is the supervisee responding to the client's experience? Does the client seem to feel understood?
2   Introjection – What characteristics of the supervisee are not attended to in the psychotherapy with the client? For example, is the client's father similar to the therapist's father or teacher?
3   Projections – Is the supervisee overly empathetic with their client rather than challenging the client's frame of reference? Does this reflect the therapist's own limitations?
4   Retroflection – What emotions or behaviors are not encouraged by the supervisee and do these indicate areas in which the therapist holds back or is troubled?
5   Enmeshment – What role does the client play in the supervisee's fears, plans, and desires? One therapist who had difficulty with termination discovered that he was relying on his clients to fulfill his needs to feel important.

Even though supervisees may be in, or have been in, personal psychotherapy, some disturbing issues may only become apparent when supervisees present their therapeutic work to an attuned supervisor. It is in the supervisory dialogue that issues of reactive countertransference are revealed and, if contractually appropriate, resolved.

Peer Group Supervision

When supervision is done in the presence of other professional therapists, the supervisor may choose to invite others to give their perspectives or possible treatment approaches. This often stimulates all the people in the supervision group to think about their potential interventions and the theoretical bases for those interventions. This is most effectively accomplished after the group of supervisees has had considerable professional experience; if done too soon the result may be a discussion of personal preferences rather than keeping the focus on what the client needs in their psychotherapy.

Some of the difficulties with the group feedback approach include: the discussion may be side-tracked to the interests of other trainees; the feedback may center on preferential styles; information may become repetitive; the person giving feedback may be more intent on gaining attention than providing information; and the process can be time-consuming. Some ways of making good use of the professional expertise in the group and overcoming these difficulties include setting time limits on discussion, asking supervisees not to repeat previous feedback but only add new information, or in giving each member a specific theoretical area in which to make their observations. Although group participation in supervision may be a complex supervisory task, it is extremely rewarding in that it includes all those present in developing options for the client's psychotherapy.

Advanced Phase of Supervision: Multi-Theoretical Perspective

Although discussions of ethics are central at each phase of training and supervision, the aim of supervision in this phase of professional development is for the supervisee to fully embrace a set of guiding principles to integrate multiple theoretical frames of reference, and to select various treatment options based on observations and hypotheses about a particular client. I often challenge the experienced supervisee to think about their clients from different theoretical perspectives and to talk about how they might work differently if guided by another concept. This is the phase in which the supervisee can develop their acumen by questioning both the theory they are using and how they practice psychotherapy. It is an opportunity to explore treatment options and develop flexibility in using other ways of working with clients. One of the ways I do this is to invite the supervisee into a dialogue that is shaped by the following:

1   Describe the client's overt behavior, affect, and physical reactions in detail as well as your emotional responses. Our discussion often focuses on distinguishing the difference between actual observations and countertransferential reactions.

2   Think about the observations of the client's behavior, affect, or physical reactions in terms of different theories. This discussion is often enriched when the supervisee can play with both the similarities and contradictions inherent in the use of various theories. This may lead to studying new concepts.

3   Discuss one or more hypotheses about this particular client based on a specific theory and contrast the various therapy interventions.

4   Develop a variety of possible interventions that are an outgrowth of the chosen theory.

For example, the supervisee may observe that the client encourages people to be close and when they do, the client uses various means to alternately cling to or push other people away. The concepts of secure, anxious, isolated, and avoidant attachment patterns could be used to provide the theoretical understanding that when infantile bonding is repeatedly disrupted there will be confusion and anxiety around closeness and separation in later life.

From the construct of attachment theory, the therapist can draw hypotheses based on their observations. Hypothesis A: this client's infantile bonding was inconsistently gratifying and therefore the client is perpetually anxious about separation and individuation; Hypothesis B: this client's infantile bond was disrupted because of caretakers' consistent misattunement to the infant's needs and therefore there is an urge to distance from any dependent relationship. If the therapist assumed Hypothesis B, the focus of a developmentally based, relationally oriented intervention could include following the client's lead, providing choice, consistent empathy, and patience. If the therapist had assumed Hypothesis A, the focus of the interventions could include establishing consistent affect and developmental attunement, allowing of a period of dependency, and providing the security to tolerate the disruptions inherent in any psychotherapy.

When the trainee is competent at developing alternative hypotheses and various interventions from one theoretical perspective, they can then be challenged to examine the same behavior from different theoretical perspectives with concomitant hypotheses and interventions. The supervisor can then discuss various interventions which are an outgrowth of these hypotheses. This multifaceted theoretical look at a client's behavior provides the therapist with the stimulus for thinking about an integrative, in-depth treatment plan for the client and expands the therapist's capacity to be open to new points of view.

Once supervisees have mastered the skills of psychotherapy and have confidence in themselves as psychotherapists, an intensive case study approach to supervision provides valuable learning in how to plan and carry out in-depth treatment plans for helping the clients achieve physically and mentally healthy lives. The case study method of supervision provides both the supervisor and supervisee an opportunity to study one client's therapy for several months or even years. Here the emphasis is on thoroughly understanding the psychological functioning of the client over time, how the client is open and closed to contact, what the supervisee has attended to, and possible new directions in the psychotherapy.

Guiding Principles at Every Phase of Supervision: Fostering a Value System

Throughout each phase of supervision, whether it is with a new supervisee or an experienced colleague, I strive to include aspects of professional ethics – a commitment to the welfare of our clients. Hopefully I accomplish this by both modeling and talking about several guiding principles:

1   All people are equally valuable. We psychotherapists manifest this principle when we treat our clients with kindness, when we provide them with options and choices, and when we accept them as they present themselves.

2   Humans suffer from relational disruptions, not "psychopathology". When we view someone as pathological, we lose our awareness of the person's unique creative accommodation and their attempts to manage situations of neglect, ridicule, and/or shame. It is in recognizing and authentically appreciating the other person's emotional vulnerability, relational needs, and desperate attempts at self-stabilization that we create the possibility for full intersubjective contact – a contact that heals old psychological wounds.

3   All people are relationship seeking and interdependent throughout life. When we affectively, rhythmically, and developmentally attune to our clients, constantly inquire about our clients' experience, and when we are authentically involved with our clients, we change their perspectives of what is possible in intersubjective contact. As we effect a change in one aspect of our clients' relational systems, we influence their other relationships as well.

4   Internal and external contact is essential to human functioning. In a relationally focused Integrative Psychotherapy we are always inviting the client into full contact – contact with their internal processes of body sensations, affect, memories, and thoughts. We also invite them into external contact – to communicate interpersonally with awareness and authenticity.

5   All experience is organized physically, affectively, and/or cognitively. People are always communicating a story about their life either consciously or unconsciously. Our clients' unconscious communication is embedded in their physical tensions, entrenched in their emotional reactions, and encoded in the way they make visceral and cognitive sense of their current and past situations.

6   All human behavior has meaning in some context. Problematic behaviors and disruptive relationships serve some psychological function such as

prediction, identity, continuity, and stability. Our therapeutic work involves normalizing our client's behaviors by helping them understand the contexts in which their behaviors, beliefs, or fantasies were derived.

7   Humans have an innate thrust to grow. As integrative psychotherapists it is our commitment to engage each client in a contactful relationship that vitalizes their innate thrust to grow. We do this by fostering our client's capacity for full internal and interpersonal contact. Our goal includes promoting their vitality and psychic energy that can be invested in health, creativity, and the expansion of their personal horizons.

8   The intersubjective process of psychotherapy is more important than the content of the psychotherapy. The intersubjective process involves the melding together of each person's subjective experiences, their affects, belief systems, internal relational models, implicit and explicit memories, and relational needs. Effective psychotherapy emerges in the creation of a new perspective and understanding.

Conclusion

The supervisee's use of ethical principles and their integration of multiple theoretical frames of reference in their psychotherapy practice involves acquiring information in the theory, process, and techniques of psychotherapy; assimilating the various skills necessary to form a unique way of working with each person; and being fully present with their clients. Through the resolution of reactive countertransference and life script issues the supervisee's Self becomes the most important tool in psychotherapy.

This outline of various approaches to supervision reflects my own supervision practice – a practice that has evolved and changed over the years. Although I have organized this chapter according to various phases of professional development, these descriptions of the phases of supervision do not have to be followed in a stepwise manner. It may be necessary in some cases to focus on the resolution of reactive countertransference and life script issues early in supervision, to emphasize ethical principles, or to recycle through earlier phases of supervision.

The purpose of supervision is to develop competent, ethical psychotherapists – psychotherapists who have the capacity for self-supervision and a commitment to find the most effective means of promoting the psychological and physical health of their clients.

References

Erskine, R. G. (2024). Countertransference: An Integrative Psychotherapy perspective. *International Journal of Psychotherapy*, 28(1), 47–61.

Erskine, R. G. (2025). *Relational patterns, therapeutic presence: Concepts and practice of Integrative Psychotherapy*. Routledge Mental Health Classic Editions.

Erskine, R. G., & Moursund, J. P. (2022). *The art and science of relationship: The practice of Integrative Psychotherapy*. Phoenix Publishing.

Erskine, R. G., Moursund, J. P., & Trautmann, R. L. (2023). *Beyond empathy: A therapy of contact-in-relationship*. Routledge Mental Health Classic Editions.

Perls, F., Hefferline, R., & Goodman, P. (1951). *Gestalt therapy: The excitement and growth in the human personality*. Julian Press.

Racker, H. (1968). *Transference and countertransference*. New York: International Universities Press. (Original work in Spanish, published 1960).

Stewart, L. (2010). Relational needs of the therapist: Countertransference, clinical work and supervision. Benefits and disruptions in psychotherapy. *International Journal of Integrative Psychotherapy*, 1(1), 41–50.

Žvelc, M., & Žvelc, G. (2023). *Mindfulness and compassion in integrative supervision*. Routledge.

Chapter 15

Compassion, Hope, and Forgiveness in the Therapeutic Dialogue

Compassion. The word conjures up images of Jesus healing the sick and Buddha's suffering because others in the world were suffering from hunger or oppression. The word "compassion" comes from Latin. "Com" which means "with" and "passion" which means "to suffer". Compassion then means to "suffer with" the other, "to suffer together".

Compassion involves both a physiological and an emotionally sensed experience of the suffering that others endure. It is a total sense of the other... a moving out of our own experience by being fully aware of the pain of others. Compassion is selfless. It is about the welfare of others. It may involve putting the welfare of another person above our own – much as when a hero jumps into cold water to rescue someone they do not know.

In psychotherapy compassion begins with our ethics. We are compassionate when we practice our profession with a constant perspective on ethics. In my opinion the most significant ethic of all is the commitment to our client's welfare. It is the client's welfare that guides us in all we do and say. All other ethics emerge from this central ethic that involves our commitment to make our client's welfare most important in all of our actions.

Compassion is a central element in psychotherapy. Compassion is what may have motived some of you to become psychotherapists. It is that felt sense of experiencing other people's suffering and a simultaneous desire to relieve the other's pain, anguish, or loss. Compassion is what motivates us to put our arm around a person who is grieving. We want to comfort them, to alleviate their grief. Compassion motivates me to attune to the client's affect, rhythm, and relational needs, to fully connect with them.

In my practice of psychotherapy, compassion emerges from a conviction that each person is of value in his or her unique way. Carl Rogers called this valuing of the other person "unconditional positive regard" (1951, p. 144). Martin Buber described how this aspect of compassion is based on what he called an "I-Thou" relationship (1958). Martin Buber used the Biblical word "thou" to reflect the spiritual nature of a fully contactful relationship: a relationship that is without any preconceived notions of the other; a relationship built on continually discovering the uniqueness of the other person;

DOI: 10.4324/9781003626718-15

and a relationship that attends to the other's affect and relational needs (Erskine et al., 1999).

When we foster such a contactful relationship we are naturally empathic because empathy is based on compassion. Although the words compassion and empathy are often used interchangeably in the English language, empathy often refers to the emotional connection with a specific person whereas compassion is often associated with a response to suffering of all human beings. Empathy is the word used to depict our ability to feel the emotions of another person; to experience those feelings as though they were our own. A saying attributed to the natives in America is, "You cannot really know another unless you have walked a mile in his moccasins".

Empathy is about being deeply connected to the other person's affect and experiencing what it is like to be in his or her skin. Carl Rogers, in defining the theory and practice of client-centered therapy, elaborated on this idea when he defined empathy as our capacity to feel the other person's affect; to feel the other's sadness or fear or anger or joy (1951, 1980).

The psychoanalyst Heinz Kohut in writing about Psychoanalytic Self-Psychology referred to empathy as a form of listening to the other person's phenomenological experience without any preconceived notion or judgment (1977). For Kohut empathy was about his wanting to understand the other's subjective experience while not imposing his ideas on them. When we are engaging in psychotherapy with a client, this kind of empathy occurs automatically if we have the attitude that "I know nothing about the other person's experience and so I must continually strive to understand the subjective meanings of his or her emotions and behaviors". As psychotherapists it is essential that we have these two forms of empathy, the forms that Rogers and Kohut describe: to feel the client's affect; and to strive to understand how they experience themselves.

Although empathy usually refers to our ability to feel both the emotions of another person as well as an understanding the other person's reasoning, compassion generally refers to the desire to help. This is the type of compassionate psychotherapy I described in the book *Beyond Empathy: A Therapy of Contact-in-Relationship* (Erskine et al., 1999) and also in the book *The Art and Science of Relationship: The Practice of Integrative Psychotherapy* (Erskine & Moursund, 2022).

We go beyond empathy when we attune ourselves to our clients. Attunement is our Yin to the client's Yang. Affect attunement provides the necessary reciprocity that the other needs to feel emotionally whole. Reciprocity is an important concept; it describes that the other needs something from us in response to his or her affect. I will share four examples of the reciprocity that our clients may need from us:

- When our client is sad we provide expressions of sensitivity, warmth, tenderness, and acceptance

- When our client is angry we respond by taking what they say seriously
- When our client is afraid we feel protective and may act protectively
- When our client is joyful we meet him or her with our vitality and celebration

Recently I was typing up a video transcript of a therapy session and trying to describe the compassion, empathy, and attunement that the client required in order to heal from the emotional wounds of neglect and abuse. As I typed the transcript I realized that the words I was using only slightly conveyed my compassion and empathy because the most important component of compassion was in my non-verbal behavior (Erskine, 2021). Compassion was expressed in my sustained eye contact, in the muscles of my face, in my hand gestures, in the tone of my voice, as well as in the words I was using. My eyes, face, and voice tone conveyed my full presence.

Therapeutic presence requires that we be fully "with our client's experience" as well as be "there for them", de-centered from ourselves. To be fully present we make our own concerns not important. Yet, simultaneously, we draw on all of our personal and professional experiences as a resource to further our attunement and connection with our clients. It is our presence and attunement that allows for an authentic person-to-person connection. Our clients' capacity to heal from the wounds of neglect, ridicule, or abuse is directly dependent on the quality of interpersonal contact and attunement that we provide.

Confronted by Compassion

One spring day, after returning from lunch, I discovered a women sitting on the stairs to my office. She was dressed in a rumpled skirt and blouse, and appeared to be in her mid-fifties. I noticed her stringy grey hair that was hanging over her face. Her face was red and her eyes swollen from crying. I asked her if she needed anything and she responded that she was waiting for the psychologist whose name was on the sign. I told her that I was that person and asked her why she was waiting. She said that she was "confused" and needed to talk to someone who could help her.

It was apparent that she was distressed, confused, and did not know how to phone for an appointment. I did not want to leave the women crying on the stairs, and, equally important, I did not want to talk to her. This brief encounter was unsettling to me. I had intended to use the half hour before my four o'clock client to take a nap. Yet, the way that she conveyed her anguish and confusion touched my heart. I could not ignore her request to talk. I decided to give her a few minutes before my next client and perhaps refer her to a colleague. I asked her to step into the waiting area of the office and tell me why she wanted to see a psychologist.

She rapidly told me fragments of an entangled story about her husband dying of pancreatic cancer, her wanting a divorce, her care of him during his painful illness, his physical abuse of her throughout their marriage, and her children's anger at her for staying in the marriage. She punctuated each part of the story with "I'm so confused". Although I was empathic with her, I too was confused by the profusion of information as she went from one part of the story to another and then back again. It was too much information too fast. It was difficult to stay attuned to her changing affect and discombobulated story. She continued to talk for the full 30 minutes before my next client arrived.

Unexpectedly I was drawn to her emotion-filled story in some way I did not understand. As a result I offered to see her the next day. I added that we could only have a maximum of six sessions since I would be leaving in seven weeks for a trip to Europe. I knew it was not the time to begin a psychotherapy relationship with anyone yet I spontaneously offered her the six sessions.

Later that day I wondered how I had become ensnared in such a counter-transference trap. That evening I arranged to see a trusted colleague to talk about my encounter with the woman and how, against my better judgment, I had arranged to see the women for six psychotherapy sessions. As I told the story my eyes fill with tears. I talked about how I wanted to comfort the woman – a woman with whom I did not yet have a relationship. It seemed necessary to explore the countertransference feeling I was having.

In our conversation my colleague used the word "compassion" a few times to explain my intense reactions to this woman I had just met on the stairs. We talked about the meanings and significance of compassion as well as our professional commitment to the welfare of our clients. My colleague's discussion of the concept of compassion opened a new awareness for me. That night I had an enlightening dream about protecting a woman from being physically attacked by a man. I was filled with a desire to protect and help. It was as though COMPASSION had a deep hold on me. I had felt a similar sense of deep interpersonal connection several times in both my personal and professional life but I had never thought of it as compassion – a deep desire to provide the other person with relief of his or her suffering.

The next day we began our limited series of therapy sessions. I soon realized that I was again experiencing compassion via my intense affect attunement when Agatha told me more of the details of her life story. This was the beginning of a significant therapeutic relationship that was eventually transformative in Agatha's life.

Hope

The word hope reminds me of a children's book entitled *The Little Engine that Could* (Piper, 1930). "I think I can, I think I can, I think I can" was the motto of the little engine. Some of you may know this story as well as I do if you also read it over and over to your young children. In this children's story the Little Engine eventually was able to climb the hill and finally exclaim: "I knew I could, I know I could". This is a delightful story to teach children about the importance of hope.

Webster's Dictionary has two definitions of hope: first, "a desire with anticipation", and second, "desire accompanied by expectation of or belief in fulfillment". I like this second definition because it is central to the process of psychotherapy. Our clients come to us because they have an expectation that they will change and grow. They are looking for some form of fulfillment. This is why transactional analysts often begin with a clear contract defining the client's expectations and how they will know when those goals have been fulfilled.

Hope is optimistic. It is a state of mind based on anticipation that something good will result and that events and circumstances in life will turn out well. One of the important teachings from my mother was about hope. When things were bleak and I was discouraged she frequently said, "Life always turns out, not necessarily the way you expect, but it always turns out". More than 70 years later I realize how instrumental my mother's message of hope has been in my life. Her message has served to keep me enthusiastic and enjoying the adventure of life. Several writers on psychotherapy have commented on the sense of hope.

Alfred Adler sees hope as central in our mental health when he describes the importance of goal seeking (Ansbacher & Ansbacher, 1956). He encouraged clients to make plans and to find various ways of making their plans come true. Lawrence LeShan described his research with people who were diagnosed with terminal cancer (1994). He encouraged them to dream big, to make big plans, to do what they have always wanted to do, and then to implement those plans. The patients who activated their dreams, who dared to follow their desires, lived from two to five years beyond their previously diagnosed time of death (LeShan, personal communication, May 20, 1993).

Donald Winnicott (1964) saw hope in a child's disruptive behaviors as an unconscious desire to make an impact on the adults in the child's life. If we expand on Winnicott's idea perhaps our clients' "resistance" is their desire to make an impact on us. What would happen in your practice of psychotherapy if you saw your clients' reluctance not as a "resistance" but as an unconscious desire to influence you, to encourage you to see the world from his or her perspective?

The psychologist Charles Snyder described the connection between hope and mental will power (1994). In my personal experience hope emerges most strongly when there is a crisis; because it is hope that opens me to new, creative options. My client may be despairing about the circumstances in his or her life and in that moment of crisis I'm often propelled to find some important way of connecting with that person. The crisis in our therapy relationship propels me forward with a new hope, with courage to experiment with different ways of our being together.

Hope offers us a challenge. Hope is much more than wishful thinking. Hope is not passively longing for something to happen to us. True hope is realistic. It must include real possibilities, with a clear plan on how to reach what is hoped for. An important aspect of psychotherapy includes helping clients identify their aspirations and then to find the step-by-step ways to achieve their hoped-for goals. However, our psychotherapy may also involve helping the client to be realistic about what may never happen; to let go of the illusion that someone else will change.

If the loss of hope results in depression, then hope must be an essential element in psychotherapy. Not only is hope instrumental in recovery from the psychological effects of neglect, abuse, and humiliation, hope is so central in all the psychotherapy that we do. Hope helps people recover from physical illnesses and may even prevent illness from developing in the first place because our beliefs and expectations can stimulate the body's hormones to enhance recovery from illness.

The author Alexander Pope writes about how people are blessed because "Hope springs eternal in the human breast" (1891/2007). I think he means to tell us that hope gives us a sense of liveliness filled with desire to achieve something. It is hope that gives sparkle to our lives. This zest for life is something that ancient sages have emphasized for millennia; St. Paul says, "For we are saved by hope" (Romans 8:24, King James Version). All of the world's religions emphasize hope as a necessary aspect in overcoming the drudgeries of life.

Agatha's Hidden Hope

Over the next few weeks Agatha told me many of the details of how she had been "trapped in a disastrous marriage" with a husband who both physically and sexually abused her. She had finally gone through the arrangements for a divorce when her husband was diagnosed with pancreatic cancer. Agatha gave up on the divorce and instead nursed him devotedly for the next 11 months while he continued to criticize and verbally abuse her. After he died she had a "strange mixture of missing him" and being "free of the bastard". She was confused by her "mixed-up feelings". She described how over the years she had often wanted to murder her husband but was too scared to do so because it would have "a disastrous effect" on her two children.

I discovered that I was the first person she had ever told about the abuse she had lived with every day for 33 years. She was feeling guilty about wanting to kill her husband and the murderous fantasies she had from the time she was first pregnant. Her self-criticism and guilt were intense.

Providing her some relief from the intense internal criticism seemed important before we went further in our psychotherapy. I used the word "hope" to describe her fantasies of killing her husband – "hope to have some relief from the pain your husband repeatedly inflicted on you". At first she did not understand and continued to feel guilty. In the next session she was again confused as to why she had wanted "to kill him all these years and yet I carefully nursed him to the end".

Again I described both her fantasies and actual caring behavior as hopeful, as "a way to have relief at a time when you did not have the internal resources to terminate a disastrous marriage". She told me how she would "lie in bed imagining him dead... with a knife in his balls" and would fantasize getting a divorce "if I only had the money to do so and a place to go". I explained how hope is often the unconscious motivation in people's fantasies and that hope provides us with some relief from discomfort. Agatha began to think of her fantasies as a significant desire to be free of an abusive marriage and no longer as though something was evil in her.

Our conversations about the significance of hope helped her realize that all through her married life she had longed to return to university to finish the course of study that had been interrupted when she became pregnant. In our next session she told me how she again had begun to imagine finishing her university degree.

As our sessions came to an end she was not confused. She had spent several sessions telling me the details of her painful story that she had never revealed to anyone. She was still embittered about her abusive marriage, still resentful about her children's anger at her for staying in the marriage, but she was no longer self-criticizing nor feeling guilty. Agatha was hopeful about returning to school. We decided together that she would continue our psychotherapy sessions in September.

Forgiveness

Forgiveness is letting go of resentment. It is about finding an end to our angry reactions and bitterness toward someone who has offended us. It is about freeing ourselves from the physical and mental pressure that occurs when we continue resenting someone. Forgiveness frees us to move out of the past and into the present and future with a new and different perspective. Resentment results from holding on to old angers; it is a living in the past.

It is often accompanied by fantasies of getting even or fantasies of withdrawal. Resentment includes a fantasied misperception that we hold some power over the other person. But in actuality resentment is a distraction from the disappointment and pain that occurs when there is a disruption in relationship.

When we hold on to anger at someone the body is stimulated to produce cortisol and adrenaline, two primary stress hormones that have a major effect on our behavior (Cozolino, 2006; Damasio, 1999). Our body may then become addicted to living with an overproduction of stress hormones. The addiction to stress hormones is one of the reasons why some of our clients will hold on to old resentments for many years, perhaps even after the other person is dead. The prolonged release of stress hormones within the body often interferes with both our physical and mental health. This is why forgiveness is so important in the process of psychotherapy; forgiveness brings peace to both body and soul.

With my psychotherapy clients I find that forgiveness begins when they make a conscious decision to let go of the resentment. The second step occurs when the client examines his or her own behavior and attitude toward the person he or she resents. I guide my clients into challenging themselves with the question, "How did I possibly contribute to the conflict?" This question involves a process of soul searching and facing some truths about ourselves. It consists of examining our attitudes, fantasies, and behaviors toward the person we resent. This soul searching is a central part of the Alcoholics Anonymous 12-step program. The Alcoholics Anonymous literature describes this important step as "taking a searching and fearless moral inventory of ourselves".

Some people consider that forgiveness is about forgetting, no longer remembering what occurred. Forgiveness does not mean forgetting. It involves both being fully aware of what occurred as well as taking some responsibility for what occurred. By responsibility I do not mean self-blame, I mean being soberly aware of my part in the conflict. Forgiveness does not mean that we excuse the other person for what they did. They too are responsible for their behavior. But central in forgiveness is taking responsibility for what one believes and feels. Forgiveness is based on our attitude toward the other person and about ourselves.

The third step in resolving resentment includes not only telling the truth to one's self, as in step 2, but also telling the truth to an interested other person. The truth telling to an emotionally attuned other is essential in achieving forgiveness. When confessing to another person we not only hear our own words and explanations, we observe the facial expressions and hear the voice tone and words of the other person. Such intersubjective communication often helps to calm resentment and restore internal peace.

To help clients maintain an attitude of forgiveness and not lapse back into resentment I try to convey to my clients the idea that at any moment in time we each do what we think is best given the limited perception we have of options. Later we may realize that our choice of behavior was a poor one, but, at the moment we said what we said or did what we did, it often seemed like the only choice.

Forgiveness does not mean that we have to reconcile with the other and make everything OK. It means letting go of the false idea that we have some control by remaining resentful. We can engage in the process of forgiveness even if we never talk to the other person again.

Forgiveness may take a long time. It is a process of self-awareness and the knowledge that "this resentment and anger that I feel hurts me as much, or even more, than it hurts the other". Forgiveness is based on our own attitude, not on the other's behavior. Many clients spend years in bitterness waiting for the other person to apologize for what they did. The other person may never change but we can change how we feel and respond. We can stop the fantasies of resentment. Forgiveness is a process of growing; it is not a specific event. Forgiveness requires that we **not** deny the reality of what had occurred. Forgiveness cannot be based on the other's actions or attitudes.

In 1973 I published an article entitled "Six Stages of Treatment" in which I described the last stage of therapy to be forgiveness of the other people. After I published that article I became concerned that some therapists may push clients into premature forgiveness and that the client merely adapts to what the therapist wants, or that some people may push themselves to forgive before they are internally ready. For example, some clients are quick to say "My parents did the best job they were capable of doing". In some situations this may be true and in other situations the parents did not do the best possible job. They may have been drunk, intentionally critical, inflicted physical pain, or were sexually abusive. In such situations forgiveness based on excusing the other is not transformative and growth producing; it is merely the avoidance of realizing and accepting the impact that the other has had on the individual.

Resentment Is Killing Me

When we resumed our therapy sessions in September Agatha was excited about having enrolled at the university. She was taking a special course designed to reorient old students who were returning to study. We agreed that she would come to psychotherapy weekly until the end of May. As our sessions evolved she expressed how she experienced my being supportive of her and how it gave her courage to rage at her husband's many acts of abuse.

At first it seemed important that I witness her intense rage and resentment but as the months went on her resentment did not dissipate. In fact, it seemed to become more intense. Her anger was not an interpersonally contactful form of anger. She was just enraged and unaware of what she may have needed in a healthy marriage. Over the next few sessions, whenever I could get a chance, I talked to her about the caring qualities that she needed, and were absent, in her marriage. Periodically she ignored my opinions of what she needed and would again express her intense resentments. It was as though the rage and resentment were providing some form of self-stabilization.

Eventually she began to cry about what had never occurred in her marriage and how her husband was not only abusive to her but how he was neglectful and abusive to their two children. I talked to her about the tension I could see in her face and neck when she was resentful. She angrily said "You want me to forgive the bastard but I will never forgive him". I explained that forgiveness was not about forgetting the abuse he did but it was about letting go of his influence over her and that as long as she remained resentful she was under his domination. She cried and said that she had always felt so controlled by him. As she wept her whole body relaxed.

The next session began by Agatha saying "my resentment is killing me. If I am going to survive I need to forget all the awful things he has done. I need to make a new life for me". We talked about the difference between forgetting what occurred versus not letting what occurred influence us any longer. Over the next few sessions we talked both about making a conscious decision to stop the resentment and various ways of "letting go". We talked at length about Agatha's hurt and anger at her husband as well as her responsibility in provoking some of the physical fights that she had with her husband. She concluded that she should have ended the relationship the first time he raped her, that she protected him and never told his family about the physical abuse, nor reported him to the police. She wept as she described how she spent "half a lifetime waiting for him to change". She added "now I am going to change. I am going to stop my hatred of him because this resentment is killing me. I will make a new life".

In the late winter she met a man who attended the same university course. They quickly developed a respectful and caring relationship. She was excited about her "new life". She then told me that she had a confession to make. She described how for a few years she had walked past my office twice a day and would look at the "psychologist" sign on the door and "hope". She had tears in her eyes as she talked about crossing the street to look into my window so she could see what I looked like, hoping that I would be sympathetic, kind, able to understand her, and help her create a new life.

She described the importance of expressing her anger and how I had never criticized her for her rage. She added that the most important thing was to let the anger go because the "resentment was killing me". Agatha had a sense of renewed hope that she said she had not felt since she was an adolescent.

Conclusion: Compassion, Hope, and Forgiveness

Compassion, hope, and forgiveness are central in a relationally focused Integrative Psychotherapy. These three areas of therapeutic involvement are frequently in my mind when I am listening to my client's narrative. I am continually monitoring my expressions of empathy and desire to be compassionate so that I am affectively attuned to the client's internal experiences. I want to emotionally connect with my client but I am also cautious that my expressions of compassion not overwhelm my client by invoking more emotional stimulus than he or she can internally process. Affect attunement is always a challenge because it requires a moment-by-moment emotional balance of my affect in resonance with my client's affect.

I want to infuse my clients with a sense of hope. Hope is the antidote to despair because it provides us with direction and enthusiasm. Yet, I want to make sure that I am not offering "hope" as a panacea but that the "hope" we share together is realistic and vitalizing. Hope, and the accompanying sense of well-being, is based on the realization that a fully-lived life is a process of learning and growing from each and every experience.

Forgiveness is an important ingredient in a relationally based psychotherapy. When working with my clients I want to make sure that any expressions of forgiveness are coming from the client's desire and readiness to let the emotionally consuming past be over. I do not want to suggest that they "forgive" before they are internally ready. The desire to forgive must come from the client's sense of hope, a hope to be relieved of the burden of resentment. Forgiveness is transformative when the impetus for change is the result of our client's realization that their resentment harms themselves, even more than the other.

Compassion, hope, and forgiveness. These are thee important elements of a psychotherapy relationship that are instrumental in the healing of the psychological wounds of neglect, stress, shame, and abuse. As psychotherapists we have a humbling and important mission.

References

Ansbacher, H. L., & Ansbacher, R. R. (1956). *The individual psychology of Alfred Adler.* Atheneum.

Buber, M. (1958). *I and thou* (R. G. Smith, Trans.). Scribner.

Cozolino, L. (2006). *The neuroscience of human relationships: Attachment and the developing social brain.* Norton.

Damasio, A. (1999). *The feeling of what happens: Body and emotion in the making of consciousness.* Harcourt Brace.

Erskine, R. G. (1973). Six stages of treatment. *Transactional Analysis Journal*, 3(3), 17–18.

Erskine, R. G. (2021). *A healing relationship: Commentary on therapeutic dialogues.* Phoenix Publishing.

Erskine, R. G., & Moursund, J. P. (2022). *The art and science of relationship: The practice of Integrative Psychotherapy.* Phoenix Publishing.

Erskine, R. G., Moursund, J. P., & Trautmann, R. L. (1999). *Beyond empathy: A therapy of contact-in-relationship.* Brunner/Mazel.

Kohut, H. (1977). *The restoration of the self: A systematic approach to the psychoanalytic treatment of narcissistic personality disorder.* International Universities Press.

LeShan, L. (1994). *Cancer as a turning point: A handbook for people with cancer, their families, and health professionals.* New Plume Books.

Piper, W. (1930). *The little engine that could.* Platt & Munk.

Pope, A. (2007). *Essay on man: Moral essays and satires.* (Originally published by Cassell & Company in 1891).

Rogers, C. R. (1951). *Client-centered therapy: It's current practice, implications, and theory.* Houghton Mifflin.

Rogers, C. R. (1980). Empathic: An unappreciated way of being. In *A way of being* (pp. 137–163). Houghton Mifflin. (Original work published 1975).

Snyder, C. D. (1994). *The psychology of hope: You can get here from there.* The Free Press.

Winnicott, D. W. (1964). *The child, the family, and the outside world.* Pelican Books.

Chapter 16

The Psychotherapist's Myths, Dreams, and Realities

When I was asked to I give this keynote address on the theme, "Myths, Dreams and Realities", for the 2nd World Congress of Psychotherapy (Erskine, 1999), I was reminded of Carl Jung's (1961) autobiography *Memories, Dreams, and Reflections*. I reread Jung's account of his life wherein he endeavors to tell what he calls his "personal myth" (p. 3). A personal myth is like an impressionistic painting: not as a camera would take a photograph, not an accurate representation of truth, but rather as a vivid description of emotional experience. Jung says, "The only question is whether what I tell is my fable, my personal truth" (p. 3). It is important to "tell my personal myth", not the accuracy of the facts (p. 3). Myth reflects a person's phenomenological view and individual subjective expression of life, colored by affect and various developmental perspectives. It's the story, as we live it inside our own minds, not necessarily a factual story that can be verified by someone else. Such a personal or phenomenological experience of life can only be expressed by stories. The personal myth is the stories that we tell, either to ourselves or to others. As Jung went on to say in his autobiography, "it is the interior happening" (p. 3). Our personal myth is composed of existential meaning making, our reactions, our conclusions, and our decisions that each of us make along the path of life (Erskine & Moursund, 1997).

The Psychotherapist's Myth

Why are we psychotherapists? What subjective story do we tell ourselves about why we entered this profession? In my ongoing case consultation groups, these questions are periodically the focus of supervision. Particularly in the mid-phase of a supervisory process, we examine the psychotherapist's unconscious motivation for being in the profession and/or for taking a particular therapeutic stance. It is important that we question why we specialize in certain "types" of clients and avoid clients with other characteristics, or why we favor a particular theory or school of psychotherapy. Sometimes I discover in the mature therapist with whom I am talking a little boy's or girl's

DOI: 10.4324/9781003626718-16

commitment to treating a depressed mother, saving an alcoholic father, or repairing his or her parent's marriage. These motivations are often unaware because the childhood decisions have been lost to awareness: they have become unconscious. Yet these desperate childhood attempts to make an impact on early family life often affect how the therapist practices psychotherapy years later.

Dr. James Chu, President of the International Society of the Study of Dissociation, recently wrote about his naïveté entering into the profession. He said, "I felt that if I could only be good enough for my patients through exercising kind and thoughtful care, then they would respond with positive growth in healing" (Chu, 1997, p. 7). A wonderful ideal! And then he went on to talk about his clients with dissociative identity disorder and how some of them got even more fragmented with his kind, thoughtful, and caring therapy; how some of them got angry and even vengeful because of the treatment he provided. His personal myth collided with the reality of what he faced with some of his patients.

Each of us is attracted to and remains in this profession based on our personal story. Sigmund Freud, in 1927, wrote about what propelled him as a young man. "In my youth I felt an overpowering need to understand something, something of the realities of the world in which we live and perhaps even to contribute something to their solution" (Freud, 1999). Certainly many have benefited from his discovery of these mysteries.

Myths are like metaphors. They provide an expressive communication that emphasizes our emotional and developmental perspectives. Personal myths are what make each and every one of us unique. Personal myths are the basis of the world's great literature, of poetry and of theatre. Personal myths are also the basis for psychotherapy theory. In telling our personal myths – our own story – we are continually revealing ourselves to ourselves, and if authentically expressed, we are revealing ourselves to others as well.

I would like to share a story – one of my personal myths:

When I was 12 years old, I would listen to a radio show on Sunday night called "Inner Sanctum". The program usually featured scary ghost stories or tales about creatures coming from other planets. One December night, prior to Christmas, the radio drama was about a 12-year-old boy (perhaps that's why I identified with it), who had gone shopping to buy a Christmas present for his mother. He had a limited amount of money and he struggled to buy both a present for his mother and also to buy something for himself. He found something suitable for his mother and he felt lucky that he had money left over. He was looking in the store windows and saw a toy he wanted. However, the shops were closing, so he didn't have an opportunity to spend the money. He planned on returning to the store after Christmas. It had started snowing. The snow was heavy and wet: the wind was increasing. He decided to ride the bus home, rather than endure the long cold walk. He went to the bus stop, which was crowded with people getting on the bus with all their Christmas presents. An old, homeless man stood at the bus stop asking each person to buy him a ticket so that he could sleep the night on the warm bus instead of being in the wet snow. Each of the adults refused to buy the old, homeless man a ticket. The little boy was perplexed. He hoped to use his remaining money to buy the cherished toy when the shop opened after Christmas. But he also wanted someone to buy the old man a bus ticket. No one would help the homeless man. At the last moment the boy decided to buy the old man a ticket. The 12-year-old boy got on the bus and made his way to a seat near the back. The old man was the last to get on, and when he walked down the aisle of the bus, he said in turn to each person, "bless you, bless you, and bless you". When he got to the little boy, the old man looked him in the eye and said, "God is with you". The homeless man proceeded to walk right through the steel structure of the bus and disappeared. The little boy was fascinated! And puzzled. A short ride later the bus passed a church that had a Christmas nativity display with baby Jesus, Mary and Joseph, angels, and shepherds. When he arrived home, he ran in the house saying, "Mama, tell me, is Christ really that baby in the manger, like the one in front of the church at Christmas time? Or could he be an old man on the bus?"

That story lingers in my mind and raises questions: Who is the client sitting across from me? Who is the colleague with whom I am talking? Who are the seemingly old, homeless street people that I meet? That myth, that story has stayed with me as I approach my clients and hopefully, each and every person I meet. My therapy is profoundly shaped by this personal myth! I hope that each inquiry and expression of presence and affective attunement expresses this unconditional positive regard (Rogers, 1951).

In the process of growing up every child ponders the question, as I did at age 12, "What does a person like me, do in a world like this, with people like you?" This existential question raises three dilemmas: Who am I? Who are you? And what is the quality of life? (Erskine & Moursand, 1988/1997). When those three questions are flexible and amenable to new influences, when the answers are continually upgraded by experience and change, they form our ongoing personal story – a story that includes our fond memories, our pleasant experiences, our ideals, the things that have hurt us, the things that have frustrated us, and the philosophies that serve as our guiding principles: what Alfred Adler called "The Lifestyle" (Ansbacher & Ansbacher, 1956). When these decisions and myths about self, others, and the quality of life become fixated, when they are rigid, when we hold onto them like a prejudice, they form what Fritz Perls (1973), or Eric Berne (1972) referred to as "life script". Life scripts are composed of myths and beliefs that limit spontaneity and inhibit flexibility in problem solving, health maintenance, and relating to people (Erskine, 1980; Erskine & Moursund, 1988/1997). I think it is part of a therapist's task to facilitate the client's telling of his/her life's story and to sort out and resolve what is a limiting and inhibiting life script from what is each individual's unique narrative of personal experience.

Carl Jung beautifully described this therapeutic process of unearthing the client's personal life script.

> The patient who comes to us has a story that is not told, and which as a rule, no one knows of. To my mind, therapy only begins after the investigation of the whole personal story. It is the patient's secret, the rock against which he is shattered. And, if I know his secret story, I have the key to his treatment. The doctor's task is to find out how to gain that knowledge.
>
> (1961, p. 117)

Here, Jung is talking about the realities of psychotherapy – what we actually do in clinical practice.

The Psychotherapist's Dreams

Before we go on to the psychotherapist's realities, let us examine the psychotherapist's dreams. Not our night dreams, but rather our daydreams or imaginings, the basis of our theories. For a moment, think of all of our many theories as constituting the "dreams" of our psychotherapy profession. The proliferation of theoretical concepts and ideas that have marked the past 125 years of psychotherapy may point to the usefulness of conceptualizing all of these psychotherapy theories, not so much as a true description of reality or of human nature, but perhaps much more usefully, as a collective dream, a psychological *zeitgeist*. I love to play with theories. It's stimulating for me to learn them and apply the concepts in clinical practice. I enjoy teaching, but when I try to make any therapy "truth" I get into trouble. When I think of theory as a dream, I don't argue with it anymore. I'm freed from the search for "truth" and the quest for a real description of human nature. I'm not trying to prove one theory against the other. When clients reveal dreams, we do not argue about the dream's symbols' representation of reality or whether these symbols can be proven by research. Rather, we examine the meaning of the dream in the context of the client's life experience.

When we examine theory as a dream, rather than look at it as truth, we uncover important symbols about what is occurring both consciously and unconsciously within our client and also within ourselves. Over the past century the writers of psychotherapy theories have argued over which theory is a true description of human nature. We argue over the assumptions of what constitute human difficulties and what methods ease suffering and confusion. The current eclectic mix of theories, some contradicting others, takes on a patient-centered perspective when we view theories as the author's dreams.

In the *Interpretation of Dreams* (1913), Sigmund Freud pointed out that dreams were hidden expressions of wish fulfillment, determined by the dreamer's waking life and closely related to his current involvements and problems. Ten years later in *Beyond the Pleasure Principle*, Freud (1920/ 1953–1974) changed his idea and said that dreams unmasked traumatic impression. Jung argued with Freud's premises: dreams represented neither wish fulfillment nor trauma. According to Jung, dreams inform the dreamer about the unaware condition of his inner and outer life. The dream content hints at ways by which the dreamer might solve his problems (Weiss, 1950). I frequently integrate these three theoretical ideas; two by Freud and one by Jung, as a way to examine psychotherapy theories: the solution to a current life problem that provides an opportunity to understand ourselves and our clients, a wish fulfillment, and perhaps an expression of our own traumatic memories buried in our theory. I often include in this integrative perspective Fritz Perls' concept that a dream is an existential expression (1973). This post-modern perspective dissolves the sharp line between what is real and un-real, what is provable by research and what is a coconstruction of helpful phenomenological experience – it challenges the "reality-making" of theory.

To write this speech I had to dream, to imagine. I had to conceptualize, to theorize. Theories can be viewed as our collective professional dreaming. Sigmund Freud (1927) wrote in *The Problem of Lay Analysis*, "Every philosopher, poet, historian and biographer evolves his own psychology based on individual presumptions" (p. 48). If he is correct, then perhaps each theoretical persuasion should be viewed as partly autobiographical.

I have had the privilege of knowing several authors who have written on psychotherapy theory and have read the biographies of others: some of these writers and teachers were exceptional people, each contributing his/her unique perspective on psychotherapy theory and methods. I found in many of their writings their own personal autobiography imbedded in the theory they expounded. That does not detract from the importance of that theory, but it certainly humanizes it. To view psychotherapy theory from its auto-biographical origin lessens the need to argue whether the theory is "true" or provable. Each writer describes the subjective experiences of his or her personal/professional life.

My "dream" of an effective psychotherapy is to make the relationship between client and therapist central – to provide an intersubjective space that allows for a therapeutic dialogue. Winnicott (1965) referred to this space as the facilitating environment, the domain wherein the "play" of psychotherapy occurs. Therapeutic involvement is the oscillation between two processes: de-centering and self-awareness. I usually spend a greater amount of time de-centering from my self. That is, I make my own thoughts, my own perspectives, or my favorite theories unimportant. I try to create myself as an empty vessel, to be filled by the client's phenomenological perspective. Alternately, almost simultaneously, I allow myself to free associate – to explore the many different aspects of my own life, my own therapy, super-vision, work with past clients, and all the various theories I have studied and read. I may think of the words of a song, a metaphor from history or science, or a verse from the Bible. I think that the oscillation between being de-centered and freely associating to what the client presents allows for the creation of a different theoretical perspective for each client. When with clients, I try to make this intersubjective process more central than any theory. This allows for a creative interchange in the process of psychotherapy. This is the therapeutic involvement described in *Beyond Empathy: A Therapy of Contact-in-Relationship* (Erskine et al., 1999).

I would like to share my own perspective on Sophocles' story of Oedipus Rex as an example of how one's personal story influences the use of psychotherapy theory. Sigmund Freud (1923/1961, 1924/1961), used the ancient Greek story of Oedipus Rex as a model for describing both his energetic and structural theories: the drives of libido and aggression and the influence of the id and superego on the ego. Freud's rendition emphasizes a young man's murder of his father and a sexually consummated marriage with his mother. Influenced by Freud's own personal and professional experience (Ellenberger, 1970; Levenson, 1983; Masson, 1984), this interpretation was used to illustrate the profound human experience of aggression and sexuality (Mitchell, 1988).

A relational perspective of Sophocles' story significantly alters our understanding of human nature and interpersonal dynamics. As I read this ancient Greek writer (cited in Mullahy, 1948), his trilogy is one of human relationships; of disruptions in interpersonal contact; of relationships gone awry; and desperate attempts at compensation and repair. Oedipus Rex is a tragedy of failed relationships. Sophocles portrays a tale wherein two young parents become distraught by the prediction of the Oracle of Delphi that foretells of a child killing his father and marrying his mother. Rather than seeking help to solve their fears, the parents instruct a servant to kill the child. Instead of directly killing the child himself, the servant stakes his foot to the ground and leaves him to die. A kindly old shepherd rescues the child, Oedipus, and raises him as his own son. But as this young boy grows to manhood, he yearns to find his own way in the world. Because of his maimed foot, Oedipus walks through life with a limp, symbol of the tragic wounding caused by the rupture in parental attachment.

At a crossroads Oedipus meets a stranger and the second element of this tragedy unfolds: the stranger, Oedipus' father, does not recognize him as his own son. The two men, strangers to one another, fight and Oedipus kills his father, never realizing the paternal relationship. Later Oedipus visits Thebes and lifts a curse on the city, is made the new king, and marries the dead king's wife. For many years Oedipus has no idea that the man he killed at the crossroads was his father, the King of Thebes.

This is not a story of aggression against one's father and lust for one's mother. It is a tragedy about parental abandonment, the attempt to kill a child, and the child's longing for attachment. It is a story of a mother who cannot recognize that this young man was my baby whom I had abandoned. Years later when a new plague emerges in the city Oedipus is told the facts of his parents' abandonment and he realizes that the man he killed at the crossroads was his father, the king. Oedipus is so shocked that he gouges out his own eyes, symbolizing the blindness in the family, the failure to see the importance of relationships and attachment. When we look at the myth of Oedipus Rex from a relational perspective rather than from a theory of drives, it alters our therapeutic understandings and challenges the very nature of how to practice an effective psychotherapy.

Each theoretical perspective provides an alternative view on clients' psychodynamics. When we think of all of our theories as though they are dreams, then we are faced with what we actually do with clients.

The Psychotherapist's Realities

The realities of psychotherapy require that we develop a high level of inter-personal skills to engage in complicated and sometimes painful interactions with clients, to combine empathy and attunement with understanding and the support for change. If we take a client-centered approach to psychotherapy we are faced with the questions, "What do I know about this person? What does this client need from me, now? What can I provide?" Answers to these questions are best if formed, not from a theory, but from what I know directly from each client.

To paraphrase the earlier quotation by Carl Jung, the psychotherapist's task is to find out the person's whole story: that which he or she already knows and the story that is a secret, a secret even to the client. The discovery of the client's secret is facilitated through inquiry. Inquiry is a genuine investigation into the psychological experience of the other person. Inquiry is multifaceted: it includes a respectful conversation about the client's phenomenological process, historical and transferential experience, defensive copying style, and psychological vulnerability. Phenomenological inquiry always begins with the assumption, "I know nothing about this client's experience". When I embrace this assumption, none of my theories, none of my past experiences, not even my observations tell me enough about what it's like to live in this person's skin. To engage in a phenomenological inquiry, I use questions or statements that focus on the client's internal experience: What's it like to be sitting here talking to me? What do you feel when you tell me that story? Describe what is happening in your body? What sense do you make of that?

Respectful inquiries allow the person to tell their own personal story; the narrative of his or her life. An empathic inquiry provides an opportunity for the client to express who he or she is to a willing listener. The purpose of such inquiry is primarily for the client to discover aspects of self that were previously not known or spoken about. Inquiry is focused on the client's discovering his or her internal process, not about factual information per se. Phenomenological processes often reflect expectations and, simultaneously, aspects of their history. A historical inquiry is about the client's experience of important events in his or her life: Who did what? Who said what? How did that affect you? Do you anticipate that I will do the same?

In conjunction with a historical inquiry, we may again return to a phenomenological inquiry, such as, "What's it like for you when you remember that your father treated you that way?" This frequently leads to discovering how the client coped and may reveal his or her system of psychological defenses. We may then return to either a phenomenological or historical inquiry that focuses on what decisions, conclusions, and survival reactions the person made in previous developmental phases. This inquiry is about the beliefs that form the life script. An effective inquiry often brings the client to an awareness of how they arrived at conclusions about "Who am I?" or "Who are those other people?" Examples of such conclusions are: "I'm not loveable", "Something is wrong with me", "People can't be trusted", "Other people come first". These conclusions and decisions may have helped the client cope with difficult situations at an earlier time in life. However, over time such conclusions may become rigid beliefs that stop the person from responding freely and being aware of relational needs.

The client's psychological vulnerability is the fourth area of inquiry. Vulnerability is that precious sense that all of us have of being in touch with our needs, our own sensations without having to be defended. It is that capacity to know that in this relationship I need security and validation, as I do every day of my life. In this therapeutic relationship I need to be able to rely on this therapist, but also at times I need a shared experience. I need to know that sometimes this therapist has suffered like I have suffered so that I have a sense of that human connection. Also in the therapy, as in every human relationship, there is the need for self-definition, the need to make an impact on others, and the need to have the other reach out and do something for me. Also, the need to express gratitude and affection is essential in every relationship. When those eight relational needs are addressed, the person feels valued, cared for, and loved (Erskine, 1998).

Many years ago, Harry Guntrip wrote a wonderful description of the realities of psychotherapy. He said,

> It is the psychotherapist's responsibility to discover what kind of parental relationship the patient needs in order to get better... The child grows up to be a disturbed person because he is not loved for his own sake as a person in his own right, and as an ill adult he comes to the psychotherapist convinced beforehand that this "professional man" has no real interest or concern for him. The kind of love the patient needs is the kind of love that he may well feel in due course that the psychotherapist is the first person ever to give him. It involves taking him

seriously as a person in his difficulties, respecting him as an individual in his own right even in his anxieties, treating him as someone with the right to be understood and not merely blamed, put-off, pressed and molded to suit other people's convenience, regarding him as a valuable human being with a nature of his own that needs a good human environment to grow in, showing him genuine human contact, real sympathy, believing in him so that in the course of time he can become capable of believing in himself. All these are ingredients of true parental love (agape, not eros), and if the psychotherapist can not love his patients in that way, he had better give up psychotherapy.

(Hazell, 1994, pp. 10–11)

How do we do what Harry Guntrip describes? We love them through our phenomenological inquiry, through understanding their defensive process, through valuing their vulnerability. We connect with them through affective attunement: when they are sad, we meet them with compassion; when they are angry, we take their anger seriously; when they are scared, we create that psychological holding environment that surrounds them with protection; and when they are joyful, we meet them with vitality. Those are the realities of our therapeutic process that make our dreams come true because we share our personal presence in an intersubjective arena between client and therapist.

References

Ansbacher, H. L., & Ansbacher, R. R. (1956). *The individual psychology of Alfred Adler.* Atheneum.

Berne, E. (1972). *What do you say after you say hello? The psychology of human destiny.* Grove Press.

Chu, J. A. (1997). Why we do this work. *International Society for the Study of Dissociation News,* October, 7.

Ellenberger, H. (1970). *The discovery of the unconscious: The history and evolution of dynamic psychiatry.* Basic Books.

Erskine, R. G. (1980). Script cure: Behavioral, intrapsychic, and physiological. *Transactional Analysis Journal,* 10, 102–106.

Erskine, R. G. (1998). Attunement and involvement: Therapeutic responses to relational needs. *International Journal of Psychotherapy,* 3, 235–244.

Erskine, R. G. (1999). *The psychotherapist's myths, dreams and realities.* (Cassette Recording MO4 (1 tape)). Audiotorium Netzwerk. 2nd World Congress for Psychotherapy, July 4–8, Vienna, Austria.

Erskine, R. G., & Moursund, J. C. (1997). *Integrative Psychotherapy in action.* Gestalt Journal Press. (Originally published by Sage Publications in 1988).

Erskine, R., Moursund, J., & Trautmann, R. (1999). *Beyond empathy: A therapy of contact-in-relationship.* Bruner/Mazel.

Freud, S. (1927). *The problem of lay-analysis.* Brentano's Publishers.

Freud, S. (1953–1974). Beyond the pleasure principle. In J. Starchey (Ed.), *The standard edition of the complete psychological works of Sigmund Freud* (Vol. 18, pp. 3–64). Hogarth Press. (Original work published 1920).

Freud, S. (1961). The ego and the id. In J. Starchey (Ed.), *The standard edition of the complete psychological works of Sigmund Freud* (Vol. 19, pp. 1–66). Hogarth Press. (Original work published 1923).

Freud, S. (1961). The dissolution of the Oedipus complex. In J. Starchey (Ed.), *The standard edition of the complete psychological works of Sigmund Freud* (Vol. 19, pp. 171–179). Hogarth Press. (Original work published 1924).

Freud, S. (1999). *Sigmund Freud: Conflict and Culture*. Exhibition, The Jewish Museum, New York, NY. April 18 – September 9.

Hazell, J. (Ed.) (1994). *Personal relations therapy: The collected papers of H. J. S. Guntrip*. Jason Aronson.

Jung, C. G. (1961). *Memories, dreams, and reflections*. Random House.

Levenson, E. (1983). *The ambiguity of change*. Basic Books.

Masson, J. (1984). *The assault on truth*. Farrar, Strauss & Giroux.

Mitchell, S. R. (1988). *Relational concepts in psychoanalysis: An integration*. Harvard University Press.

Mullahy, P. (1948). *Oedipus: Myth and complex. Oedipus Rex*. (Trans. SirR.Jebb). Hermitage Press.

Perls, F. (1973). *The Gestalt approach and eye witness to therapy*. Science & Behavioral Books.

Rogers, C. R. (1951). *Client-centered therapy: Its current practice, implications, and theory*. Houghton-Mifflin.

Weiss, E. (1950). *Principles of psychodynamics*. Grune Stratton.

Winnicott, D. W. (1965). *The maturational processes and the facilitating environment: Studies in the theory of emotional development*. International Universities Press.

Index

For Product Safety Concerns and Information please contact our EU
representative GPSR@taylorandfrancis.com
Taylor & Francis Verlag GmbH, Kaufingerstraße 24, 80331 München, Germany

* 9 7 8 1 0 4 1 0 4 0 7 0 5 *